RESCUING PSYCHOANALYSIS FROM FREUD

The History of Psychoanalysis Series

Professor Brett Kahr and Professor Peter L. Rudnytsky (Series Editors)

Published and distributed by Karnac Books

Other titles in the Series

RESCUING PSYCHOANALYSIS FROM FREUD

And Other Essays in Re-Vision

Peter L. Rudnytsky

KARNAC

First published in 2011 by
Karnac Books Ltd
118 Finchley Road, London NW3 5HT

British Library Cataloguing in Publication Data

A C.I.P. for this book is available from the British Library

ISBN: 978 1 85575 873 5

Edited, designed and produced by The Studio Publishing Services Ltd
www.publishingservicesuk.co.uk
e-mail: studio@publishingservicesuk.co.uk

Printed in Great Britain

www.karnacbooks.com

CONTENTS

ACKNOWLEDGEMENTS

Psychoanalysis, like scholarship, is at once an eminently solitary and an exquisitely social undertaking. Among those colleagues whose friendship and counsel have sustained me during my clinical *Lehrjahre* are Salman Akhtar (Philadelphia), Rosemary H. Balsam (New Haven), Sara Boffito (Milan), Carlo Bonomi (Florence), Franco Borgogno (Turin), Vera J. Camden (Cleveland), Arnold M. Cooper (New York), Aleksandar Dimitrijevic (Belgrade), Giselle Galdi (New York), Antonella Granieri (Turin), Fred L. Griffin (Dallas), Steven Groarke (London), Axel Hoffer (Brookline), Wendy Jacobson (Atlanta), Brett Kahr (London), Christine Miqueu-Baz (London), Anna Ornstein (Brookline), Paul H. Ornstein (Brookline), Warren S. Poland (Washington), Esther Rashkin (Salt Lake City), David M. Sachs (Bala Cynwyd), Bennett Simon (Jamaica Plain), Judith E. Vida (Sunland), and Robert S. Wallerstein (Belvedere).

The recent rough economic seas would have been even more hazardous had Pamela Gilbert not been at the helm of the English Department at the University of Florida, where my students annually rekindle my passion for teaching. I have twice been privileged to be a Visiting Scholar at the Psychoanalytic Studies Program at Emory University, for which my heartfelt thanks go to Sander

L. Gilman, Robert A. Paul, Kevin Corrigan, and Claire Nouvet. I likewise cherish my associations with the Tampa Bay Institute for Psychoanalytic Studies and the Institute of Contemporary Psychoanalysis in Los Angeles. The nobility of the profession of social work has been incarnated for me by Susan C. Horky. Matthew J. Snyder has fought valiantly in the trenches of *American Imago*.

Lectures based on chapters in this book have been presented at the following venues: for Chapter One, a case conference series, Department of Clinical and Health Psychology, University of Florida, June 2006; "Freud at 150—Evaluating His Impact on Psychology and Our World", a symposium sponsored by Divisions 39, 24, 29, and 32 at the convention of the American Psychological Association, New Orleans, August 2006; a conference of the Sándor Ferenczi Society, "Clinical Sándor Ferenczi: Mind, Body, and the Bridge Between", Baden-Baden, Germany, August 2006; a Grand Rounds, Tulane University Medical School, New Orleans, December 2006; and (in Italian) at the Postgraduate School in Clinical Psychology, University of Turin, November 2007; for Chapter Two, "Sándor Ferenczi Returns Home", a conference in Miskolc, Hungary, November 2008; the Chicago Psychoanalytic Society, September 2009; and at the Ferenczi House in Budapest, June 2010; for Chapter Four, "The Good-Enough Winnicott", a symposium sponsored by The Freud Museum and The Winnicott Clinic, London, October 2005; The Psychoanalytic Center, New Orleans, December 2006; a colloquium sponsored by the PhD programme in Clinical Psychology, City College of New York, March 2007; an Emory University Psychoanalytic Studies Program colloquium, October 2008; and at the Spring Scientific Meeting of the Korean Association of Psychoanalysis, Seoul, May 2010; for Chapter Five, the Atlanta Psychoanalytic Society, December 2009; and (in Italian) at the Postgraduate School in Clinical Psychology, University of Turin, June 2010, and at the H. S. Sullivan Institute of Analytic Psychotherapy and the Florentine Association of Interpersonal Psychoanalysis, Florence, June 2010; for Chapter Seven, "Psychoanalysis and the University: The Clinical Dimension", a conference of the Psychoanalytic Studies Program, Emory University, November 2007.

Earlier versions of Chapter One appeared in 2008 in the *American Journal of Psychoanalysis, 68*: 117–127, and in Italian translation (2007) in *Il vaso di Pandora: Dialoghi in psychiatria e scienze umane*, 15: 29–46. A version of Chapter Three was published in 2006 in *Psychoanalysis and History*, 8: 123–157, while the Appendix appeared first in 2008 in *The American Psychoanalyst*, 42(2): 6–7, 15–16. I am grateful to all those who have hosted me in person and in print.

ABOUT THE AUTHOR

Peter L. Rudnytsky is Professor of English at the University of Florida, a visiting scholar in the Psychoanalytic Studies Program at Emory University, and the editor of *American Imago*. Honorary Member of the American Psychoanalytic Association and Corresponding Member of the Institute of Contemporary Psychoanalysis in Los Angeles, he is a licensed clinical social worker with a private practice in Gainesville. He is the author of *Freud and Oedipus* (1987), *The Psychoanalytic Vocation: Rank, Winnicott, and the Legacy of Freud* (1991), *Psychoanalytic Conversations: Interviews with Clinicians, Commentators, and Critics* (2000), and *Reading Psychoanalysis: Freud, Rank, Ferenczi, Groddeck* (2002), for which he received the Gradiva Award in 2003. In 2001 he received the Local Educators' Award from the International Forum for Psychoanalytic Education, and in 2004 he was the Fulbright/Freud Society Scholar of Psychoanalysis in Vienna. His numerous edited books include *Transitional Objects and Potential Spaces: Literary Uses of D. W. Winnicott* (1993), *Freud and Forbidden Knowledge* (1994), *Ferenczi's Turn in Psychoanalysis* (1996), *Psychoanalyses/Feminisms* (2000), *Psychoanalysis and Narrative Medicine* (2008), and *Her Hour Come Round at Last: A Garland for Nina Coltart*, published concurrently with the present volume by Karnac in the History of Psychoanalysis Series.

Nearly twenty-five years ago, a fellow historian urged me to read a new book, entitled *Freud and Oedipus*, written by a then fledgeling American scholar with impeccable Ivy League and Oxbridge credentials. I imbibed the young Peter Rudnytsky's début volume with gusto, impressed not only by the depth and breadth of erudition, but also by the fresh style of writing and by the richness of conceptualization. I had a strong sense that the author of *Freud and Oedipus* had many more fine thoughts awaiting publication; therefore, it did not surprise me when Rudnytsky published another substantial book only a few years later, the now classic study, *The Psychoanalytic Vocation: Rank, Winnicott, and the Legacy of Freud*. I knew already that Dr Rudnytsky possessed a magisterial command of the Freud literature, but after reading his newer offering, I came to appreciate that he also knew his Rank, and his Winnicott, and his Kohut, and his Guntrip, and even his Lacan, with the same degree of profound understanding.

I realized that as a result of these publications, both clinicians and historians of psychoanalysis would have to welcome and embrace a new and weighty contributor. But I did *not* have the foresight to realize that Peter Rudnytsky would, in years to come, create, almost single-handedly, a whole new genre of scholarship. Certainly, numerous Freud scholars had preceded him. But virtually *no one* had written about the history of the Independent tradition in psychoanalysis. I think that one can safely claim that Rudnytsky inaugurated the study of the Independent group as a genuine arena for academic engagement. Whether by writing sweeping psychobiographical studies of the pioneers of Independent psychoanalysis, beautifully conveyed in his Gradiva Award-winning volume *Reading Psychoanalysis: Freud, Rank, Ferenczi, Groddeck*, whether by publishing interviews with Enid Balint, Charles Rycroft, Peter Lomas, and other survivors of the post-Winnicott generation, or whether through his printing of hitherto neglected archival materials, such as the indispensable interview with Clare Winnicott conducted by fellow medical historian Michael Neve, Rudnytsky had opened up a new vein. In researching the Independent tradition, Rudnytsky established the close links to Freud, and he delineated a veritable "through-line" which traces a particular path within psychoanalysis from Freud to Ferenczi to Rank to Winnicott to Guntrip to Coltart, and beyond, one which had become in danger of being eclipsed, in part because the Independents have always eschewed the creation of cult followings.

Professor Rudnytsky has made primary contributions to many different sub-fields within the history of psychoanalysis, contributing, *inter alia*, to Freud studies, to Ferenczi studies, and to Winnicott studies, in particular; in doing so, Rudnytsky has helped to create an intellectual trajectory of the Independent tradition not only in British psychoanalysis (the long-standing home of the "Independent Group"), but also in other countries and during other time periods. Over the past two decades, Rudnytsky has sculpted an intellectual history of Independent thinking within the broader, longer history of psychoanalysis, and he has done so with erudition, with grace, and with an unusual clarity of vision.

In his latest offering, *Rescuing Psychoanalysis from Freud and Other Essays in Re-Vision*, Peter Rudnytsky, now a venerable professor with more than a dozen books to his credit, treats us to a very mature work of psychoanalytical history which offers an engagement with the Independent tradition from Sigmund Freud to Donald Winnicott, from Margaret Little to Nina Coltart, from the consulting rooms of Vienna to the classrooms in Atlanta, Georgia, where Rudnytsky has taught as a Visiting Scholar in residence on the pioneering Psychoanalytic Studies Program at Emory University.

Peter Rudnytsky has inaugurated the "Introduction" to his book of essays by wondering, "What might it mean to view the history of psychoanalysis from an Independent perspective?" As a scholar, as a historian, and, more recently, as a clinician, Rudnytsky has devoted much of his distinguished professional career to careful readings of psychoanalysis and its foundational texts, and to original researches on this topic; he has done so with a remarkable freedom of thought, unfettered by a desire either to worship Freud and his followers or to bash them. One might claim Rudnytsky as the independent scholar of the Independents, exploring not only the light but also the shadow of the heroes and heroines within this historical cluster, introducing us to a Winnicott ravaged by a painful divorce and a Coltart traumatized by the death of both of her parents in a train crash, a Winnicott and a Coltart who, in spite of their private agonies, created, nevertheless, path-breaking bodies of original work.

As one reads through Rudnytsky's rich, layered, textured, and engaging chapters, one quickly discovers oneself to be in the presence of a narrator who has the capacity to guide us through the maze of psychoanalytical history with much intimate knowledge, with a bravery required to state the unpopular, and with a quality approaching genuine objectivity. By engaging with Rudnytsky in his nuanced analyses, we feel intellectually refreshed.

Naturally, Rudnytsky has begun his exploration with an examination of Sigmund Freud, exploring the paradox of Freud as the Independent *revolutionary* who created psychoanalysis, and Freud as the *saboteur* who often assassinated his most creative, Independent-minded colleagues. In spite of his allegiance to Freud, and in spite of his love for Freud, Rudnytsky can also dare to embrace Freud critically in true independent spirit. In the "Introduction" to *Rescuing Psychoanalysis from Freud and Other Essays in Re-Vision*, Rudnytsky has quoted from the writings of Max Graf, the distinguished Viennese musicologist, pioneering applied psychoanalyst, and father of Herbert Graf (better known as "Little Hans"), citing Graf's summation of the relationship between Sigmund

Freud and Alfred Adler. Graf had referred to Freud as the "head of a church" who "banished" Adler for his heresy. Commenting on this observation, Rudnytsky has noted,

> It is because Freud, despite being the inventor of psychoanalysis, too often failed to heed its most important lessons that my sympathies lie predominantly with Adler and the other courageous souls who cherish what Freud gave us "as a new tool for investigative work, which every physician should use for independent research". [pp. xxiii–xxiv]

Rudnytsky thus poses a provocative challenge, but one which he substantiates in convincing chapters.

Ever since the publication of Dr Ernest Jones's magisterial biographical triptych of Sigmund Freud, scholars have struggled to provide an accurate assessment of the founder of psychoanalysis and his legacy. On the whole, historians have portrayed Freud either as a genius of Christ-like, Einsteinian proportions who battled against the evil forces of sexual repression and psychiatric cruelty, or as a duplicitous charlatan who fabricated his data while snorting cocaine. Even a first-year student of undergraduate-level psychoanalytical studies would recognize these polarized evaluations of Freud as prototypical examples of idealization and denigration, two very primitive qualities of mind which, as Melanie Klein has reminded us, characterize much of infantile thinking.

From this point on, Rudnytsky provides us with an engrossing conundrum, acquainting us with a Freud who, in spite of having invented psychoanalysis, may not have understood his own creation in all its respects as well as some of his more liberal-minded colleagues. Through his stunning examinations of the neglected contributions of such marginalized figures as Wilhelm Stekel, and through his earlier work on Sándor Ferenczi (once marginalized and now, as a result of the efforts of Rudnytsky and others, hugely respectable, if not venerable), we begin to encounter a Freud who often shot himself in the foot, executing some of his best comrades, thereby threatening his own creation of psychoanalysis with conservatism and, ultimately, with orthodoxy. As a scholar who has lived creatively in the spaces between academia and psychoanalysis, Peter Rudnytsky fears neither charges of heresy nor threats of excommunication. Instead, he writes with a remarkable honesty, allowing him to elucidate his vision of how we might rescue psychoanalysis from Freud himself, daring to question what he has described as Freud's "sovereign authority over psychoanalysis".

In Chapter One, "Inventing Freud", Rudnytsky encapsulates his philosophy of psychoanalytical historiography most helpfully:

> To those who reject Freud out of hand, I would say that his discovery of psychoanalysis is indeed one of the supreme achievements in all of human history, worthy to be set beside the scientific revolutions of Copernicus and Darwin. To those who retain an excessive devotion to Freud, conversely, I would say that not only did he get many things wrong but that he was so tragically flawed as a human being that he nearly destroyed his beloved creation because—being as much an insecure Narcissus as an incestuous Oedipus—he could see in it only a reflection of his own image. [p. 7]

In this respect, Rudnytsky offers us his "Independent" assessment of Freud, revealing his capacity to love Freud's work, to worry about Freud's character, and to bristle at Freud's treatment of his own baby.

By the time we immerse ourselves in Chapter Two, " 'Infantile thoughts': reading Ferenczi's *Clinical Diary* as a commentary on Freud's relationship with Minna Bernays", we meet Rudnytsky as historian and as ethicist, and we soon realize that Freud's relationship with his sister-in-law cannot be dismissed as mere gossip, or as only a family secret, but, rather, that Freud's extramarital affair functioned as a deeply uncomfortable piece of knowledge which impacted directly on his relationships with both Carl Gustav Jung and Sándor Ferenczi, and perhaps disastrously so. In the chapters which follow, on Wilhelm Stekel and Donald Winnicott, we encounter the further dangers of what Rudnytsky has described so cunningly as "the Scylla of Freud-bashing and the Charybdis of Freudolatry", exploring the ways in which both Stekel and Winnicott have suffered unfairly from marginalization within the putative psychoanalytical mainstream, and how questions of centres and peripheries might be challenged. Although Stekel and Winnicott have each inspired their own historico-biographical and critical literatures, they remain for many psychoanalytical clinicians the objects of huge suspicion, as do Sándor Ferenczi, Otto Rank, Otto Gross, Georg Groddeck, Wilhelm Reich, Theodor Reik, Karen Horney, Erich Fromm, and a host of other pioneering figures who could not fit comfortably into traditional institutional frames. Rudnytsky embraces quite a number of these individuals as an "honour roll of dissidents", who, in spite of difficulties in their own private lives, or perhaps because of them, made enormous contributions to the study and treatment of the human mind, which suffer the threat of repression or extinction.

In loving spirit, Rudnytsky greatly laments that the men and women who devised "the common project" of psychoanalysis, and who bound themselves to one another in their love for psychoanalysis, ultimately became its assassins and its victims. One's heart sinks when one realizes, as Rudnytsky has done, that "In recounting the stories of their relationships to Freud, Stekel, Jung, and Ferenczi all recall one or more searing moments in which their hitherto unbounded affection and admiration suffered a grievous injury" (p. 62). It remains a great sadness in the history of human relations that Freud and Stekel, for example, began as deep admirers, and as creative co-contributors, and yet ended either by hurling vicious schoolboy epithets at one another, or, as in the case of Stekel, by internalizing them. How tragic that Freud, who applauded Stekel, who needed Stekel, and who even provided analytical sessions for Stekel, should have come to regard him, ultimately, as little more than a swine. Perhaps Freud deserves Rudnytsky's charge that Freud first seduced, and then abandoned, many of those who contributed so plentifully to his cause.

In the final chapters, Rudnytsky offers his readers a selection of more contemporary exegeses, exploring first the work Dr Donald Winnicott, examining the interplay between Winnicott's marital crisis and his theoretical contributions. Rudnytsky's essay on Winnicott reads rather like a good mystery story, filled with cunning detective work, treating us to an elegant synthesis of biography, theory, and textual analysis. Rudnytsky then explores the life and work of his own psychoanalytical heroine, the late British clinician Dr Nina Coltart, whom Rudnytsky has described as the most independent of the Independents, and as the historical figure with whom he would most like to have had an analysis. Peter Rudnytsky recently published an entire *Festschrift* to Coltart, which he edited with Coltart's sister, Mrs Gillian Preston, entitled *Her Hour Come Round at Last: A Garland for Nina Coltart*, which merits careful study. But here, in an elegant encapsulation of the spirit of that delicious *Festschrift*, Rudnytsky rescues Coltart from the threat of obscurity, a fate that has befallen many seminal Independent Group analysts who never sought to clone disciples.

Having begun his academic career in the field of Renaissance studies, Rudnytsky integrates his knowledge of Freud and Shakespeare in a most organic fashion, and he has concluded his book of essays with a deft study of *King Lear*. With great creativity, Rudnytsky has drawn most unexpectedly upon two doyennes of British Independent thought, Miss Ella Freeman Sharpe and Dr Margaret Little, comparing and contrasting their own approaches to *King Lear*. By examining William Shakespeare's supreme tragedy through the historical lineage of Freud, Sharpe, Little, and Rudnytsky himself (with the Independent-minded American psychoanalyst Professor Arnold Cooper inserted for a transatlantic perspective), we can enjoy a mini-history of the maturation of psychoanalytical theory from Vienna to London, from the early twentieth century to the early twenty-first century, from Oedipal readings to pre-Oedipal readings of texts, and much more besides.

In the final codetta to this *magnum opus*, Rudnytsky calls upon universities to provide more secure homes for psychoanalysis, urging the creation of integrated clinical training and academic PhD programmes in psychoanalysis. Rudnytsky shares the chagrin of many who regret that psychoanalytical trainings have remained for far too long the province of private guilds and clubs that have not yet become fully integrated into the mainstream of higher education. In a clarion call of truly independent-style thinking, Rudnytsky proclaims that Freud erred when he created psychoanalysis as a "movement" rather than as a "discipline". Perhaps Freud had no other choice during the late 1890s and early 1900s, but now, psychoanalysis has every opportunity to enter the academy in a more egalitarian, transparent fashion . . . and indeed it must. As Rudnytsky exclaims, "It is time for psychoanalysis to dream big dreams again".

As the long-standing editor of *American Imago*, a journal founded by Sigmund Freud and Hanns Sachs in 1939, Peter Rudnytsky has facilitated the scholarship and the careers of numerous authors at all stages of their professional development over a long period of time. For those familiar with Rudnytsky's work as editor, one celebrates the fact that he has not only internationalized the horizons of the journal, but he has sought contributions from clinicians, critics, academics, journalists, artists, patients, and so forth, editing and revitalizing this landmark journal in an exciting fashion. Rudnytsky brings those same fine qualities to bear upon the construction of his new book, *Rescuing Psychoanalysis from Freud and Other Essays in Re-Vision*. But, herein, Rudnytsky writes not as an editor or as a facilitator of others; he writes, instead, in his own very personal, very audible voice, in carefully crafted, joyfully engaging prose. He represents a truly independent voice in psychoanalysis. I find it a pleasure to listen.

Professor Brett Kahr
Series Co-Editor
London, June 2011

An independent perspective on the history of psychoanalysis

> "... a recognition, implicit in the expression of every experience, of other kinds of experience which are possible ... "
>
> (T. S. Eliot, "Andrew Marvell", 1921)

What might it mean to view the history of psychoanalysis from an independent perspective? I think it must begin with delineating a tradition of thinking and writing that provides a context for the collective achievement of the Group of Independent Analysts in the British Psychoanalytical Society (otherwise known as the Middle Group), of which D. W. Winnicott remains the pre-eminent figure, although its intellectual architect, as well as the originator of the term "object-relationship psychology", was W. R. D. Fairbairn (1944). At a deeper level, however, my project also requires the elaboration, not only declaratively but also procedurally, of a sensibility from which the historical terrain can be surveyed. Finally, this scholarly sensibility should be congruent with a relational or intersubjective approach to clinical practice.

In two previous books, *The Psychoanalytic Vocation* (1991) and *Reading Psychoanalysis* (2002), I have sought to make the case that the paradigm shift away both from drive theory and from Freud's male-centred perspective that is now broadly agreed to characterize modern psychoanalysis was first comprehensively articulated in the mid-twentieth century by the adherents of the British Middle Group, and I have traced the antecedents of the contemporary "relational turn" back to the work of Ferenczi, Rank, and Groddeck, whom I esteem as the most brilliant and prescient of Freud's first-generation disciples. In the present book, I pay a return visit to two of the brightest stars in the independent constellation, Ferenczi and Winnicott, Ferenczi being the indispensable progenitor not only of object relations theory but also of self psychology, and train my scholarly lens for the first time on other less conspicuous orbs, including Nina Coltart and Margaret Little, whose emanations have likewise touched me with singular immediacy.

To a greater extent than in either of these earlier books, however, I expand my focus here from historical inquiry to the articulation of what I have termed "a psychoanalytic *Weltanschauung*" (Rudnytsky, 1991, Chapter One) that is distinctively independent. I encapsulate my definition of this sensibility in my title, *Rescuing Psychoanalysis from Freud*. What I mean by this phrase is inseparable from the notion of revision, or re-vision, which also forms a leitmotif of these essays. When spelled with a hyphen, "re-vision" means taking a fresh look at something, whether prompted by the celebration of the one hundred and fiftieth anniversary of Freud's birth, as I do in the opening chapter, or as the result of the discovery of new primary sources or major additions to the scholarly literature, as in my chapters on Stekel and Winnicott, or simply as a consequence of the way that one's understanding of a phenomenon changes with one's own intellectual and emotional development, as I have tried to demonstrate in my chapters on Ferenczi and *King Lear*.

In addition to being essays in "re-vision", however, the chapters in this book are avowedly revisionist in the sense that they adopt a sceptical attitude towards all forms of psychoanalytic orthodoxy, particularly those which entail excessive deference to the authority of charismatic figures. Whenever he told the story of his relationship with Freud, Jung recalled his irrevocable moment of disillusionment, which came during their 1909 trip to America when

Freud refused to continue with the analysis of one of his own dreams with the words, "I could tell you more, but I cannot risk my authority" (Billinsky, 1969, p. 42). Whatever one may say about their theoretical disagreements, Jung is surely right to question Freud's placing of his own authority above the search for truth, and, in so doing, he upholds the core ideals of psychoanalysis, notwithstanding their betrayal by Freud himself. That this primordial confrontation between Freud and Jung has continued to haunt the history of psychoanalysis is attested by Esther Menaker's (1989) account of her experience as a young woman in Vienna beginning analysis with Anna Freud in 1930. Obeying the admonition to communicate whatever was uppermost in her mind, Menaker asked "what proved to be a very provocative question: 'What troubles me about analysis'", she said, "'is that there are so many splinter groups: Jung, Adler, Rank. If you are all searching for the truth of human personality, why can't you work together?'" To this Anna Freud unhesitatingly replied, "'Nothing is as important to us as the psychoanalytic movement'" (p. 40).

Just as Jung was permanently disenchanted by Freud's cloaking of his humanity beneath a mantle of authority, so, too, Menaker reports that she was "appalled" by the answer given by Anna Freud, and that even six decades later, she has "never forgotten that moment", which brought home the realization that "the movement and maintaining its cohesiveness were more important than the truth" (1989, p. 40). These prototypical encounters with Freud and his daughter constitute traumas not simply for the two seekers directly involved, but for all those who have been oppressed by the legacy of authoritarianism in psychoanalysis.

From Breuer to Bleuler, from Ferenczi to Fromm, from Stekel to Sullivan, the noblest (if sometimes also the most troubled) spirits in psychoanalysis have been revisionists and, therefore, independents in the expanded definition I am giving to this term. To an even greater extent than Jung, Adler became an anathema to Freud for having dared to stand up for intellectual freedom in psychoanalysis. As Max Graf, the musicologist and father of Little Hans, writes in his classic essay, "Reminiscences of Professor Sigmund Freud" (1942), Adler understood that Freud "had created a new technique, the product of real genius: this technique was a new tool for investigative work, which every physician should use for independent research" (p. 473). Adler compared Freud's "technique for exploring the unconscious with the technique of great artists, which pupils would take over but which they would have to adapt to their given personalities". Thus, "Raphael used Perugino's technique, but he was not copying Perugino", and may in the end even have surpassed his master. But when Adler sought to persuade Freud to bestow autonomy on the pupils in his studio, he "would not listen. He insisted that there was but one theory, he insisted that if one followed Adler and dropped the sexual basis of psychic life, one was no more a Freudian". For Freud, therefore, psychoanalysis was not a method but a doctrine, allegiance to which he was prepared to enforce by excommunication if necessary. "In short," Graf sorrowfully concludes, "Freud—as the head of a church—banished Adler: he banished him from the official church".

It is because Freud, despite being the inventor of psychoanalysis, too often failed to heed its most important lessons that my sympathies lie predominantly with Adler and the other courageous souls who cherish what Freud gave us as "a new tool for investigative work, which every physician should use for independent research". Although my interest in psychobiography leads me to explore how the achievements of creative thinkers and writers have their roots in the soil of personal experience, I do so paradoxically in order to emancipate myself from a cult of personality and to gain a more nuanced appreciation of the ideas and works of art that are my ultimate concern. Thus, in undertaking to rescue psychoanalysis from Freud, my purpose is above all to distinguish between owing fealty to Freud, who was an incontestably great but tragically flawed human being, and being a practitioner of psychoanalysis as a way of thinking and living, which each of us must incarnate for himself or herself. To go down the latter path is to cultivate a spirit of constructive criticism even toward what one loves most in psychoanalysis.

Beginning with Freud, the chapters that follow chart a roughly chronological progression through Ferenczi and Stekel, then to Winnicott, and to Winnicott's younger colleagues in the Independent group, Coltart and Little. Although it is only a side issue here, the chapters on Ferenczi and Stekel touch on Freud's relationship to his sister-in-law, Minna Bernays, a subject of great controversy I hope to address more comprehensively in a future book. My chapter on *King Lear*, which draws extensively on Little and compares her understanding of psychotic anxieties to the more circumscribed approach to Shakespeare's play of Ella Freeman Sharpe, leads me to argue for the essential similarity between the skills I have honed in my capacity as a literary critic and those I now also deploy in my work as a clinician. The seventh chapter, like the first, was originally written for a specific occasion—in this instance, a conference at Emory University on the integration of the academic and clinical worlds of psychoanalysis—and I have taken the liberty of interweaving an autobiographical narrative with my vision of a future for psychoanalytic studies. Circling back to issues raised in the opening chapter, I conclude by appending an interview I conducted in January 2008 with Eric R. Kandel, after we had both been made Honorary Members of the American Psychoanalytic Association, in which I concur with the Nobel Laureate's insistence that psychoanalysis as a theory of mind must rest on a sound scientific foundation if it is to thrive in the twenty-first century, while intimating my conviction that it must retain a hermeneutic dimension as a therapeutic art.

In a recent paper, Michael Parsons (2009a) has articulated some of the principles that guide him and other members of the Group of Independent Analysts in the British Psychoanalytical Society in their clinical practice: (1) they tend "to organize their analytic identities around underlying intellectual and human values rather than particular analytic doctrines" (p. 222); (2) they recognize that "unless analysts find personal meaning in their work, there will be no personal meaning in it for patients either" (p. 224); (3) they favour "a vernacular style, using everyday language in speaking and writing about analysis" (p. 225); (4) because they emphasize "the interrelation of external and internal reality", they believe it to be "important to locate the experience of the analysis in the historical context of the patient's life as a whole" (p. 228); and (5) they know that fostering "such an analytic climate depends more on how analysts listen than on the things they say" (p. 229).

Since respect for individuality is integral to independent analysts, it is only to be expected that I should differ from Parsons on at least one point. In my own view, an emphasis on "what differentiates human beings and makes them unique" is not, as Parsons supposes, antithetical to recognizing "how they exemplify general principles" (2009a, p. 223). When I end my interview with Kandel by invoking what I have called, in the last chapter of *Reading Psychoanalysis*, the "dream of consilience", I am affirming that it is not necessary to choose between defining psychoanalysis as an art or as a science. What is indispensable is to know when and in what respects it should be thought of as one or the other. Indeed, it is the burden of my argument—here no less than in my earlier books— that it is the enduring achievement of the tradition of which Parsons is himself a distinguished contemporary representative to have made psychoanalysis at once more attuned as a therapy to the uniqueness of every human being and a more intellectually robust theory, with "general principles" that can withstand the attacks of its detractors.

Despite this one area of disagreement, I hope my perspective on the history of psychoanalysis—and the sensibility on display in these pages—will be deemed to be consonant with the principles set forth by Parsons. I try to write clearly, read closely, listen deeply, think open-mindedly, and pay attention to both internal and external reality. If I have succeeded in catching glimpses of my own unconscious between the lines of these essays, perhaps the reader will be able to extract some personal meaning from them as well.

For Cheryl

Inter-assured of the mind

(John Donne, "A Valediction: Forbidding Mourning")

CHAPTER ONE

Inventing Freud

"It feels good as it is without the giant,
A thinker of the first idea".

(Wallace Stevens, "Notes Toward a Supreme Fiction", 1942)

In one of her masterful clinical papers, Nina Coltart says of a florid fantasy produced by an otherwise reticent elderly male patient that it caused her to feel that "if Freud had not existed, it would have been necessary to invent him" (1991a, p. 154). Coltart's allusion to Voltaire's satirical joke about God provides the jumping-off point for my reflections on the one hundred and fiftieth anniversary of the year of Freud's birth.

Above all, by her witty comparison of Freud to God, Coltart pays tribute to what she regards as the undeniable truth of Freud's key ideas as these are borne out in her consulting room. When another patient, one with ulcerative colitis, described to Coltart how much he enjoyed aggressively driving his new sports car, a Triumph, she responded by suggesting that "he identified with the car as if it were his powerful penis, with which he could control, hurt, and frighten people" (1996b, p. 105). To this he cried, "'Don't be so *disgusting*! . . . How you can say such mad things I don't know, and expect me to swallow them'". The man went on to complain that women who wanted him to wear a condom during intercourse did not realize how 'it makes me feel completely cut off', which, as Coltart reminded him, was precisely the phrase he had used to convey how much he missed his car when it needed to go to the garage for repairs. "'Oh, shut up, shut up', he shouted, catching my drift, 'that was nothing—just a screw loose!'" Then, after the patient recounted how he had felt "'just wonderful—empty and clean'" after he had "'*cleared it all out*'" and "'produced this *huge* amount of money'" he had hoarded to pay for his "'lovely car'", Coltart proceeded to compare these experiences "to withholding his shit till he was utterly constipated", following which his "mother's enema would produce a huge clear-out". At this intimation of an equation not simply between his car and his penis but also between money and faeces, the patient's protests again increased in vehemence as "he bounced and kicked angrily on the couch": "'There you go!' he screamed. 'You torture me with your rubbish. You've got a mind like a sewer'" (p. 106).

For my money—or its corporeal equivalent—the entire debate over Freud's legacy comes down to whether one chooses to align oneself with this patient who angrily rebuffed Coltart's "disgusting" interpretations or with the perspective of Coltart herself, for whom the patient's "very language 'gave the game away' over and over again"—though he remained unable to hear the double meanings in his own words—and in whose estimation "it was as if his secondary processes had peeled away and we were face to face with the language of primary process" (1996b, p. 104) in her analysand's exceptionally vivid communications.

In intellectual disputes it is always risky to accuse one's opponents of resistance, since this can be a way of evading legitimate criticism and substituting sheer bullying for rational discourse.[1] Still, if Freud's teachings have any enduring value, it is above all

---

[1] For an attempt to show the presence of defensiveness in Frederick Crews's polemics against psychoanalysis, see my essay "Wrecking Crews" (1999b).

because he asked us to take seriously the concept of a repressed unconscious, a portion of our minds that cannot be apprehended directly and that it is inherently discomfiting to be forced to confront. The virtue of the clinical vignette furnished by Coltart is that it allows us to catch the unconscious on the wing, as it were, along with the defence mechanisms that seek to prevent the repressed thoughts from emerging into the patient's consciousness; and since one colorful example is worth a thousand pale abstractions, I believe it should suffice to convince any impartial person that we do indeed live in a world that, if not created by Freud, in fundamental respects obeys the laws that bear his name.

The primary meaning I wish to give to the notion of "inventing Freud", therefore, is wholly positive, in that it underscores the extent to which Freud taught us things that must be conceded to be true. But there is a second, more ambiguous sense to my title. And that is that there is no escaping the enormous divergence of opinions, both popular and learned, about Freud. To put it even more strongly, each of us creates Freud in his or her own image. In psychoanalytic parlance, whatever we may think about Freud necessarily involves the workings of projection and transference, and is, thus, bound to reveal as much about *us* as it does about *him*.

I have so far proposed two variations on the theme of "inventing Freud": the first underscores how much of what Freud has to say continues to command our assent, while the second acknowledges the unavoidable degree of subjectivity in any judgements about so controversial a figure. But there is a third change I should now like to ring on the phrase, with its implicit comparison of Freud to God, and that concerns the analogy between psychoanalysis and religion—and Christianity in particular.

Here, again, there is an initial sense in which this parallel can be viewed in a positive light. Whatever one may think about Freud, it has to be recognized that his ideas struck many of his earliest followers with the force of a revelation. Witness Wilhelm Stekel's rapturous effusion, "I was the apostle of Freud who was my Christ!" (1950, p. 106), or Theodor Reik's recollection of the dinner given by Freud's followers in 1913 to celebrate the publication of *Totem and Taboo*: "We were, I am sure, more than twelve at the table, but something must have reminded me of Christ and His apostles at the last Supper" (1957, p. x).[2] Even today, I think, almost every-one who devotes his or her life to psychoanalysis has had some-thing akin to a conversion experience, most often arising from an encounter with the works of Freud. Certainly, as the author of a book entitled *The Psychoanalytic Vocation* (1991), and as one now undertaking clinical training in my sixth decade, I share with Michael Parsons the conviction that "psychoanalysis is a vocation in so far as the analyst finds in it the way of being which most profoundly articulates who he is", and this is a process of self-discovery that by its very nature "takes time" (2000, p. 34).[3]

There is, to my mind, something noble about the concept of a vocation, and it is a measure of Freud's greatness that for more than a century so many people have felt their lives to be transformed by his work. The subjective experience of faith, however, does not suffice to establish the truth of one's ideas. That which I have affirmed about the impact of Freud could be echoed by the follow-ers of Joseph Smith, L. Ron Hubbard, or any other charismatic founder of a sect. Thus, as with the notion of "inventing Freud", the comparison of psychoanalysis to a religion shades from having a positive sense into being simply a way of describing an ideology in which a certain number of people happen to believe fervently.

But there is a third, more sinister, component to the comparison of psychoanalysis to a religion, and to the likening of Freud to God, that cannot be minimized in taking stock of Freud at one hundred and fifty. This is the degree to which Freud looked at himself as someone with sovereign authority over psychoanalysis. Whereas, at his best, Freud could be as inspiring as Jesus, at his worst he arro-gated to himself the infallibility of a Pope. Indeed, in April 1913, Freud quipped to Ludwig Binswanger that the reason Adler and Jung had broken away from him was "precisely because they too wanted to be Popes" (Binswanger, 1956, p. 9), implying that he wished to reserve the title of Supreme Pontiff for himself.

---

[2] For more extended discussion of the parallels between psychoanalysis and religion, and between Freud and Christ, see my *Reading Psychoanalysis* (Rudnytsky, 2002, pp. 193–206).

[3] See, however, the cautionary reflections of Allen Wheelis (1956). That Wheelis's vignette of "Larry", reprinted as the last chapter of his first book (1959), is based directly on his own experience is clear from Wheelis's last book, *The Listener* (1999, pp. 108–117).

The timing of Freud's remark to Binswanger is significant. For, while the seeds of Freud's authoritarianism must have been deeply embedded in his personality, they burst into full bloom at the time of the schisms, first with Adler and Stekel in Vienna, and then with Jung in Zurich. In 1909, Freud began the first of his five lectures at Clark University by disavowing any credit for having discovered psychoanalysis, ascribing this honour to the treatment of Anna O. in the early 1880s by Josef Breuer, his senior colleague on the *Studies on Hysteria*. Freud writes, "If it is a merit to have brought psycho-analysis into being, that merit is not mine. I had no share in its earliest beginnings" (1910a, p. 9). Five years later, however, in "On the history of the psychoanalytic movement", Freud's once-becoming modesty gives way to an insistence that only he is entitled to determine what is and is not psychoanalysis. He now proclaims in the opening paragraph that "psychoanalysis is my creation", and "even today no one can know better than I do what psychoanalysis is, how it differs from other ways of investigating the mind, and what should be authenticated with its name or is better designated otherwise" (1914d, p. 7).

"Psychoanalysis is my creation": there could scarcely be a more brazen assertion of sovereignty over an intellectual domain. Embittered by the series of defections, Freud here shows his true colours, but his underlying bad faith is laid bare by a letter of 28 September 1910, to Eugen Bleuler, Jung's superior at the Burghölzli hospital in Zurich, whom Freud had avidly courted for the psychoanalytic cause. In this letter explaining his motives for founding the International Psychoanalytic Association, Freud affirmed, "I wish to state that one identifies psychoanalysts too much with my person", and, hence, he had concluded that "the time has come to withdraw personally and show our opponents how foolish it is to believe that psychoanalysis rests upon my personal existence and will pass with me" (Alexander & Selesnick, 1965, p. 2). In his response, Bleuler assured Freud that he "certainly [did] not underestimate his work", which Bleuler ranked "with that of Darwin and Copernicus" (p. 5), but he declined to affiliate himself with Freud's new organization. He elaborated his criticisms of Freud's tendency to expel those whom he regarded as ideologically suspect in a letter of 11 March 1911: "'Who is not with us is against us,' the principle 'all or nothing' is necessary for religious sects and for political parties. I can understand such a policy, but for science I consider it harmful". Bleuler continued, "I recognize in science neither open nor closed doors, but no doors, no barriers at all".

Although Freud's defenders have sought to excuse his conduct as "forced upon him by circumstances beyond his control", to wit, "the obstinate emotionally biased rejection of contemporary psychiatrists and the jealousies and fanaticism prevailing among some of his own followers" (Alexander & Selesnick, 1965, pp. 4–5), the institutional structure of his movement was, in fact, a magnified projection of Freud's authoritarian personality.[4] It was Freud's original intention to appoint Jung president for life, though he had to yield to the protests of his Viennese followers and agree to limit Jung's term to two years, albeit with the prospect of indefinite re-election. Thus, Freud's "withdrawal" was no more than a charade enabling him to entrust the reins of power to Jung, his chosen successor, who could wield authority publicly, leaving Freud free to pull the strings behind the scenes in their private correspondence.

By an irony of fate that illustrates the core of truth in Freud's ideas, however, Jung, far from relishing his role as heir apparent, chafed under Freud's domination, and eventually broke with him in a most acrimonious manner. In his 1914 polemic, Freud summed up the lesson he had learned by lamenting that, in Jung, he had "lighted upon a person who was incapable of tolerating the authority of another, but who was even less capable of wielding it himself, and whose energies were relentlessly devoted to the furtherance of his own interests" (1914d, p. 43). Jung, on the other hand, never wavered from his critique of Freud for "placing personal authority above truth" (1963, p. 158), as epitomized by Freud's refusal to continue with the analysis of one of his own dreams during their 1909 travels in America.[5]

---

[4] For a profound, and superbly researched, study of how, "through the presence of a superego complex", the institutions of psychoanalysis "have a tendency to betray the very analytical spirit for whose promotion they have been devised", see Reeder (2004, p. 10).

[5] As I will discuss in the following chapters, Freud's dream had to do with his relationship with his sister-in-law Minna Bernays, the illicit nature of which was independently argued by Peter Swales (1982) and which remains the greatest skeleton in the psychoanalytic closet. In my view, Freud's need to guard the secret of this affair, which was almost certainly consummated in 1900 and, thus,

Whereas in my discussion of the vignette involving Nina Coltart and her patient with ulcerative colitis I argued that the patient's protests were indicative of unconscious resistance, in the confrontation between Freud and Jung my sympathies are almost entirely on Jung's side. The theoretical issues over which they clashed are ultimately less important than are the human dynamics of their relationship. And it is not to minimize any of Jung's failings to say that I think he was fundamentally right in his assessment of Freud's personality. The notion that the president of what purports to be a scientific body should be expected either to bow to, or to wield, authority is preposterous, and Freud's failure to realize this bears out the justice not only of Jung's critique but also of Bleuler's when he told Freud that science recognizes "neither open nor closed doors, but no doors, no barriers at all".

Thus, what I believe is called for in assessing Freud's legacy on this anniversary occasion is not one but two lectures, or rather, the same lecture addressed to two different audiences. To those who reject Freud out of hand, I would say that his discovery of psychoanalysis is indeed one of the supreme achievements in all of human history, worthy to be set beside the scientific revolutions of Copernicus and Darwin. To those who retain an excessive devotion to Freud, conversely, I would say that not only did he get many things wrong but that he was so tragically flawed as a human being that he nearly destroyed his beloved creation because—being as much an insecure Narcissus as an incestuous Oedipus—he could see in it only a reflection of his own image.

It is because I take my stand as neither a Freud-basher nor a Freud-worshipper that I deem it imperative to distinguish between being a "Freudian", which I am not, since my allegiance is not to the great but fallible human being who was Sigmund Freud, and being an adherent of psychoanalysis, which I proudly am, since I am convinced that it has the potential to fuse the truths of art and science to offer an unsurpassed window into the human mind. Psychoanalysis has changed profoundly since Freud's death in 1939. And it is because I revere critical thinking that, when it

coincides both with his break from Wilhelm Fliess and with the inception of the psychoanalytic movement, exacerbated his innate authoritarian tendencies and made him even less responsive than he would in all likelihood otherwise have been to his followers' demands for emotional intimacy and reciprocity.

comes to sorting out my allegiances among the various schools of psychoanalysis, I find myself least in sympathy with those associated with such figures as Melanie Klein and Jacques Lacan, who, notwithstanding the brilliance of their contributions, are not only dogmatic in their cognitive styles but present their innovations merely as extensions of the Freudian system, while I am most enamoured of precursors such as Sándor Ferenczi and D. W. Winnicott, who have made it possible for contemporary scholars and practitioners to forge an identity that is indubitably psychoanalytic without being narrowly "Freudian".

In this lecture addressed to both Freud-bashers and Freud-worshippers, I would also say the following. To the idolators, I would make the point that Freud's greatest defect is not that he erred in some of his cherished convictions—such as Lamarck's notion of the inheritance of acquired characteristics, or Haeckel's thesis that ontogeny recapitulates phylogeny—but, rather, as Patricia Kitcher has argued, that "he bet his theories on quite specific future discoveries in other disciplines and then ignored the mounting evidence that these discoveries would never be forthcoming" (1992, p. 212). Whether in his personal relationships or in the intellectual domain, that is, Freud found it almost impossible to admit that he could be wrong and to change his mind when he should have known better. As a result, he was often unscientific in his way of working, since science is essentially a formalized set of procedures designed to induce the investigator to remain open to new evidence even when it refutes his hypothesis, and, thus, to be able to say "I'm sorry" on an intellectual level.

To the iconoclasts, conversely, my message is not to turn a blind eye to the extent to which Freud's core tenets—including the existence of unconscious mentation, the distinction between primary and secondary processes, the role of defences in coping with anxiety, and the enduring effects of experiences in infancy and childhood—have been vindicated by scientific research.[6] It is, above all, in the areas of attachment theory, pioneered by Harry Harlow in ethology and John Bowlby in psychoanalysis, and of neuroscience, as exemplified by such contemporary Nobel laureates as Eric

---

[6] For a comprehensive review of the empirical evidence that has corroborated a range of psychoanalytic concepts, see Westen (1998).

Kandel and Gerald Edelman, that the findings have been most robust. Although the waning of interest in psychoanalysis on the part of many departments of psychology could once be said to have been a barometer of its declining cultural prestige, the shoe is now on the other foot. As a cover story in *Newsweek* (Adler, 2006) has lately reminded us, "Freud is *not* dead", and those programmes that continue to ignore psychoanalysis and to think that the scientific study of psychology can be confined to cognitive–behavioural paradigms are now the ones that are behind the times and in danger of falling victim to their own smugness and insularity.

Within psychoanalysis itself, the most fundamental cleavage at the present time is between those who, in Arnold Cooper's words, believe that "the scientific development of psychoanalysis depends solely on findings derived from the psychoanalytic situation", and those who, like Cooper himself, are convinced that "interpretations will be strengthened by the knowledge that they are in accord with scientific data" (1985, p. 83). Despite the prestige of some of those who continue to insist that psychoanalysis is answerable only to itself, this position is, in my judgement, a counsel of despair, a last refuge of the dogmatism that has been the bane of Freud's legacy, though it is steadily being eroded by the tides of history.

What, then, is the current status of psychoanalysis in our increasingly globalized culture, and what are its prospects for the future? In my own view, the cracks in the institutional foundation for which Freud was himself largely responsible, and which became exacerbated in the United States by the restriction of clinical training to physicians for most of the twentieth century, have for the most part been repaired, and the house that Freud built is now soundly equipped to face the challenges of the twenty-first century.

Adapting Freud's schema (1923a), we may consider psychoanalysis to be (1) a method of interpretation; (2) a form of treatment; and (3) a theory of mind. With respect to psychoanalysis as a method of interpretation, I can securely avouch that it has outlasted its detractors and remains alive and well, not only in the humanities, but also in the social sciences. As Lionel Trilling wrote as long ago as 1940,

> the Freudian psychology is the only systematic account of the human mind which, in point of subtlety and complexity, of interest

and tragic power, deserves to stand beside the chaotic mass of insights which literature has accumulated through the centuries. [p. 32].

There are no grounds for retracting this statement today. And if psychoanalysis remains the reigning psychological theory employed by scholars in the fields of art and literature, why should we settle for anything less when it comes to human beings, who are hardly less complex and mysterious than the greatest imaginative masterpieces?

The use of psychoanalysis as a therapy for mental illness is far more controversial. But any form of treatment that relies even partially on the spoken word and on the formation of a relationship between therapist and patient is indebted to Freud, however little it may otherwise have in common with psychoanalysis. As Masud Khan has contended,

> the greatest invention of Freud will always be the invention of this unique human situation where a person can explore the meaning and experiential realities of his life, through a relationship with another, and yet not be intruded upon or manipulated in any way that is not true to his own self and values. [1972, p. 127][7]

Most present-day psychoanalysts are by no means opposed to prescribing medication when it is truly required, but they recognize that even a severely disturbed patient is above all experiencing—in Harry Stack Sullivan's phrase—"problems in living" (1953, p. 295) that cannot be remedied unless another human being is willing to take the time and trouble simply to listen.

Nor do psychoanalysts seek to dissuade people from obtaining the help they need from other forms of psychological therapy. Indeed, for certain conditions, such as addictions and phobias, there may be great benefit from time-limited treatment modalities, in which the goals are clearly defined from the outset and success is measurable. Results do matter, and those who pay for treatments

---

[7] It is a tragic irony that this ideal of the psychoanalytic situation as a sacrosanct forum for self-exploration so beautifully articulated by Khan was grievously betrayed in practice by Khan himself.

are entitled to judge their efficacy by whatever standards they deem appropriate.

But psychoanalysis does differ from other forms of therapy, precisely in not setting predetermined goals or measuring outcomes exclusively by empirical yardsticks. In analysis, one thing always leads to another, and the reason why a person initially seeks treatment may turn out to be no more than the thread that leads to the unravelling of the entire fabric of a life. As Jonathan Lear has written, "psychoanalysis is the one form of therapy which leaves it to analysands to determine for themselves what their specific goals will be. Indeed, it leaves it to them to determine whether they will have specific goals" (1995, p. 21).

The utility of psychoanalysis as a method of treatment is closely allied to its status as a theory of mind. Psychoanalysis today, in consonance with Freud's vision, is scientific, in so far as it relies upon science to address those questions that are within the purview of science to answer. But psychoanalysis goes beyond science in also being concerned with questions of value and meaning to which there are no objective answers. The neurophysiology of dreaming is a matter for scientific investigation; the meaning of last night's dream is not. Thus, psychoanalysis is not inimical to modes of cognitive–behavioural therapy that, within their limits, are powerful and effective. But it stands resolutely opposed to the array of forces in our society—let us call them collectively the pharmaceutical–insurance complex—that seek to reduce human beings to the lowest common denominator and to assess the worth of everything according to a utilitarian calculus.

As a discipline that bridges art and science, the subjectivity of interpretation and the objectivity of empirical research, psychoanalysis is uniquely positioned to promote what E. O. Wilson (1998) has termed "consilience", the dream of the unity of all knowledge that goes back to the Enlightenment.[8] As Wilson reminds us, the Marquis de Condorcet wrote his *Sketch for a Historical Picture of the Progress of the Human Mind* in 1794, at the height of the Reign of Terror during the French Revolution. Thus, this paean to human

---

[8] See my extended discussion of this theme in the final chapter of *Reading Psychoanalysis* (Rudnytsky, 2002).

reason was not oblivious to the violence and irrationality that threatened to destroy its hopes. Now, as I contemplate the future prospects of psychoanalysis in our age of neuroscience, my innate optimism is tempered by anxiety about the twin catastrophes of global warming and nuclear war that hang like the sword of Damocles over this good earth. Whether life as we know it will continue for another one hundred and fifty years seems to me less certain than it once did. But if it does, I have no doubt that people will continue to be shaped by their experiences in childhood, to have secret histories of desire that reveal their natures most truly, and to be riddles unto themselves because a portion of their minds always remains unconscious. In the event that humanity is here at all, I am confident that audiences will again be gathered in 2156 and beyond to commemorate the birth of the founder of psychoanalysis and to invent Freud for themselves.

CHAPTER TWO

"Infantile thoughts": reading Ferenczi's *Clinical Diary* as a commentary on Freud's relationship with Minna Bernays

"We should not forget that the young child is familiar with much knowledge, as a matter of fact, that later becomes buried by the force of repression".

(Sándor Ferenczi, "The dream of the 'clever baby'", 1923)

1

To juxtapose Freud's relationship with Minna Bernays and Ferenczi's *Clinical Diary* might well be described as a metaphysical conceit in Dr Johnson's famous pejorative definition of such comparisons as "the most heterogeneous ideas yoked by violence together" (1781, p. 14). For, I must concede at once, the name of Freud's sister-in-law is never mentioned in the private journal kept by Ferenczi in 1932, the year before his death.

In order to render plausible my ensuing argument, therefore, let me circle back to the beginning of the story and offer some guideposts by way of orientation. I start with the premise that, if Freud did engage in a sexual affair with Minna, four years younger than his wife, Martha, and his own junior by nine years, the effects of this primordial boundary violation would not have been confined to Freud's "private" life, but would, rather, have extended to the professional sphere in manifold ways, and would, indeed, haunt the entire history of psychoanalysis. By examining the image of Freud fashioned by the Hungarian disciple who has become an inspirational figure for contemporary relational and independent analysts,[1] we shall gain an inkling of the far-reaching impact of Freud's alleged transgression, which—if proved true—would constitute not simply adultery, but also incest in both a psychological and a biblical sense.[2]

My second premise is that, whatever the role one ascribes to fantasy in psychic life, it makes a profound difference whether or not this affair was consummated in reality. For, by Freud's own theory, it is only to be expected that human beings will entertain forbidden thoughts. To acknowledge such desires in a psychoanalytic context would not be compromising. But if Freud acted on these impulses, especially with a member of his own family, to confess what he had done would have had catastrophic consequences for his reputation and put an end to any hopes of founding a movement to advance his radical ideas about sexuality and the unconscious. Thus, in the scenario I am envisaging, Freud did engage in an affair with his sister-in-law, and this left him with an all-consuming secret—something, in the words that Freud was fond of quoting from Goethe's *Faust*, he could not tell the boys. It was the strain of keeping concealed what he most longed to reveal that caused this conflict arising in Freud's domestic life to disturb his relations above all with Jung and Ferenczi, the two colleagues who sought to know him best, with ever-widening ripples in the pool of psychoanalytic history.

---

[1] On Ferenczi as a touchstone not only for analysts who identify themselves as relational but also for those who consider themselves independent, the former being predominantly, though not exclusively, American, and the latter British, see the eloquent paper by Michael Parsons (2009a) and the responses by Anthony Bass (2009), Emanuel Berman (2009), and Warren Poland (2009), and Parsons's reply (2009b) to these commentaries.

[2] The Book of Leviticus makes explicit the prohibition against sexual intercourse between a man and his sister-in-law: "Neither shalt thou take a wife to her sister, to vex her, to uncover her nakedness, beside the other in her life time" (18:18; King James Version).

We come now to the bedrock question of whether Freud did enter into a liaison with Minna Bernays. Although I have come to believe that he did, to make that case properly would require book-length treatment and must be deferred to a future occasion. By way of a down payment, however, I can outline why I find the evidence to be compelling. The fundamental point to be grasped is that there is not *one* indispensable source of information concerning this affair, but *two*, and these are *entirely independent* of each other. Thus, if even one of these sources were deemed to be credible, then the evidence for Freud's affair would already be very strong; but if both were to stand up under rigorous scrutiny, then I submit that the case would have been proved beyond any reasonable doubt.

The first source of information is *internal* and comes from Freud's own writings, especially "On dreams" (1901a) and his analysis of the "aliquis" parapraxis, found in Chapter Two of *The Psychopathology of Everyday Life* (1901b), as well as other passages in the same book, all of which were written in the fall of 1900, after Freud returned to Vienna from his summer travels, first with Martha and then with Minna. It was on the basis of a brilliant exegesis of these texts that Peter Swales (1982) first advanced the thesis that Freud and Minna consummated their affair in the summer of 1900, following which Freud—like the allegedly recently re-encountered but in actuality non-existent "young man of academic background"[3] (Freud, 1901b, pp. 8–9) who misremembered a line from Virgil's *Aeneid*—evidently feared he had impregnated Minna and sent her to a sanatorium where she probably underwent an abortion.

The second source of information concerning Freud's affair with Minna Bernays is *external* and turns on the testimony of Jung, who, in an interview given to the American theologian John Billinsky in 1957, but not published by Billinsky until 1969, reported that during his first visit to Freud in Vienna in 1907, he had learnt from Minna

---

[3] The similarity of this description to that of Freud's interlocutor in "Screen memories"—"a man of university education, aged thirty-eight" (Freud, 1899a, p. 309)—who is universally recognized to be none other than Freud himself, combined with Freud's statement in the *Psychopathology* that he had "renewed his acquaintance" (Freud, 1901b, p. 8) with the perpetrator of the "aliquis" slip, can, in my view, be construed as Freud's private signal that he is continuing the disguised self-analysis begun in "Screen memories" in his fictional dialogue with "Herr Aliquis".

that "Freud was in love with her and that their relationship was indeed very intimate" (Billinsky, 1969, p. 42).[4] Although I shall, in the ensuing chapter, show the essential integrity of Jung's evolving narratives of his relationship with Freud, the key point for my present purposes, as I have indicated, is simply that these two sources—the *internal* and *external*—are altogether *independent* of one another, and, hence, there is no sense in which Swales relies on Jung in advancing his arguments.

In view of the highly charged nature of the material, it is not surprising that even distinguished scholars and analysts have lost their bearings in dealing with Freud and Minna. In their annotations to Ferenczi's pivotal self-analytic letter to Freud on 26 December 1912, for example, the editors assert that "an attempt was made by Peter Swales . . . to verify Jung's claim that Freud and Minna Bernays had an intimate relationship" (Brabant, Falzeder, & Giampieri-Deutsch, 1993, p. 455). But, for the reasons I have set forth, this way of putting things is seriously misleading. Even more egregiously, Elisabeth Young-Bruehl (1988) derides Swales for presenting "an absurd theory, for which there was no documentary proof, only an old rumor launched by Carl Jung and Swales's strange construal of one of the dreams Freud had analyzed in *The Interpretation of Dreams*" (p. 449). In point of fact, however, *The Interpretation of Dreams* was published in November 1899, *before* the crucial summer of 1900, and Swales does not rely on *any* dreams from that work in mounting his case. Thus, what is "absurd" is not Swales' theory, but the attempt of Young-Bruehl—who has confused *The Interpretation of Dreams* with "On dreams"—to pontificate on a topic about which she is woefully uninformed.[5]

---

[4] The published version of Jung's interview with Billinsky is only the tip of the archival iceberg. In a letter dated 20 February 1970 to Franz Jung, Billinsky stated, "May I say in all frankness that I gave only excerpts of your father's remarks and not the whole story as your father told it to me". In unpublished contemporaneous notes of the interview, Billinsky quotes Jung as having said explicitly, "I learned that Freud was in love with her and had sexual relations with her". I am grateful to Peter Swales for sharing with me these documents, given to John Kerr by Billinsky's son after his father's death. Also indispensable is Jung's 1953 interview with Kurt Eissler, derestricted by the Freud Archives at the Library of Congress in 2003.

[5] Among many others to have engaged in irresponsible Swales-bashing is Elisabeth Roudinesco, who opines: "Taking as a point of departure a confidence

Without claiming to have proved that Freud and Minna had an affair, I hope I have said enough to show why I have come to believe that they were indeed "very intimate". There are two further pieces of historical detritus that also merit consideration. The first is the by-now notorious 1898 Swiss hotel log documenting that Freud signed in with Minna Bernays as his "wife", which led to a front-page story in the *New York Times* (Blumenthal, 2006) when the article by Franz Maciejewski (2006) reporting this discovery was published in *American Imago*. Although the fact that they shared a room does not mean that Freud and Minna necessarily engaged in sexual intercourse, and I concur with Swales that the relationship was not consummated until 1900, the hotel log incontrovertibly establishes Freud's capacity for duplicity about his domestic arrangements; and surely he and Minna could not have spent the night together as man and wife without at least entertaining the fantasy of being married to one another.

The second piece of unexpectedly resurfaced material is found in Ferenczi's letter to Freud of 26 December 1912, the editorial commentary on which I have criticized as inaccurate. In this letter, Ferenczi broaches for the first time the idea of being analysed by Freud,[6] and recounts two dreams—one having to do with a black cat that repeatedly jumps on him, the other with a severed erect penis on a saucer—analysing the former in depth. As such, these dreams may be regarded, in Ernst Falzeder's words, as the *"initiating* dream[s] of the analysis" (1997, p. 418), though Ferenczi's three "slices" of formal analysis with Freud, amounting to no more than eight weeks in total, did not take place until 1914 and 1916.[7] As

---

that Jung claimed to have gathered from the mouth of Minna Bernays, he utilized it to 'prove' that Freud had had a sexual liaison with his sister in law" (1994, p. 109). But Swales does *not* take Jung as "a point of departure", and, as with Young-Bruehl's use of the phrase "old rumor", Roudinesco simultaneously misrepresents Swales and casts aspersions on the integrity of Jung.

[6] "It was and is my intention, if you can grant me time (hours), to go into analysis with you—perhaps two weeks (maybe three) for now" (Brabant, Falzeder, & Giampieri-Deutsch, 1993, p. 450).

[7] Falzeder is actually describing not the dreams in Ferenczi's letter of 26 December 1912, but the dream of the occlusive pessary, sent as a manuscript to Freud on 8 September 1914, shortly before his first "slice" of analysis, and

Carlo Bonomi has observed, moreover, this letter also "represents a turning point in the transferential relationship between the two men" (1997, p. 159). Partly because of his enmity toward Jung, and partly because he was engulfed in the maelstrom of his personal turmoil, Ferenczi makes the fateful pronouncement, "*mutual analysis* is nonsense", and abjures his desire for reciprocal emotional intimacy with his revered teacher in favour of the wish to be analysed by Freud, whom he now proclaims, subserviently, to be "right in everything" (Brabant, Falzeder, & Giampieri-Deutsch, 1993, p. 449).

After he informs Freud about the dream of the black cat, "*You* and your sister-in-law play a role in this dream", Ferenczi adds in parentheses "(next to it: Italy, a four-poster bed)" (Brabant, Falzeder, & Giampieri-Deutsch, 1993, p. 451), drawing a sketch not reproduced in the English edition. Ferenczi concludes his analysis of the dream by comparing Freud's relationship with Minna Bernays to his desire for Elma Pálos, fourteen years his junior and the daughter of his mistress, Gizella Pálos, a married woman eight years Ferenczi's senior.[8] As is by now common knowledge, this

---

published as the dream of a "patient" the following year (Ferenczi, 1915). There are many links between the "initiating dreams" of 1912 and 1914. Falzeder connects the dream of the occlusive pessary with Freud's dream of dissecting his own pelvis in *The Interpretation of Dreams*: "In both Ferenczi's and Freud's dreams, there is an operation, performed by the dreamer on the lower part of his own body; in both cases the associations link this operation with self-analysis, resulting in a publication" (1997, p. 423). Similarly, Bonomi ties the dream of the severed penis back to Freud's dream of self-dissection, noting that the figure of Louise N., to whom Freud presented a copy of H. Rider Haggard's *She* and whose request to read one of Freud's own works instead occasioned the dream, "was very probably Minna Bernays" (1997, p. 162; see also p. 160). (Significantly, Freud cites Goethe's aphorism on not revealing one's secrets to boys in this connection.) In its intertwined layers of public and private meaning, in which Ferenczi figures outwardly as the analyst of someone else but is seen by the initiated reader to be the patient analysed by Freud, "The dream of the occlusive pessary" replicates what I have termed the "narcissistic formation" of Freud's quintessential self-analytic text, "Screen memories" (see Rudnytsky, 1987, pp. 76–82).

[8] In 1912, Ferenczi was thirty-nine, Gizella forty-seven, and Elma almost twenty-five. See the thoroughly researched (and lavishly illustrated) biographical narrative by Berman (2004). Complementing the magisterial work of Bonomi, a comprehensive treatment of the Freud–Ferenczi relationship has been offered by Forrester (1997).

triangle was the central romantic entanglement of Ferenczi's life: he had fallen in love with Elma after taking her into analytic treatment in 1911, only to hand her over to Freud when their marriage plans collapsed. Swayed by Freud's unyielding preference for the mother over the daughter, Ferenczi renounced Elma and finally married Gizella in 1919, her ex-husband inauspiciously dying on their wedding day.

In his self-analytic letter, Ferenczi recalls how, at the age of fourteen, in what Bonomi calls an "acoustic primal scene" (1997, p. 182), he had been "terribly shocked to hear that my father, unsuspecting of my presence, had told my mother that so-and-so had married a whore" (Brabant, Falzeder, & Giampieri-Deutsch, 1993, p. 453). Ferenczi interprets the last portion of his dream as "a kind of defiant apology", addressed simultaneously to his father and to Freud. Just as he himself longs for Elma, so his father, by saying the word "whore", had symbolically acted on his illicit desires; but so, too, in Ferenczi's mind, did Freud betray his wife with her sister. Ferenczi makes explicit the analogy between his father and Freud:

> Only you have moved to the position of father, your sister-in-law to that of mother. [Father also said [=acted=] "whore". = You once took a trip to *Italy* with your sister-in-law (*voyage de lit-à-lit*) (naturally, only an infantile thought!).] [p. 453; all punctuation in original]

If this "initiating dream" makes manifest Ferenczi's transference to Freud, it does so, as Judith Dupont has remarked, in surprising fashion, in that "Freud is in place of the father and Minna (not Martha) in place of the mother" (1994, p. 303). The upshot of Ferenczi's double indictment is the plea that he should be allowed to gratify his passion for his mistress's daughter without fear of castration because both his biological and spiritual fathers are no less guilty than he: "The infantile 'wish-fulfillment' of the dream would thus be as follows: 'I satisfy my forbidden sexual desires; they won't cut off my penis after all, since "adults" are just as "bad" as "children""" (Brabant, Falzeder, & Giampieri-Deutsch, 1993, p. 453).

2

Ferenczi does not disclose how he learnt that Freud "once took a trip to *Italy*" with his sister-in-law, and, indeed, he immediately disavows his insinuation that there was anything untoward in their relationship by calling it "only an infantile thought". But if one seeks to reconstruct how Ferenczi, in 1912, came to acknowledge harbouring even a fantasy about Freud's affair with Minna, it seems likely that the seed was planted during the 1909 voyage to America on which he accompanied Freud and Jung. During their travels, the three men analysed each other's dreams; and, as Jung informed Billinsky (1969), when Freud refused to continue, with the declaration, "'I could tell you more, but I cannot risk my authority'", the dreams that caused him to respond so defensively "were about the triangle—Freud, his wife, and wife's younger sister" (p. 42). More specifically, the dreams had to do with Freud's "intimate relationship with his sister-in-law", about which Jung had been informed by Minna two years earlier, though Jung insists that Freud "had no idea that I knew" about this most compromising of secrets.

Neither in his interview with Billinsky nor in his more circumspect public recounting of the same events in *Memories, Dreams, Reflections* (1963) does Jung deign to mention that Ferenczi was also on board the *George Washington* that brought the psychoanalytic plague to America. As a consequence, however, Ferenczi must have been, in Bonomi's words, "cast in the role of a secret listener to Jung's analysis of Freud", that is, the auditor of another "acoustic primal scene" (1997, p. 186) preceding the overtly sexual one in his dream of the black cat. And since Ferenczi was there to witness Jung's unavailing attempts to get Freud to open up about his tabooed love affair with Minna, it does not seem far-fetched to imagine that this preternaturally gifted analyst might well have divined the true nature of the gauntlet that Jung was throwing down to Freud, even if the name of Minna Bernays was never uttered by either of the Oedipal antagonists during their *agon* at this crossroads in the history of psychoanalysis.

The reconstruction I have proposed of how Ferenczi came to have his "infantile thought" about Freud and his sister-in-law entails a corollary: after the trip to America, Ferenczi possessed *unconsciously* the great secret about Freud of which Jung was *consciously* aware, although Jung, unlike Ferenczi, was never able to bring himself to speak about it openly to Freud.[9] It is, therefore, no coincidence, but, rather, a profoundly determined "secret symmetry" that Ferenczi's most radical self-analytic letter, announcing his desire to enter analysis with Freud, was written in December 1912, the same month in which the long-simmering tensions in the Freud–Jung relationship finally boiled over into an irrevocable breach.

Once the reader is attuned to Ferenczi's unconscious knowledge of Freud's relationship with his sister-in-law, various details in their correspondence following the return from America take on an uncanny resonance. As a backdrop, it is important to note the following remarkable parallel: just as Freud's younger sister Anna had married Eli Bernays, his wife's elder brother, so, too, Ferenczi's younger brother Lajos married Gizella's younger daughter Magda, Elma's sister, in 1909 (Berman, 2004, p. 504). Thus, in addition to being Ferenczi's patient, beloved, and eventual stepdaughter, Elma was also (at least by poetic license) his sister-in-law! What is more, although Freud's triangle involves two sisters and Ferenczi's a mother and daughter, this distinction does not preclude their situations from being unconsciously conflated by both men. Martha was like a mother to Minna, while Ferenczi had an elder sister named Gizella, which was also the name of Freud's first love, Gisela Fluss, about whom he wrote at the age of sixteen to his school friend, Eduard Silberstein, "it seems that I have transferred my esteem for the mother to friendship for the daughter" (Boehlich, 1989, p. 17: letter of 4 September 1872; see Forrester, 1997, p. 60). In the midst of Ferenczi's vacillations, Freud wrote to Gizella Pálos on 17 December 1911: "his choice is depreciated by the consideration that he is automatically swinging from his mother to his sister, as

---

[9] The one hint given by Jung to Freud that he was aware of his liaison with Minna Bernays can be found in his commentary on his own dream of the "two skulls" in *Memories, Dreams, Reflections* (1963), to which he turns immediately after recounting his disillusionment with Freud's "placing personal authority above truth" (p. 158) during the trip to America. Irked by Freud's insistence that "secret death wishes were concealed in the dream", Jung admits to having prevaricated and told Freud that these wishes were directed towards "'My wife and my sister-in-law'" (p. 159), which could readily have been taken by Freud as a veiled allusion to his secret affair. See John Kerr's perceptive interpretation (1993, pp. 267–268) of this exchange, and Chapter Three, n. 13, below.

was once the case in his earliest years" (Brabant, Falzeder, & Giampieri-Deutsch, 1993, p. 320), thereby positioning himself and Gizella, as John Forrester has elucidated, "as the old father and mother", while casting Ferenczi and Elma "as brother and sister, both abandoning the mother for each other" (1997, p. 59).

Given that Ferenczi was, in his own phrase from the *Clinical Diary*, a "reverent spectator" (1985, p. 184: entry of 4 August 1932) of Jung's abortive effort to analyse Freud on the trip to America, what shall we make of it when, in a letter on 30 October 1909, he reports to Freud that Gizella had given her "Non-Plus-Ultra" coffeemaker, "which announces *the end of the brewing process with a kind of bird's chirping*", to Ferenczi's brother-in-law, the husband of his eldest sister, and that he had interpreted this to Gizella as a "symptomatic action" through which "she had clearly made known her inclination to give her love to the *brother-in-law*" (Brabant, Falzeder, & Giampieri-Deutsch, 1993, p. 90; underlined in blue pencil in original)? The likelihood that Ferenczi is obliquely alluding to Freud's "inclination to give his love to the *sister-in-law*" increases when we read, in Ferenczi's letter of 9 July 1910, of the "decided progress" in his "analytic association with Frau G.":

> As the "ménage à trois" on the George Washington became a significant experience for me and provided the occasion for unshackling my infantile complexes, so did the visit of a sister from Italy prove to be a ferment for Frau G., which activated her heretofore inadmissible impulses of jealousy, hate, etc. [Brabant, Falzeder, & Giampieri-Deutsch, 1993, p. 186]

Here, Ferenczi expressly links his "ménage à trois" with Jung and Freud on the *George Washington* with an erotic triangle involving Gizella—the perennial object of his "affectionate" current—and a female relative. In 1910, it is Gizella's younger sister, Saroltà, and not yet her daughter Elma, who represents the "sensual" object of Ferenczi's polarized desire, but this variation on the Oedipal theme brings Ferenczi's libidinal constellation into complete alignment with Freud's.[10] If Ferenczi were unconsciously aware of Freud's

---

[10] Freud's first two papers on love, "A special type of choice of object made by men" (1910h) and especially "On the universal tendency to debasement in

love for his sister-in-law, this would help to explain the multiple parallels between his letter about Sarolta and his analysis of the dream of the black cat in his letter of 26 December 1912. Sarolta, like Minna Bernays, is associated with Italy; Ferenczi speaks here of his "infantile complexes", and there of his "infantile thought". Above all, Ferenczi activates "impulses of jealousy, hate, etc." in Gizella by his attraction to her sister, as Freud could not have failed to do with Martha, however stoutly she turned a blind eye to what was going on between her husband and Minna.

We have it on record that Ferenczi did not merely fantasize about Sarolta. As he wrote to Freud on 18 November 1916, "I couldn't resist having my way with her, at least manually", during a visit from Sarolta the preceding day; and he recalls an earlier encounter between them that went even further: "That's the way my actual neurosis before the trip to Rome began. I permitted myself inter-course with a prostitute—then with Sarolta—, the syphilophobia came as a punishment" (Falzeder & Brabant, 1996, p. 155). Since Ferenczi and Freud were in Rome together for two weeks in September 1912, and following that trip Ferenczi confessed to a fear that he had contracted syphilis (Brabant, Falzeder, & Giampieri-Deutsch, 1993, p. 412: undated letter probably from October 1912), it seems safe to conclude that Ferenczi had sexual intercourse with Sarolta in September of 1912, only one month after he had "severed the last thread of the connection" to Elma (Brabant, Falzeder, & Giampieri-Deutsch, 1993, p. 402: letter of August 8, 1912).

That Ferenczi lived out Freud's fantasy does not permit us to say anything about what Freud himself may or may not have done with Minna. But once one has been persuaded by the combination of internal and external evidence that she and Freud did have an affair, it becomes fascinating to contemplate not only the homolo-gies between Freud's incestuous triangle and Ferenczi's but also the vicissitudes in Ferenczi's desire for the sister-in-law. And I think it

---

the sphere of love" (1912d), seem to be based in no small measure on the saga unfolding in Ferenczi's letters, as well as on what Freud knew about the anti-monies of desire from his own experience. Swales (1982) takes as his epigraph Freud's declaration that "whoever is to be really free and happy in love must have surmounted his respect for women and come to terms with the idea of incest with his mother or sister" (1912d, p. 186).

makes eminent sense to hypothesize that what Dupont has called "Freud's uncontrolled countertransference departure from neutrality in his championing of Gizella over Elma" (1994, p. 302) may be connected to his history with the sisters Bernays. Having tasted the forbidden fruit of his desire for Minna, I would propose, Freud was averse to allowing any of his "sons" to emulate the "sexual megalomania"[11] that he believed to be his prerogative alone as the primal father of psychoanalysis; and this is what prompted Freud to behave as unanalytically as he did in relentlessly pressuring Ferenczi to marry the mother rather than the daughter.

3

Having completed my long preamble, I come at last to the *Clinical Diary* in the hope of vindicating my metaphysical conceit. Since it is clear from Ferenczi's letter of 26 December 1912 that he had learnt, probably during the 1909 trip to America, that Freud had gone on a *"voyage de lit-à-lit"* with Minna Bernays, is there any way that the *Diary*, though nowhere mentioning Freud's relationship with Minna, might, none the less, be taken as a commentary on it, thereby casting light not only on its "psychical reality" for Ferenczi, but also on the underlying question of its "material reality" for Freud himself?[12]

---

[11] Freud offers this phrase in his 9 January 1908 letter to Karl Abraham as a key to the 1895 "specimen dream" of Irma's injection in Chapter 2 of *The Interpretation of Dreams*, adding with respect to the women figuring therein, "I have them all!" and "there would be one simple therapy for widowhood" (Falzeder, 2002, p. 21). As Patrick Mahony pointed out long ago, it is striking that Minna Bernays, whose fiancé, Iganz Schoenberg, died in 1886—and who could therefore be viewed as a widow—"remains the only member of the Freud family who is not mentioned in *The Interpretation of Dreams*, and as a matter of fact she does not appear once throughout the *Standard Edition*" (1979, p. 23). This omission can only be deliberate, given that Freud described Minna to Fliess in 1894 as his "closest confidante" (Masson, 1985, p. 72) apart from Fliess himself, and she became a member of his household in 1896. In *Totem and Taboo*, Freud states that in the primal horde "the jealousy of the oldest and strongest male prevented sexual promiscuity" (1912–1913, p. 125), adding that the "violent and jealous father . . . keeps all the females for himself and drives away his sons as they grow up" (p. 141).

[12] On the distinction between "psychical reality" and "material reality", see Freud (1916–1917, p. 368).

In an extensive entry on 31 March 1932 about mutual analysis, Ferenczi addresses the complications that can ensue when an analyst enters into such an arrangement with a patient who is himself an analyst, and who then chooses to repeat the experiment with his own patients. Ferenczi writes, "when a mutually analyzed patient (himself an analyst) extends the mutuality to his own patients, then he must reveal the secrets of the primary analyst [*Uranalytiker*] (that is to say, mine) to his own patients" (1985, p. 74).

In this passage, Ferenczi explicitly names himself as the "primary analyst" whose secrets might be revealed to his patients' patients through, as it were, a chain letter of mutual analyses. But, given that Ferenczi was himself not only Freud's patient but also the one who, beyond all others, in Bonomi's words, was "unavoidably attracted by the verbal tombs of the master, and unconsciously driven to excavate them" (1997, p. 161), it could equally well be said to be *Freud* who occupies the position of the "primal analyst", and whose secrets *Ferenczi* is, therefore, exposing in conducting mutual analyses with his own patients, as well as in writing about these daring innovations in his *Clinical Diary*.

At the heart of the critique of Freud that Ferenczi offers in the *Diary* is the conviction that an authoritarian attitude on the part of the analyst has the effect of infantilizing the patient. As Ferenczi writes on 7 May, when the analyst becomes unduly "pedagogical", he becomes simultaneously "more and more impersonal (levitating like some kind of a divinity above the poor patient)", and, as a result, the analyst does not suspect that "a large share of what is described as transference is artificially provoked by this kind of behavior", rather than being entirely "created by the patient" (1985, p. 93).[13]

---

[13] That this passage is directed at Freud is clear from the echoes of Ferenczi's 17 March entry, the only time in the *Diary* where he refers overtly to his experience as Freud's patient:

My own analysis could not be pursued deeply enough because my analyst (by his own admission, of a narcissistic nature), with his strong determination to be healthy and his antipathy toward any weaknesses or abnormalities, could not follow me down into those depths, and introduced the "educational" stage too soon. [1985, p. 62]

Because of his own experience of having been traumatized by his analysis with Freud (that is to say, by their entire relationship), Ferenczi identifies with *all* patients who have been mistreated by their parents or analysts. Drawing on his work with a female patient, "B.", he writes on 23 July, "It is unbearable for children to believe they alone are bad because they react to torture with rage", whereas adults "always are and always feel they are in the right" (1985, p. 167). Ferenczi then shifts to the first person: "so it is of some consolation when I succeed in making my respected father [*Herr Vater*] or teacher lose their tempers, making them admit indirectly that they are not any less subject to 'weaknesses' than their children". As we have seen, the desire to prove that "'adults' are just as 'bad' as 'children'" had previously fuelled Ferenczi's 1912 dream of the black cat, where he had sought to avoid being castrated for his love for Elma Pálos by citing the (real or symbolic) marital infidelities of his father and Freud. Thus, in reverting to the theme of making his father-figures "admit indirectly that they are not any less subject to 'weaknesses' than their children", Ferenczi is himself commenting "indirectly" on Freud's dangerous liaison with Minna Bernays.

Of all the concepts advanced by Ferenczi during his final period, none is more closely identified with Ferenczi himself than that of the "wise baby" (see Vida, 1996).[14] Near the end of the *Diary*, Ferenczi writes of a female patient, "G.", who was subjected to a "*sudden* shock (swift, unforeseen) when she observed her parents having intercourse" (1985, p. 202). As a consequence, she under-

---

In his climactic final entry of 2 October 1932, moreover, Ferenczi casts Freud as an uncaring divinity, the loss of whose protection is ultimately responsible for the pernicious anaemia that would soon cost Ferenczi his life:

> In my case the blood-crisis arose when I realized that not only can I not rely on the protection of a "higher power" but *on the contrary* I shall be trampled under foot by this indifferent power as soon as I go my own way and not his. [p. 212]

[14] Originally introduced in a brief communication of 1923, the concept receives its fullest elaborations in Ferenczi's classic papers, "Child analysis in the analysis of adults" (1931) and the posthumously published "Confusion of tongues between adults and the child" (1949), as well as in the *Clinical Diary*.

went a deep regression that led her to declare, "'I am so dreadfully alone, of course I haven't been born yet, I am floating in the womb'". Ferenczi elaborates:

> The patient became terribly intelligent; instead of hating her mother or father, she penetrated by her thought-processes their psychic mechanisms, motives, even their feelings so thoroughly . . . that she could apprehend the hitherto unbearable situation quite clearly. . . . The trauma made her emotionally embryonic, but at the same time wise in intellectual terms, like a totally objective and unemotionally perceptive philosopher. [p. 203]

Everything that Ferenczi says about "G." applies equally to himself, particularly to his relationship with Freud and disavowed awareness of Freud's illicit involvement with Minna Bernays. Like his patient, Ferenczi casts himself in the dream of the black cat in the role of a child whose father, "unsuspecting of my presence", exposes him to a primal scene. Also like "G.", Ferenczi, in his final diary entry on 2 October 1932, after his disastrous last meeting with Freud in Vienna and the ensuing debacle with his paper, "Confusion of tongues between adults and the child" (1949), at the Wiesbaden Congress, describes himself as having experienced a "further regression to being dead" and facing the danger of "not yet being born" (1985, p. 212). And no less than his patient, who is "dreadfully alone", Ferenczi confesses to feeling "abandoned by colleagues" who are cowed by their fear of Freud.

In his entry of 17 August, Ferenczi continues his meditation on "G." by remarking that she is "quite despairing" of his lack of analytic understanding because, in the patient's words, "'even he'" calls her marriage "'happy'", even though "'nothing could be further from my thoughts'"; after "'this reality was forced on me . . . the way to normal development was blocked: instead of loving and hating I could only identify with people'" (1985, pp. 204–205). Although Ferenczi never mentions his erotic triangle with Gizella and Elma Pálos in the Clinical Diary, this passage comments implicitly on Ferenczi's marriage to Gizella, a "reality" that had been "forced on" him by Freud, who then insisted on regarding this outcome as "happy", even though Ferenczi continued to chafe at the way it had prevented him from fulfilling his "normal development" with the younger woman who could have borne him children.[15] Indisputably, Ferenczi struggled with an inhibition in his capacity for both "loving and hating", and he rebuked himself in his final entry in the *Diary* for having chosen the path of "'identification' with the higher power"—namely, Freud—at the cost of having erected his personality on a "false and untrustworthy" foundation, a self-betrayal that Ferenczi believed to be responsible for his life-threatening illness.[16]

At the core of Ferenczi's theoretical disagreements with Freud during his final period was his effort to rehabilitate Freud's pre-1897 emphasis on "the traumatic factors in the pathogenesis of neurosis" that, as Ferenczi wrote in "Confusion of tongues", had been "unjustly neglected in recent years" (1949, p. 156). From his chastened perspective in the *Clinical Diary*, Ferenczi ruefully judged his long association with Freud—despite all that it had brought him personally and professionally—to have amounted to a massive cumulative trauma (see Khan, 1963). The practical lesson of Ferenczi's renewed attention to the importance of real experiences, whether those of children with their parents or of patients with their analysts, is that one ought to give credence to the perceptions of those who have been abused, especially when the perpetrators compound their original violations by seeking to convince their victims that what has been inflicted on them is only a figment of their overly florid fantasies.

In my reconstruction of the history of psychoanalysis, although Freud's relationship with Minna Bernays is rooted in his early experiences with two "mothers"—his young biological mother and the Czech nurse whom he described to Fliess as "his teacher in sexual

---

[15] On the tendentiousness of Freud's three published narratives of his relationship with Ferenczi, culminating in his disingenuous assertion in "Analysis terminable and interminable" (1937c) that Ferenczi "married the woman he loved" (p. 211), see my discussion in *Reading Psychoanalysis* (Rudnytsky, 2002, p. 112–119).

[16] On Ferenczi's confession of his "impotent rage" towards both his mother and Freud in his letter of 26 December 1912, see again my *Reading Psychoanalysis* (Rudnytsky, 2002, pp. 122–123), where I go on to detail (pp. 133–134) how Winnicott's (1960a) concept of the True and False Self epitomizes his affinity with Ferenczi.

matters" (Masson, 1985, p. 269: letter of 4 October 1897)—and inevitably laden with unconscious meanings, once he took the irrevocable step from the wish to the deed, their affair became for Freud a radioactive secret, which had at all costs to be encased in lead. This imperative not only shaped Freud's articulation of an analytic persona in both theory and practice, but also led to his defensive manoeuvres to safeguard his "authority" by repelling the longings of Jung and Ferenczi to get to know him as a human being. But what was a secret in Freud's personal life became for the psychoanalytic movement what Nicolas Abraham and Maria Torok (1987)—Hungarian-born analysts whose work is deeply indebted to Ferenczi—have termed a *phantom*. According to their conception, as Esther Rashkin has lucidly expounded:

> symptoms in specific patients might not be related to a conflict or trauma which they themselves have experienced and repressed, but could originate with someone else—usually a parent—who had concealed a secret so shameful that its contents had to be preserved intact lest their exposure threaten the integrity of the entire family. This secret, which the parent either repressed or simply kept silent about, would be transmitted unknowingly, and without ever being explicitly stated, through ciphered behaviors, affects, and language, directly from the parent into the unconscious of the child. [2006, p. 378]

As placed in a wider context by Abraham and Torok's compelling theory, Ferenczi's dismissal in 1912 of his awareness of the true nature of Freud's relationship with Minna Bernays as "only an infantile thought" is the effect of the phantom "transmitted unknowingly, and without ever being explicitly stated . . . directly from the parent into the unconscious of the child". Or, in Ferenczi's own language from the *Clinical Diary*, if he, like his patient "G.", is a traumatized "wise baby", "emotionally embryonic but at the same time wise in intellectual terms", this regression to a primitive state of mental functioning—far from invalidating his "fantasy" of what is going on between the parental couple—enables him to discern "their psychic mechanisms, motives, even their feelings so thoroughly" that he "could apprehend the hitherto unbearable situation quite clearly".

On 27 September 1932, in his first letter to Freud following the Wiesbaden Congress, the mortally ill Ferenczi writes:

You can tell by the length of the reaction time the depth of the shock
with which our conversation in Vienna before the Congress came
to me. Unfortunately, such things are always connected to bodily
ailments in me, so that my trip to the south of France by way of
Baden-Baden was and is, actually, a "voyage de lit-à-lit". [Falzeder
& Brabant, 2000, p. 443]

To convey the "depth of the shock" resulting from the trauma of his
final encounter with Freud, Ferenczi resorts to the same ambiguous
French phrase he had not used since his sublime self-analytic letter
of 26 December 1912. In the lexicon of Abraham and Torok, this is
an instance of *cryptonomy*, which Rashkin defines as a "new rhetorical figure" introduced by these analysts "to explain how the words
constitutive of the unspeakable secret are themselves sealed off
from awareness in one generation while they are phantasmatically
transmitted to the next" (2006, p. 378). Thus, beneath Ferenczi's
overt allusion to his own beds of affliction there lies, unbeknown
even to himself, a second level of meaning that summons the phantom of Freud's "unspeakable secret", the exposure of which would
indeed "threaten the integrity of the entire [psychoanalytic]
family".

Thus, with the aid of the *Clinical Diary*, we can conclude that
Ferenczi's 1912 "infantile thought" about Freud and Minna's
"voyage de lit-à-lit", in addition to what it reveals about Ferenczi's
"psychical reality", may also furnish an unexpectedly credible piece
of evidence concerning the "material reality" of this primordial
boundary violation in the history of psychoanalysis—Freud's adultery, which also constitutes incest, with his sister-in-law, Minna
Bernays.

CHAPTER THREE

Rescuing psychoanalysis from Freud: the common project of Stekel, Jung, and Ferenczi

"Prejudice is the hangman of Truth".

(Wilhelm Stekel, *Autobiography*, 1950)

N o event is more enthralling to psychoanalysts than the recovery of a lost object. Jaap Bos is, therefore, to be commended for having made available the first English translation of Wilhelm Stekel's seminal 1926 monograph, "On the history of the analytic movement", completed the previous June in response to Freud's *Autobiographical Study*, but borrowing its title from Freud's polemic of 1914 prompted by the defections of his two leading Viennese disciples, Adler and Stekel, as well as of Jung, his heir apparent in Zurich.[1] Grateful though I am to Bos for his labours on Stekel's behalf, however, I cannot agree with his theoretical

---

[1]Although Bos uses "analytical" in his version, I prefer the American spelling "analytic". For the sake of greater accuracy, I have provided my own translations from Stekel's essay, though page references to both the German and English versions are included for the reader's convenience.

perspective, either in his introductory essay (2005), published in *Psychoanalysis and History*, or in the article (2004) he co-authored with Leendert Groenendijk in the *International Journal of Psychoanalysis*.[2] Thus, I propose to begin by clarifying the nature of these disagreements. Then, I shall draw on my work in progress on Freud's relationship with Minna Bernays to show how the testimony of Jung and Ferenczi converges on certain key points. I shall use this material to argue, contrary to Bos, that it is the proper task of the historian to search for truth.[3] Following these two preliminary sections, I shall proceed to my main order of business: juxtaposing Stekel's critique of Freud with those offered by Jung and Ferenczi. Finally, after having established the existence of a collective diagnosis concerning what Ferenczi, in the heading to his 4 August 1932 entry in the *Clinical Diary*, called the "personal causes for the erroneous development of psychoanalysis" (1985, p. 184), I shall contend that this consensus, reached independently by Stekel, Jung, and Ferenczi, leads each of them to embark on the common project of rescuing psychoanalysis from Freud.

1

My disagreements with Bos exist on multiple levels, but the most fundamental concerns the relevance of biography to the study of the history of psychoanalysis in general, and to the interpretation of Stekel's "On the history of the analytic movement" in particular. Although Bos (2005) professes himself to be an advocate of a

---

[2] Both these texts are now included in Bos and Groenendijk's book, *The Self-Marginalization of Wilhlem Stekel* (2007). Although now conceding my priority in discovering that it was Stekel and not Jung who first drew Freud's attention to *Gradiva*, Bos (p. 32, n. 13) manages to avoid including in his bibliography either the essay (Rudnytsky, 1994) where I first reported that finding, or the 2006 article in *Psychoanalysis and History* that formed the original version of this chapter. For additional perspectives on Stekel in English, see Stanton (1988), Kuhn (1998), and especially Clark-Lowes (2001). Strikingly, there is no chapter on Stekel in the classic compendium *Psychoanalytic Pioneers* (Alexander, Eisenstein, & Grotjahn, 1966).

[3] On coherence, correspondence, and pragmatism as the criteria of "truth", see Charles Hanly's (2009) précis of the philosophical position of "critical realism", with which I would, in large measure, associate myself.

"dialogic approach" (p. 95), the dialogue in question is, for him, purely one between texts and not at all between the human beings who are the authors of those texts. Thus, he writes in his conclusion, "to identify in Stekel's *discourse* a desire to be acknowledged by Freud is not the same as ascribing a psychological motive, nor is it the same as psychoanalyzing the psychoanalyst".

But how can a "discourse" have a "desire"? In seeking to preclude readers from "ascribing a psychological motive" to an author and, thereby, to limit interpretation to a rhetorical analysis of "discursive processes" (2005, p. 95), Bos overlooks that in order to experience desire, it is necessary first to have a body, and a text, as a disembodied play of signifiers, can *express* a human desire, but cannot be its source or cause. Bos elaborates his position in the article co-authored with Groenendijk in the *International Journal*. There, the Dutch scholars acknowledge that in the texts arising from Freud's self-analysis (a category in which they expressly include only *The Interpretation of Dreams* and *The Psychopathology of Everyday Life*), "the personal is very much intertwined with the epistemological", and that to read them competently an "intimate knowledge of the narrator's life is required" (2004, p. 716). Having conceded this fundamental point, however, Bos and Groenendijk try to blunt its force by contending that there is

> an unintended consequence to this tying of the self to its own accounts, which could be called the autobiographical trap: all accounts lose their innocence and are forever referred back to the autobiographical self since no one can escape the self. Consequently, ever since Freud it has become common practice to demand from people that they reveal their autobiographical self in their accounts. [p. 717]

As I have argued in *Freud and Oedipus* (1987), however, "*all* Freud's psychoanalytic writings may be read as fragments of his interminable self-analysis" (p. 7; italics added), not simply those dating from 1900 or 1901. Thus, I concur with Bos and Groenendijk that the "personal" is inextricably intertwined with the "epistemological" in psychoanalysis, though it is surely an "intimate knowledge" of the life of Freud the *author* rather than of Freud the *narrator* that is required. But where they go most seriously astray is in insinuating that an acceptance of this subjective dimension of theory formation is an "unintended consequence" of a psychoanalytic hermeneutic stance, and in referring to it as a "trap". It is, likewise, incorrect that anyone "demands" from authors that "they reveal their autobiographical self". From a psychoanalytic perspective, such self-revelations are not primarily under the sway of one's conscious volition—in the manner of Rousseau striving to convince the reader of his sincerity in the *Confessions*—but are, rather, bound up in a dialectical process whereby it is precisely an individual's attempts at self-concealment that inadvertently expose his or her most intimate truths.

Thus, when Bos and Groenendijk go on to affirm that "the autobiographical trap has implications for the position of the interpreter as well—he, too, cannot escape his own discourses" (2004, p. 717), I again agree with their logic, but not with their assumption that this constitutes a *refutation* of the need to attend to the subjective dimension of psychoanalytic texts. On the contrary, to extend the web of often inadvertent self-implication to include the interpreter of a text is simply to recognize that the reader—like the analyst in a clinical situation—does not enjoy a position of absolute mastery, but is, rather, embedded in an intersubjective matrix in which all understanding remains provisional and the quest for self-knowledge can never be complete. In the words of Hans-Georg Gadamer, "We are always within the situation, and to throw light on it is never complete. . . . To exist historically means that one's knowledge of oneself can never be complete" (1960, p. 269; see Rudnytsky, 1987, pp. 51–52).

My methodological disagreements with Bos and Groenendijk come to a head in their assessment of Stekel, whom they describe as having been "quick to draw the conclusion that nobody could escape the autobiographical trap, not even—or perhaps, in particular, not—the master himself", and, indeed, as having been "perhaps the first in what has become a whole industry of discovering Freud beneath Freud" (2004, p. 717). Ironically, it is again only their condescending tone—conveyed through such words as "quick", "trap", and "industry"—that prevents Bos and Groenendijk from realizing that they have actually paid Stekel a very high compliment.[4]

---

[4] In thus inadvertently praising Stekel's acumen as an interpreter of Freud, Bos and Groenendijk (2004) single out the 1 January 1911 meeting of the Vienna

In "discovering Freud beneath Freud", that is, Stekel lays bare the existence of Freud the man within the texts that bear his name. What is more, he dares to suppose that Freud, too, is a human being to whom the teachings of psychoanalysis apply as much as they do to his disciples or patients. In so doing, Stekel implicitly challenges Freud's authoritarianism, and, thereby, he deserves to be honoured as "perhaps the first" to have undertaken the heroic mission of rescuing psychoanalysis from Freud.

Bos's aversion to psychological interpretation leads him to underestimate vastly the importance of the text that it is his merit to have recovered from oblivion. Indeed, in his opinion, Stekel's "On the history of the analytic movement" "does not record anything that we do not already know by now" (2005, p. 88). But nothing could be further from the truth. Stekel, for instance, reprints the entire transcript of the "Conversation on smoking" from what was, in fact, the very first meeting of the five-person Psychological Wednesday Society—originally published on 28 January 1903 in the *Prager Tageblatt* (Mühlleitner, 1992, p. 320)—in the course of which the character called "The Master", whom Stekel expressly identifies as Freud, declares, "A clever girl who is known to me smoked passionately. Asked about it, she defended herself in a charming poem. In a nutshell, its meaning was: 'I smoke so much because I am kissed so little'" (1926, p. 544; 2005, p. 104). From this statement, we are now able to say that Freud continued to refer to Anna von Lieben, his most important early analytic patient—to whom he gave the pseudonym of "Frau Cäcilie M." in *Studies on Hysteria*—in the present tense as late as 1903, even though she had

---

Psychoanalytic Society, in which "Freud presented a dream of his own" and Stekel was the only discussant "who dared allow the dream to point back to Freud" (p. 717). But, in addition to inaccurately citing Volume 2 instead of 3 of Nunberg and Federn's *Minutes* (1974) as their source, Bos and Groenendijk make a graver error, since the autobiographical nature of Freud's "dream about Savonarola" is pointed out by the editors in a footnote, but is nowhere intimated by Stekel. He does, however, allege that the dream is "a typical masturbation dream", and takes issue with Freud by arguing, first, that "every symbol is bisexual" and, second, that Freud's continued flirtation with Fliess's theory of periodicity exhibits "a tendency to divert the interpreter of the dream away from psychological interpretation" (pp. 183–184).

died in 1900.[5] A no less savoury historical titbit is Stekel's account of his retort to Freud at the 1911 Weimar Congress, when the latter compared Schreber to an eagle because "only eagles are permitted to look into the sun without being punished". As Stekel informs his readers, he "aroused incessant storms of laughter" when he responded, "Freud too has an eagle [*Adler*] in Vienna who dared to look into the Freudian sun unpunished" (1926, p. 565; 2005, p. 121).

These additions to the psychoanalytic archive suffice to refute Bos's claim that Stekel's text "does not record anything that we do not already know". Even more important than such items of "objective" data, however, are Stekel's impressions as a participant–observer in the early history of the psychoanalytic movement; and here again, I find Bos's commentary to be misguided in the extreme.

To begin with, although Bos emphasizes that it is not his "aim to establish the truth or falsehood of Stekel's narrative", this does not prevent him from declaring, "some of Stekel's assertions in this paper are demonstrably incorrect" (2005, p. 83). What, then, does Bos allege to be Stekel's falsehoods? The first is that Stekel claimed that his presentation at the 1910 Nuremberg Congress, in Bos's words, "resulted in the creation of a research committee that was to collect dream symbols", whereas from a letter from Freud to Ferenczi on 25 February 1910, "we learn that Freud had the intention of asking Stekel to form such a committee months before the congress". But if Stekel had no advance knowledge of Freud's scheme, which was formulated with the avowed purpose of

---

[5] On Anna von Lieben, see the definitive article by Peter Swales (1986), to whom I am indebted for alerting me to Freud's mention of her in the "Conversation on smoking". According to Swales, Freud's treatment of von Lieben, whom he dubbed his "teacher" (*Lehrmeisterin*), extended from 1889 to 1893; the poem in question appeared in a volume published posthumously in 1901. In a footnote, Swales observes that von Lieben "supposes in one of her poems that frequently women smoke cigarettes because, in truth, they yearn to be kissed", though he cautions that "whether she herself smoked, I cannot say" (p. 74, n. 60). Thanks to Stekel, we can confirm that Anna von Lieben indeed "smoked passionately". That the "Conversation on smoking" was the subject of the first meeting of the Wednesday-night group is affirmed by Stekel in his *Autobiography* (1950, p. 166). Besides himself and Freud, the other participants were Max Kahane, Rudolf Reitler, and Alfred Adler, all five of whom were physicians.

curbing Stekel's influence, how can he be blamed for supposing that the idea arose only after the Nuremberg Congress? This is an indictment of *Freud's* machinations, not of Stekel's good-faith report of what he believed to be true. Later in his article, Bos seizes on "a subtle but significant difference" (p. 87) between two accounts by Stekel of Freud's behaviour at the Nuremberg Congress, where his Viennese followers had met in secret to try to combat his plan to install Jung as president for life of the newly formed International Psychoanalytic Association. When Freud unexpectedly burst in on the meeting, Stekel writes in the "History" that "tears welled up in his eyes" (1926, p. 557; 2005, p. 115), whereas in his posthumously published *Autobiography*, Stekel recalls that "tears were streaming down his cheeks" (1950, p. 129).

Unlike Bos, I fail to see why this minor difference in wording between two accounts composed nearly a quarter of a century apart is "significant".[6] With utter consistency, both in the *Autobiography* (1950, p. 129) and in the "History", Stekel quotes Freud as having said of the representatives of "official science", " 'They begrudge the coat I am wearing' " (1926, p. 557; 2005, p. 115). It is not disputed that Freud was crying on both occasions while making a reference to losing the clothes on his back, and what Swales would call Stekel's "mnemonic integrity"[7] is, accordingly, beyond question. Indeed, in his 4 August 1932 entry to the *Clinical Diary*, Ferenczi recalls the "somewhat ridiculous" emotion with which Freud, "almost with tears in his eyes" (1985, p. 184), thanked Stanley Hall for the honorary doctorate bestowed on him by Clark University in 1909, thereby lending credence to the portrait of Freud that emerges from Stekel's recollections.

Compounding Bos's failure to see that "On the history of the analytic movement" contains a treasure trove of new insights and

---

[6] In his *Autobiography*, Stekel inaccurately assigns the controversy over the scheme to appoint Jung as lifetime president of the International Psychoanalytic Association to the 1911 Weimar Congress, but the substance of his narrative is otherwise unchanged from the "History".

[7] I borrow this phrase from an unpublished manuscript by Swales (2005) on Jung's 1953 interview with Kurt Eissler, derestricted in 2003 by the Freud Archives, which supports Swales' thesis that Freud engaged in a love affair with his sister-in-law, Minna Bernays. See Chapter Two, n. 4, above.

information, and his unwarranted attacks on Stekel's veracity in matters of fact, is his misrepresentation of the spirit in which Stekel wrote his text. In Bos's (2005) opinion, the "History" is an "extremely bitter and spiteful" work (p. 82). Insisting that Stekel shows himself to be "extremely vengeful toward Freud", while harbouring "the need to express his gratitude", Bos characterizes the "History" as "a strange mixture of overstatement and self-pity" (p. 84).

What is Bos's evidence for these aspersions? He cites Stekel's description of Freud as a person who "persecuted and taunted me and tried to harm me in a narrow-minded way" (2005, pp. 82–83; see Stekel, 1926, p. 564; 2005, p. 120). According to Bos's own article, however, Stekel's judgement of Freud is accurate. Bos himself reminds us of Freud's letter to Stekel's American ally, Samuel Tannenbaum, describing Stekel as "a terrible man", and it is Bos who paraphrases another letter from Freud to Smith Ely Jelliffe in which he "confessed to the latter that he doubted his intentions merely because he spotted him once in the company of Stekel" (2005, p. 86; see Stekel, 1926, p. 570; 2005, p. 125). Indeed, Bos concedes that Stekel's belief that Freud regarded him as "one of his worst enemies" was "not an exaggeration", adding that Freud "developed a complete and absolute aversion to Stekel".

But, given the validity of Stekel's perception of Freud as someone endowed with a "pathological degree of vengefulness" (1926, p. 564; 2005, p. 120), the full brunt of which he himself had borne, Bos's contention that Stekel's work is "extremely bitter and spiteful" can be dismissed as unfounded. On the contrary, there is no reason to question Stekel's declaration in his opening paragraph:

> I am not vengeful and am able to forgive very easily because I have looked with favor on what is universally human in many responses even in times when psychoanalysis was still an unknown concept to me. [1926, p. 539; 2005, p. 99]

It was, after all, Stekel who reached out to Freud after the latter underwent surgery for cancer of his jaw in 1923, and Freud who rebuffed this overture of reconciliation. Later, when Freud arrived in England as a refugee, whither he had been preceded by Stekel, it was again Stekel who, in 1938, "wrote him a letter expressing the wish to bridge our antagonisms" (1950, p. 284), to which Freud did not reply. Notwithstanding a litany of bitter experiences, Stekel in his "History" quotes the tribute he paid in his 1907 pamphlet, *Nervous Anxiety States*, to "the one who showed me this way and to whom I owe the new light that has illuminated much for me that was formerly dark . . . the great soul expert, Professor Sigmund Freud" (1926, p. 547; 2005, p. 106). He reaffirms in closing, "In spite of everything that Freud has done to me, I am still grateful to him and perhaps value him more highly than do many of his satellites who give themselves out to be his best friends" (1926, p. 575; 2005, p. 129).

According to Bos, the mixed judgement that Stekel passes on Freud amounts to "a strange mixture of overstatement and self-pity". Far from engaging in either "overstatement" or "self-pity", however, what Bos reprehends as Stekel's "strange mixture" of emotions is rather his exemplary solution to the problem of transference to Freud still faced by labourers in the psychoanalytic vineyard. How do we escape at once the Scylla of Freud-bashing and the Charybdis of Freudolatry? How do we acknowledge our debt to this towering genius while not turning a blind eye to the human failings that wounded an incalculable number of people and made him, in the aptly chosen words of Isidor Sadger, "not merely the father of psychoanalysis but also its tyrant" (1930, p. 34; 2005, p. 40)?[8]

In today's world, Freud's authority is no longer exercised through his personal charisma but solely through the enduring power of his texts as well as through the institutions (the International Psychoanalytic Association, the Freud Archives, etc.) that act in his name. As I have contended in the opening chapter, the

---

[8] I take this phrase from another recently rediscovered text, Sadger's memoir, *Freud: Persönliche Errinerungen*. Because of the deficiencies of the English edition by Alan Dundes (Sadger, 2005), I have translated all quotations and include the page numbers to both the German and English versions. Despite their mutual antipathy, the portraits of Freud drawn by Stekel and Sadger closely resemble one another. Sadger, who challenges Stekel's description of the Nuremberg Congress as "no less objectionable than Freud's" (1930, p. 60; 2005, p. 79), seems clearly to have read Stekel's "History". Compare my characterization of Freud as "at once the founder and betrayer of psychoanalysis" in *Reading Psychoanalysis* (Rudnytsky, 2002, p. 205).

paradigm shift wrought in recent decades by progressive forces has largely succeeded in emancipating psychoanalysis from the baleful aspects of his legacy. But the situation was altogether different for Stekel and the other first-generation pioneers for whom Freud was a living and often fearsome presence. As Bos himself admits, Stekel "desperately wanted Freud to understand him" (2005, p. 85). In a footnote, Bos quotes (p. 90) from Stekel's letter of 22 January 1924, written in response to Freud's callous rejection of Stekel's appeal for a rapprochement following the diagnosis of Freud's life-threatening cancer:

> You see only the wrongdoings that have been done to you, and you overlook the mistakes that you have made. Had you acknowledged the sources from which the rivalry between your students arose in time, you could have retained many useful hands. *It was not only a struggle of the pretenders to the throne, but a competition for your love. It had more to do with jealousy for your heart than a claim on your head.*
> [italics added]

Here, Stekel sounds the depths of the tragedy of Freud's failed relationships to many of his most gifted disciples. Beneath the struggle waged by the "pretenders to the throne" of Freud, the Oedipal father, there lies their "jealousy" for the "heart" of Freud the narcissistic mother. It is this desire for love and recognition from someone to whom they owed so much, but which Freud refused to dispense unconditionally—instead demanding fealty to himself and his doctrines as the price of his approbation—that ultimately drove Stekel, Jung, and Ferenczi (as well as Fliess, Breuer, Adler, Tausk, and Rank, among others) to distraction and dissension.[9]

Although Bos pays lip service to Stekel's need to be understood by Freud, his commitment to a purely rhetorical notion of dialogue prevents him from taking the implications of this need seriously.

---

[9] In addition to these well-known names, one should not forget Max Kahane, one of the original members of the Psychological Wednesday Society, about whom Stekel remarks that "the way he spoke about Freud cannot possibly be reproduced here" (1926, p. 570; 2005, pp. 124–125). Sadger, too, singles out the brutality of Freud's repudiation in 1908 of "this sagacious, deserving and highly respected colleague", whose only "crime" was that "he had known the great man when he was still a little student at the Gymnasium, that is to say, while still in his tattered boots" (1930, p. 36; 2005, pp. 43–44).

He observes that Stekel "did not want to put himself on a par with Freud, and never wanted to claim that he was a genius, yet in all his writings he attempted to prove that he was at least his equal" (2005, p. 91). For Bos, this attempt to claim equality with Freud is another indication of Stekel's penchant for "overstatement" and "self-pity". In my view, however, when Stekel writes, "I do not want to measure myself against Freud. I have never presumed to do so. I want only justice. I received much from Freud. I have given him at least as much, if not more" (1926, p. 571; 2005, p. 126), he properly concedes Freud's intellectual superiority while courageously standing up for his own right to be regarded as Freud's equal *in human terms*. Indeed, in his quotient of fundamental decency, Stekel may well have been the more richly endowed spirit of the two.

This return to Bos's insistence on excluding the human being behind the texts from his commentary on Stekel's "On the history of the analytic movement" brings me to a final respect in which I disagree with his theoretical perspective. In discussing what he terms the "dialectic of antagonism" (2005, p. 90) between Freud and Stekel, Bos advances the view that "because the marginal position is a position in its own right", Stekel's "marginalization was a beneficial, not a destructive, factor in the construction of his position in the psychoanalytic community" (p. 91). Extending this principle, Bos adds that "marginalization is a process that takes place with the full consent of the marginalized".[10]

A *beneficial* factor? A process with the *full consent* of the marginalized? This is preposterous. Does Bos suppose that Stekel was joking when he protested that Freud "and his pupils outdo each other in the ridiculing and depreciating of my works", and that "no man wants to be depicted before the entire public as a man who has gone astray" (1926, p. 575; 2005, p. 129)? Or that it gratified Stekel

---

[10] Elaborating this position in the introduction of their book, Bos and Groenendijk (2004) assert that marginalization "presupposes active cooperation of two parties", and, thus, should be distinguished from "stigmatization" or "disciplining" (p. 5). But this is Humpty-Dumpty logic: because marginalization "presupposes" co-operation, if Stekel was "marginalized", then the process must have been benign and voluntary. It is an entirely different matter to say that, once a subject has been marginalized, this "can result in a position that has *positive* values" (p. 4), as in Hegel's master–slave dialectic.

to be the object of Freud's "irreconcilable hate" and the edict that he "was not allowed to be quoted" (1926, p. 570; 2005, p. 125) in books and papers by other analysts? Or to be told that he was "not a scientific researcher" (1926, p. 549; 2005, p. 109)?

Because of his fallacious premise that Stekel is to blame for his own ostracism, Bos cannot fathom that what Stekel, as late as 1926, still hoped to receive from Freud was, if not love, at least a measure of genuine respect and recognition. "What Stekel demanded from Freud," he maintains, "was a continuation of the antagonistic dialectic that had driven their relationship" (2005, p. 94). But even this misguided interpretation cannot be squared with Bos's postmodernist opposition to "ascribing a psychological motive" to the authors of texts. "The marginalization of Stekel is not," he iterates in his conclusion, "in my opinion, a problem of personalities" (p. 95).

2

In the course of my research on Freud's relationship with Minna Bernays, I have been struck by the convergence of the testimony provided independently by Jung and Ferenczi on a number of key points. Although Bos doubts whether "it is the task of the historian to straighten out biases and misconceptions" (2005, p. 81), in my view, this time-honoured aspiration remains integral to the historian's *raison d'être*, however difficult it may be to realize in practice. The quest for truth proceeds simultaneously on two tracks—one of objective facts, the other of subjective interpretations.

To take a single paradigmatic example, in a 1957 interview with the American theologian John Billinsky (1969), Jung stated that during their trip to America in 1909, Freud "developed severe neuroses" that took the form of "psychosomatic troubles" and "difficulties in controlling his bladder" (p. 42). This interview, which Billinsky did not publish even in abbreviated form until 1969, is also the source for Jung's assertion that, on his first visit to Vienna in 1907, he had been told by Minna Bernays that "Freud was in love with her and their relationship was indeed very intimate".[11]

---

[11] See again Chapter Two, n. 4, above, where I have observed that in the summary that Billinsky committed to paper in Zurich immediately following

As Jung confided to Billinsky, the dreams that Freud had on the trip "were about the triangle—Freud, his wife, and wife's younger sister", and it was in the course of Jung's attempt to analyse one such dream that Freud uttered the fateful words, "'I could tell you more, but I cannot risk my authority'".

As I conceded in the previous chapter, it is again beyond my scope here to muster all the evidence that Freud engaged in a sexual liaison with Minna Bernays. But establishing the credibility of Jung's testimony is essential to that larger project, just as it is to my immediate concern with what Jung, Ferenczi, and Stekel have to tell us about Freud's character. For my present purposes, it suffices to focus on Jung's remark concerning Freud's "difficulties in controlling his bladder", about which scepticism has been voiced by Harold Blum:

> Freud was apparently also affected by a prostate or bladder condition. Jung claimed that he had an episode of urinary incontinence, with fears of recurrence. As Freud had already had indications from Jung and Sabina Spielrein, and as Freud was to further learn, Jung's reliability and ethics left much to be desired and questioned. [1998, p. 46]

In this passage, the Director of the Freud Archives moves from subtly questioning Jung's avowal that Freud "had an episode of urinary incontinence" while visiting the United States to casting a wholesale aspersion on Jung's "reliability and ethics".

Thus, it becomes of considerable interest to note that Ferenczi, in the pivotal entry of 4 August 1932 to his *Clinical Diary*, recalls "the two hysterical symptoms" he had "observed" in Freud: "(1) the fainting in Bremen, (2) the incontinence on Riverside Drive" (1985, p. 184). The fainting spell in Bremen took place just before the expedition to America, on which, as we recall from the previous chapter, Ferenczi had accompanied Freud and Jung; and since Ferenczi, like Jung, attests to Freud's "incontinence on Riverside Drive", we

---

the interview, he quotes Jung as saying, "I learned [from Minna Bernays] that Freud was in love with her and had sexual relations with her". In addition to removing any ambiguity in what is meant by "very intimate" in the published text, Billinsky's reticence attests to his desire to shield Freud, at least partially, from Jung's revelations.

have not one but *two* witnesses—one writing in a private journal in 1932, the other speaking to an interviewer in 1957—who independently recollect that Freud lost control of his bladder in New York City in 1909.[12]

In light of this incontrovertible evidence, which was available to Blum at the time he published his article, for him to hedge by saying that Freud "was *apparently* also affected by a prostate or bladder condition", and that this was merely something *"claimed"* by Jung, is grasping at straws. With as much certainty as can ever be ascribed to a historical event, we *know* that this happened! Blum's impugning of Jung's "reliability and ethics", which is presented as though it followed logically from the preceding sentences, is, thus, nothing more than a smear.[13]

In this example, we see the inseparability of the objective and the subjective dimensions of the historian's quest for truth. The

---

[12] Jung also disclosed this incident in a 1955 interview with Saul Rosenzweig, who shows in his indispensable book, *Freud, Jung, and Hall the King-Maker* (1992, pp. 64–67), that it can be dated to 2 September 1909. Just as Jung prolonged the conversation with Billinsky, telling him, "Sit down, sit down. Don't worry about the time. I am the one to tell you when the time is up" (Billinsky, 1969, p. 41), in order to unburden himself of his story concerning Freud and Minna, so, too, Rosenzweig reports of Jung's response when he broached the topic of the 1909 voyage to America: "At first Jung appeared a bit reluctant but the hesitancy was brief, and he soon was rather eagerly discussing the topic. He appeared to be deriving some special satisfaction from the disclosures he was making about Freud" (1992, p. 64). That breaking the seal of these long-held confidences should have been a cathartic experience for Jung is understandable, and the similarity in his behaviour with Rosenzweig and Billinsky—an initial reluctance to speak about a sensitive matter followed by an opening of the floodgates—gives the accounts of both interviewers the ring of truth.

[13] Blum continues in the following sentence: "Prior to his death, Jung admitted having lied to Freud about dream associations concerning death wishes to Freud" (1998, p. 46). To be sure, in *Memories, Dreams, Reflections*, Jung acknowledges that he "deceived" Freud and "told him a lie" in associating to a dream, and that this conduct "was morally not unobjectionable" (1963, p. 164). But, as I have highlighted in Chapter Two, n. 9, above, Jung is here tacitly communicating his knowledge of Freud's affair with Minna Bernays, and there is, accordingly, a great deal going on beneath the surface of this interaction. Blum, moreover, fails to consider that Jung's willingness to confess his duplicitous behaviour in the past, and, thus, to show himself in an unfavourable light, may actually *augment* his credibility in the present, rather than the reverse.

objective dimension involves piecing together the facts about a particular episode—here, Freud's "urinary incontinence"—by sifting through the relevant testimony along with any other documentary evidence that might be available.[14] The subjective dimension ensues when one seeks to construct a narrative that elucidates the significance of a given concatenation of facts and reports, which may or may not be consistent with one another.

Although questions of meaning, unlike questions of fact, are inherently open-ended and unresolvable, I regard it as axiomatic that any interpretation that flies in the face of the empirical evidence—while it may warrant examination for what it reveals about the interpreter—should be disregarded in so far as the subject at hand is concerned. In this instance, because Jung and Ferenczi can be shown to have been telling the truth about a decisive event in their relationship with Freud, there is every reason to lend credence to their judgements as to its purport. Conversely, because Blum cavalierly treats a matter of ascertainable fact as though it were no more than Jung's opinion, one is entitled to discount his pronouncements on Jung's character. Indeed, Blum's pro-Freudian bias accounts for his unwarranted scepticism about Jung's credibility in the first place.

Likewise indisputably true is Jung's recollection to Billinsky of the sentence with which Freud in 1909 had refused to proceed with the analysis of one of his dreams, "'I could tell you more, but I cannot risk my authority'". Nevertheless, in the course of a turgid polemic attacking Jung's allegation of an affair between Freud and Minna Bernays, Kurt Eissler—Blum's predecessor as Director of the Freud Archives—observes that this statement "sounds strange from [Freud's] mouth" (1994, p. 131). Had Jung not quoted it in a letter to Freud without eliciting any objection, Eissler adds, "I, for one, would have doubted its authenticity" (p. 132). Even so, he speculates, "one sometimes does not correct or refute a statement because to do so would require drawn-out explanations or lead to unending wrangles".

---

[14] As corroboration of the veracity of Jung's report, Rosenzweig (1992, pp. 65–66) cites the disjointedness of, and complaints of fatigue in, Freud's letter to his family in Vienna on 2–3 September 1909. This text is now available in Tögel's (2002, pp. 303–306) edition of Freud's travel letters.

The letter to Freud in which Jung reminded the latter of what he had said to him in New York City in 1909 was written on 3 December 1912, and it precipitated the denouement in their relationship.[15] The magical thinking to which Eissler resorts in order to try to wish away an utterance repeatedly cited by Jung as having been ultimately responsible for his break with Freud would be risible were it not so mean-spirited. Blinded by the presumption that he knows what "sounds strange" coming from Freud, even the appearance of the offending remark in the posthumously published Freud–Jung correspondence does not suffice to induce Eissler to admit that Freud must have said it in the first place.

Unfortunately for Eissler, no less than for Blum, Ferenczi's testimony again vindicates the accuracy of Jung's recollection. In a letter to Freud on 19 October 1911, accompanying a letter from Emma Jung that he was indiscreetly forwarding to Freud, Ferenczi admits that Jung's wife "could be partly right in her assertions (where she talks about your antipathy toward giving completely of yourself as a friend)". But, Ferenczi adds, "it is certainly false that it is your 'authority' that you want to protect" (Brabant, Falzeder, & Giampieri-Deutsch 1993, p. 412). Although Emma Jung's letter is now lost, Ferenczi here alludes unmistakably to Freud's words in New York, which Jung must have repeated to his wife, who in turn quoted them back to Ferenczi in her letter. Thus, as with Freud's incontinence, Jung is shown to have told the truth to Billinsky about what took place in the confrontation between him and Freud, while Eissler's demurral, like Blum's, is exposed as an example of the "Jung-bashing" that originated with Freud himself and has too often been perpetuated by the psychoanalytic establishment.

3

It is in the context of this congruence between the accounts of Freud offered independently by Jung and Ferenczi that I now approach

---

[15] The fact that more than three years elapsed before this event was brought up by either Freud *or* Jung attests to the capacity of both men to bury the traumatic moments in their relationship. This long silence in turn renders it plausible that Jung could never bring himself openly to confront Freud with what Minna Bernays had told him in 1907 about her intimacy with her brother-in-law. See also notes 31 and 34, below.

the reading of Stekel's "On the history of the analytic movement". Even more important than their consistency in matters of fact, however, is the agreement between Ferenczi, Jung, and Stekel in what they have to say about Freud the man, and what the insights of these disillusioned colleagues still have to teach us about the "personal causes for the erroneous development of psychoanalysis".

The nub of Jung's critique of Freud, given its widest dissemination in *Memories, Dreams, Reflections*, is that, in calling a halt to the analysis of his dream in New York, he "placed personal authority above truth" (1963, p. 162). In the exchange of letters that followed Freud's second fainting spell in Jung's presence (this one in Munich in November 1912), Jung was incensed above all by Freud's refusal to take seriously its significance as a neurotic symptom. Recalling his earlier fainting spell in 1909, Freud wrote to Jung on 28 November 1912:

> My attack in Munich was no more serious than the similar one at the Essighaus in Bremen. . . . According to my private diagnosis, it was migraine (of the M. ophthalm. type), not without a psychic factor which unfortunately I haven't time to track down now. . . . A bit of neurosis that I ought really to look into. [McGuire, 1974, p. 524]

Seizing on Freud's guarded admission of a "psychic factor" in his two fainting spells, Jung unleashed the resentments he had accumulated over many years in his response on 3 December:

> My very best thanks for one passage in your letter, where you speak of a "bit of neurosis" you haven't got rid of. This "bit" should, in my opinion, be taken very seriously indeed. . . .

> As for this "bit of neurosis," may I draw to your attention to the fact that you begin *The Interpretation of Dreams* with the mournful admission of your own neurosis—the dream of Irma's injection—identification with the neurotic in need of treatment. Very momentous.

> Our analysis, you may remember, came to an end with your remark that you "could not submit to analysis *without losing your authority*." These words are engraved on my memory as a symbol of everything to come. But I have not had to crawl to the cross.[16] [p. 526]

---

[16] I have modified the translation of the final sentence, since the version in McGuire's English edition, "*I* haven't had to eat my words, however," misses

Finally, after Freud had drawn attention to a minor slip in one of Jung's intervening letters, Jung exploded in still greater wrath on 18 December 1912:

> I admit the ambivalence of my feelings towards you. . . . I would, however, point out that your technique of treating your pupils like patients is a *blunder*. . . . You go around sniffing out all the symptomatic actions in your vicinity, thus reducing everyone to the level of sons or daughters who blushingly admit the existence of their faults. Meanwhile you remain on top as the father, sitting pretty. For sheer obsequiousness nobody dares to pluck the prophet by the beard and inquire for once what you would say to a patient with a tendency to analyze the analyst instead of himself. You would certainly ask him: *"Who's* got the neurosis?"
>
> . . . I am not in the least neurotic—touch wood! I have submitted *lege artis et tout humblement* to analysis and am much the better for it. You know, of course, how far a patient gets with self-analysis: *not* out of his neurosis—just like you. [p. 535]

These passages should be very familiar to students of psychoanalysis, but they repay continued reflection. It is clear that Jung is in the grip of intense emotions, and his insistence that he is "not in the least neurotic" does not deserve to be taken seriously. At the same time, it is imperative to recognize that Jung's anger does not automatically invalidate his critique of Freud, and that what he has to say is corroborated by both Ferenczi and Stekel.

Jung reproaches Freud for the hypocrisy inherent in taking it upon himself to be the analyst of others despite never having been analysed himself, especially when his behaviour—culminating in his most recent fainting spell—had proved that he suffered from a neurosis for which therapy was plainly indicated. As late as 1932, as we have seen, when Ferenczi renders his final verdict on Freud in his *Clinical Diary*, he recalls the same events of 1909—the fainting spell in Bremen and the urinary incontinence in New York—that, reinforced by the fainting spell in Munich, Jung believed had

---

Jung's scathing irony in the image of "crawling to the cross"—referring to a Jew who undergoes conversion and baptism—to describe Freud's being overtaken by neurosis in his fainting episodes.

exposed the chinks in Freud's character armour. What is more, the judgements passed by Ferenczi, based on his observations going back more than two decades, are identical to those that Jung had reached in the letters he wrote to Freud at the time of their break.

In his diary entry, "Personal causes for the erroneous development of psychoanalysis", Ferenczi remarks of Freud:

> The anxiety-provoking idea, perhaps very strong in the unconscious, that the father must die when the son grows up explains his fear of allowing any one of his sons to become independent. At the same time, it also shows us that Freud as the son really did want to kill his father. Instead of admitting this, he founded the theory of the parricidal Oedipus, but obviously applied only to others, not to himself. Hence the fear of allowing himself to be analyzed. [1985, pp. 184–185]

Having just recalled Freud's "two hysterical symptoms" of fainting and incontinence, Ferenczi, like Jung, links them to Freud's "fear of allowing himself to be analyzed". He amplifies this point in contemplating the advantages he had once derived from "following blindly":

> the calm, unemotional reserve; the unruffled assurance that one knew better; and the theories, the seeking and finding of the causes of failure in the patient instead of partly in ourselves. The dishonesty of reserving the technique for one's own person; the advice not to permit patients to learn anything about the technique. [p. 185]

Ferenczi concludes his indictment of the man whom he had once venerated so deeply with the sentence: "In his conduct, Fr[eud] plays only the role of the castrating god, he wants to ignore the traumatic moment of his own castration in childhood; he is the only one who does not have to be analyzed" (p. 188).

As one of the Viennese followers whom Freud always kept at arm's length, Stekel, in all likelihood, had no knowledge of his fainting episodes in either Bremen or Munich, nor had he been on the voyage to America. But the fact that Stekel arrived, on the basis of his own experiences, at the same conclusions as Jung and Ferenczi, who had been his adversaries in psychoanalytic politics—most notably, over Freud's scheme in 1911 to install Jung as lifetime

President of the International Psychoanalytic Association—only makes his testimony more valuable and compelling. Justly arguing that the "so-called scientific differences" between Freud and Jung were at bottom instigated by "personal rivalry" (1926, p. 569; 2005, p. 124), Stekel, no less than Jung and Ferenczi, deemed it "Freud's tragedy that he has never been analyzed himself. He needed it just as much as many of his pupils" (1926, p. 571; 2005, p. 126).

In an incisive appraisal of the dispute in the Vienna Psycho-analytic Society, chiefly between Freud and Stekel, over whether or not masturbation had harmful physical effects, Groenendijk (1997) has revived Marianne Krüll's (1979, p. 190) hypothesis that Stekel's rejection of Freud's theory of "present-day neurosis"[17] in favour of the theory that any ill effects of masturbation should, rather, be attributed to psychic conflicts was disturbing to Freud for personal reasons. It was so, Groenendijk contends, because it would have forced Freud, "who described himself as a sufferer from neuras-thenic and anxiety neurotic symptoms", to "reexamine the biologi-cal explanation of his complaints", as a result of which "a further exploration of the depths of his soul would be necessary" (1997, p. 90). But since "Freud had never been analyzed by anyone else", Groenendijk elaborates, and the prospect of undergoing therapy with Stekel was intolerable to him, he coped with this dilemma by insisting on the rightness of his theory and ultimately expelling Stekel from the Vienna Society.[18]

---

[17] I prefer to use the literal translation "present-day neurosis" instead of the customary "actual neurosis" for Freud's German term *Aktualneurose*.

[18] Because of his focus on the topic of masturbation, Groenendijk sees the struggle between Freud and Stekel over the editorship of the *Zentralblatt für Psychoanalyse* as having been no more than a "pretext" (1997, p. 88) used by Freud to expel Stekel when the time came. In support of this construction, he cites Stekel's statement in the "History" that "Freud could never forgive me for being the one who pointed out the harmlessness of masturbation" (1926, p. 549; 2005, p. 108). Groenendijk, however, overlooks that Stekel also says, with res-pect to his defeat of Freud over the *Zentralblatt*, "Now came the great event, the humiliation, for which Freud has never forgiven me" (1926, p. 567; 2005, p. 122); and he reiterates, "to this day Freud has not forgiven me for being at that time the stronger one" (1926, p. 557; 2005, p. 115), to characterize his leadership of the Viennese opposition to installing Jung as permanent President of the Inter-national Psychoanalytic Association. There is, thus, no reason to think that the

Although Groenendijk does not mention Jung in his article, his commentary throws into sharp relief the parallels between Stekel's confrontation with Freud over masturbation and Jung's attempts to get Freud to acknowledge the psychogenic component of his fainting spells and urinary incontinence. In a 1953 interview with Kurt Eissler, Jung uses indirect discourse to recount in detail what took place after Freud's episode of urinary incontinence in New York in 1909:

> Then we had to hail a taxi, and it was very embarrassing. He was frightfully smitten by it and said, "You see, I am senile." And so on! And I said, "Nonsense! You are not senile! That is simply a neurosis!" Then we talked about it and he said, "Why? How should that be a neurosis? That is a paralysis!" I said, "No, that is not a paralysis, it is a regular neurosis!" "Yes, but what could be the reason?" I said, "But I beg to inform you, Professor, with respect, everybody thinks—knows—that you are terribly ambitious!" He said, "*I*?! Ambitious?! Anything but that!"[19] [Eissler, 1953, pp. 8–9]

Just as Stekel, by challenging Freud's theory of present-day neurosis, forced him to consider the possibility that what Groenendijk has called his "neurasthenic and anxiety neurotic symptoms" may not have been the physiological consequences of the masturbation

---

dispute over masturbation dealt a more grievous blow to Freud's relations with Stekel than did Stekel's willingness to stand up to him on political and editorial matters. For my own discussion of how not only the theme of masturbation but also the conflict over the *Zentralblatt* led Freud to view Stekel with unbridled contempt and loathing, the aftershocks of which continued to reverberate in his dealings with both Ferenczi and Groddeck, see *Reading Psychoanalysis* (Rudnytsky, 2002, pp. 146–151).

[19] This interview was derestricted by the Freud Archives in 2003. Privileged access had been previously granted by Eissler to Deirdre Bair, who quotes this same extract (which she renders in dialogue form without informing the reader of this alteration) in her biography of Jung (2003, p. 164). Bair, however, confuses (pp. 116–117) what happened on Jung's first and second visits to Vienna, and her scholarship is untrustworthy also in other respects (see note 22 below). (I omit Eissler's two interjections, "Ja," in my own quotation.) That Eissler did not acknowledge the relevance of the interview he himself had conducted with Jung in 1953, which amplifies Jung's other narratives of his relationship with Freud and bolsters his claim that Freud engaged in an affair with Minna Bernays, only renders Eissler's assault on Jung's credibility more disingenuous.

to which he had undoubtedly resorted after the virtual extinction of sexual relations with his wife Martha in the mid-1890s,[20] but were, rather, the manifestations of acute psychological distress, so, too, Jung, even more boldly, told Freud to his face that his incontinence was not an organic "paralysis" but instead a "regular neurosis", which called for analytic investigation. Indeed, as Jung went on to inform Eissler, it was following his urination in his trousers that Freud began to present the dream, involving his wife and his sister-in-law, the analysis of which he then interrupted with the momentous words, "'My dear Jung, I cannot risk my authority!'" (p. 10).[21]

Unlike Freud himself, Stekel, Jung, and Ferenczi had all been analytic patients, at least to a limited extent. The "analyses" of Stekel and Ferenczi were with Freud himself, whereas Jung's was with Maria Moltzer, a nurse and the daughter of a wealthy Dutch distiller in his Zurich group with whom he appears to have

---

[20] Peter Gay (1988) has produced a memorandum in which Freud recorded that he engaged in "successful coitus" (p. 163)—presumably with his wife—in 1915. We likewise know that Anna Freud was born in December 1895, despite Freud's having confided to Fliess in August 1893 that he and Martha were "now living in abstinence" (Masson, 1985, p. 54). Notwithstanding these two exceptions, a series of explicitly or implicitly autobiographical comments—from the letter to Fliess in 1893, through the analysis of the Signorelli parapraxis originally published in 1898 and reprinted in 1901 as the first chapter of *The Psychopathology of Everyday Life*, to the bleak portrait of bourgeois marriage in "'Civilized' sexual morality and modern nervous illness" (1908d), to Emma Jung's letter in November 1911 reminding Freud of his admission that his marriage "had long been 'amortized'" and "there was nothing more to do except—die" (McGuire, 1974, p. 456)—makes it clear that sexual intercourse, "successful" or otherwise, became a rare event quite early in Freud's married life, and there is no reason to think that his passion for Martha was rekindled in the ensuing decades.

[21] That Freud's "difficulties in controlling his bladder" formed the prelude both to telling Jung his dream about the sisters Bernays and to his remark about not losing his authority is also implied, though not stated explicitly, in Jung's interview with Billinsky (1969, p. 42). When he repeats the same story for public consumption in *Memories, Dreams, Reflections* (1963), Jung obscures these connections, omitting any mention of Freud's involvement with Minna Bernays (p. 162) and veiling the exact nature of his "very troublesome symptoms" (p. 170) on the American journey; but all the elements can be pieced together by the informed reader.

engaged in a love affair.[22] Jung's relationship with Moltzer would, by contemporary standards, constitute a major boundary violation, and both Ferenczi's and Stekel's therapies were likewise not only too brief but also too compromised by their personal ties to Freud to pass muster in our more straitlaced era. Stekel writes in his *Autobiography* that what he called his "treatment" with Freud, which took place in 1901 or 1902, "lasted not more than eight sessions" (1950, p. 107). With commendable modesty, and obviously unaware of Jung's protestations to the contrary, he notes that "Freud, Adler, Jung, and Stekel were never analyzed" (p. 236). This argument goes hand in hand with Stekel's view that only physicians should be permitted to be analysts and that medical training is a more important qualification than undergoing a personal analysis for the practice of psychoanalysis.[23]

---

[22] On Jung's involvement with Moltzer, see Freud's letter to Ferenczi on 23 December 1912: "The master who analyzed him can only have been Fräulein Molzer [sic], and he is so foolish to be proud of this work of a woman with whom he is having an affair" (Brabant, Falzeder, & Giampieri-Deutsch, 1993, p. 446). He likewise wrote to Jones three days later: Jung "broke loose furiously, proclaiming that he was not neurotic at all, having passed through a φα [psychoanalytic] treatment (with the Molzer? [sic] I suppose, you may imagine what the treatment was), that I was the neurotic" (Paskauskas, 1993, p. 186). That Jung was sexually involved with Moltzer is corroborated by Jolande Jacobi, who told the oral historian Gene Nameche, "Then I heard from others, about the time before he met Toni Wolff, that he had a love affair there in the Burghölzli with a girl—what was her name? Moltzer" (quoted in Bair, 2003, p. 713, n. 23). Disregarding Jung's own insistence in December 1912 that he had been analysed, and Freud's nomination of Moltzer as the most likely person to have been his analyst, Bair inexplicably claims that "if Jung ever had any sort of formal (or informal) psychoanalysis", it was only with Wolff in 1914 (p. 249).

[23] Stekel's position on the necessity of personal analysis is inconsistent. His statement in the *Autobiography*, "The contention that every psychotherapist must be analysed to be good is, however, unsound" (1950, p. 236), contrasts with his assertions in *Advances and Technique in the Interpretation of Dreams* (1935) that "it is as impossible for a man to analyze himself as it is for a man to play chess against himself" and "every analyst should himself have been analyzed, if only as a preliminary to his practicing dream interpretation" (quoted in Bos & Groenendijk, 2004, p. 724). Citing these passages, as well as Stekel's observation in the same work that "Freud in *The Interpretation of Dreams* overlooks important complexes where his own dreams are concerned", Bos and Groenendijk conclude that Stekel believed that he had been "properly trained by Freud" and that he accordingly "had equaled the master because he understood better than Freud his inner psychological condition" (p. 725).

Notwithstanding Stekel's recognition of the incompleteness of his experience as a patient, however, the fact remains that he had exposed his intimate life to Freud, just as both Jung and Ferenczi— unlike not only Freud but also such luminaries as Abraham and Rank—could plausibly affirm that they had been analysed by someone other than themselves. In response to Jung's criticism that "your technique of treating your pupils like your patients is a *blunder*", Freud defended himself on 22 December 1912 by observing:

> In Vienna I have become accustomed to the opposite reproach, to wit, that I concern myself too little with the analysis of my "students." And it is quite true that since Stekel, for example, discontinued his treatment with me some ten years ago, I have never said one word to him about the analysis of his own person. [McGuire, 1974, p. 537]

In Freud's estimation, therefore, what Stekel had undergone with him *did* amount to an "analysis", which he had refrained from exploiting in the intervening decade when their relations as colleagues were often strained. Despite the nobility of these sentiments professed to Jung, however, when Fritz Wittels sent Freud a copy of his biographical study, *Sigmund Freud: His Personality, His Teaching, and His School* (1924), Freud responded on 15 August 1924 that "your relationship to Stekel remains the blot that depreciates the value of your work in personal as well as in factual respects", adding, in what can only be taken as a thinly veiled comment about what he had learnt about Stekel himself in his analysis and is, therefore, a violation of physician–patient confidentiality, "One day when I am no more—my discretion will also go with me to the grave—it will become obvious that Stekel's assertion about the harmlessness of unrestrained masturbation is based on a lie" (E. Freud, 1960, p. 352).[24]

---

[24] As Paul Roazen (1971, p. 212) remarked decades ago, the English translation of this letter inverts the meaning by inserting the phrase "my alleged claim of" in brackets after "Stekel's assertion about". It is, of course, Stekel and not Freud who regarded masturbation as harmless, and Freud is here using his privileged information as Stekel's analyst to impugn the soundness of the latter's theoretical position. In the *Autobiography*, Stekel discloses that he had originally consulted Freud on account of "sexual problems" (1950, p. 107; see 1926, p. 540; 2005, p. 100), and that he became "no longer a man" (1950, p. 123)

Being more indulgent than Jung, Stekel confined himself to describing it as "Freud's tragedy that he has never been analyzed", and at least in the "History" he did not accuse him of hypocrisy on this score. He does, however, take Freud to task for exhibiting a "pathological degree of vengefulness", and, doubtless having in mind his statement in *The Interpretation of Dreams* that "my emotional life has always insisted that I should have an intimate friend and a hated enemy" (1900a, p. 483), Stekel points out that Freud, "according to his own confessions, had the urgent need to have an enemy", and, indeed, he always "creates an enemy" whenever a potential rival "obtains too much recognition" (1926, p. 565; 2005, p. 121). Even more astutely, he chastises Freud's penchant for diagnosing Fliess, Adler, and other estranged colleagues as paranoiacs, branding this "a naked delusion of persecution" (1926, p. 569; 2005, p. 124) on Freud's part. Stekel was, likewise, one of the first to call attention to Freud's "unspeakable pride and stubbornness", which led him to demand "complete submission" (1926, p. 566; 2005, p. 122) from others as the price for gaining his acceptance, as a signal feature of his character.

Ferenczi, whose experience of analysis with Freud was somewhat more extensive than Stekel's, amounting to a total of some eight weeks in three "slices" during 1914 and 1916, compounded by

---

for two years during his unhappy first marriage. Through a juxtaposition of material from the *Autobiography* with the case history of "NM" in Stekel's *Impotence in the Male* (1920), Bos and Groenendijk (2004) have convincingly demonstrated that "NM" is really Stekel himself. As they report, we learn of "NM" that he "practices masturbation on a daily basis" from the time he entered the Gymnasium and that he suffered "hysterical impotence" (p. 722) at the age of seventeen. Thus, both masturbation and impotence were abiding personal issues for Stekel, of which Freud would have been aware, and Freud's comment to Wittels impugning Stekel's belief in the "harmlessness of uninhibited masturbation" must be understood as a below-the-belt hit against his erstwhile patient. As I have argued in *Reading Psychoanalysis* (Rudnytsky, 2002, pp. 146–151), when Freud in 1921 responded to prepublication drafts of *The Book of the It* sent to him by Groddeck by dourly remarking that he was reminded of the "warning example" of "a certain W. Stekel" (Schacht, 1977, p. 63), one of the principal reasons for this comparison is almost certain to have been that Groddeck not only depicts masturbation as the primordial manifestation of human sexuality, but also reports his own autoerotic experiences with astonishing frankness.

his confessional outpourings in innumerable letters, concurs with Jung in coming to see Freud's refusal to surrender his authority in the analytic situation as a form of hypocrisy: "In his conduct, Fr[eud] plays only the role of the castrating god . . . he is the only one who does not have to be analyzed". Yet, just as Ferenczi comes to the realization that "the personal causes for the erroneous development of psychoanalysis" lie in Freud's character, so, too, Stekel instances Freud's unwillingness in his *Autobiographical Study* to recant any of his views on present-day neurosis, even though they had not stood the test of time, as a defect of his character with far-reaching implications for psychoanalytic theory: "Freud has a characteristic that does him great harm and inhibits the development of analysis, and yes, has even forced it onto false tracks: *He is unable to admit that he has erred!*" (1926, p. 547; 2005, p. 107). And Jung, thinking back in *Memories, Dreams, Reflections* to the lessons he had learnt from his encounter with Freud, concludes, "I had seen that neither Freud nor his disciples could understand what it meant for the theory and practice of psychoanalysis if not even the master could deal with his own neurosis" (1963, p. 171).

Ferenczi's comparison of Freud to a "castrating god" resonates with central themes in both Stekel and Jung. Immediately following the passage in which he calls it "Freud's tragedy that he has never been analyzed", Stekel resumes his commentary on Freud's refusal to admit his mistakes:

> The greatness of a man is measured not only in his intellectual ability; it is also measured in his capacity to recognize himself, to admit mistakes, to improve himself, to be able to forgive and—to forget. Freud is unable to forget. He therein resembles his god, the furious Jehovah, who allowed the sinful company of Korah to sink into the earth and who plunged his best child Job into deepest misery in order to test his trustworthiness and his faith. [1926, p. 571; 2005, p. 126]

That Korah led the rebellion of the Israelites against Moses and Aaron, only to be swallowed up by the earth in divine retribution (Numbers 16), lends a second level of meaning to Stekel's allegory, since Freud in *The Moses of Michelangelo* (1914b) had already implicitly equated himself with Moses "struggling successfully against an inward passion for the sake of a cause to which he has devoted himself" (p. 233). In what he took to be Michelangelo's depiction of Moses' suppression of his wrath at the idolatrous worshippers of the Golden Calf (Exodus 19–32: 19), that is, Freud saw an idealized image of what he regarded as the overcoming of his own justified anger at the defections of his faithless followers in both Vienna and Zurich.[25]

For Stekel, then, Freud is a "furious Jehovah" in whom can also be traced the lineaments of the implacable Moses. Jung, it will be recalled, in his eruption of 18 December 1912, chastised Freud for wanting to "remain on top as the father, sitting pretty", and lamented that "nobody dares to pluck the prophet by the beard" in order to ask him, "'Who's got the neurosis?'" In far happier times, on 17 January 1909, Freud had written to Jung, "We are certainly getting ahead: if I am Moses, then you are Joshua and will take possession of the promised land of psychiatry, which I shall only be able to glimpse from afar" (McGuire, 1974, p. 197). Freud's align-ment of himself with Moses and of Jung with Joshua is one of the innumerable paternal metaphors used by both men to define their relationship, with the added twist that, since Joshua was regarded typologically as a precursor of Christ, Freud is equating himself with the Old Testament patriarch destined to be superseded by Jung, the New Testament Joshua–Christ.

But whereas during the period of their collaboration Freud looked upon Jung's Christianity as not only an advantage but, indeed, as a prerequisite for anointing the latter as his successor as the leader of the psychoanalytic movement, by the time of their break their divergent religious identities became one of the chief sources of friction between them. Thus, when in his letter of 18 December 1912, Jung protests, "You see, my dear Professor, as long as you hand out this stuff, I don't give a damn for my symptomatic actions; they shrink to nothing in comparison with the formidable

---

[25] That "Freud had identified with Moses and was striving to emulate the victory over passions that Michelangelo had depicted in his stupendous achieve-ment" has been recognized by his biographers since Jones (1955, pp. 366–367). As Malcolm Macmillan and Peter J. Swales (2003) have documented, Freud's reading of Michelangelo's statue is based on the mistaken assumption that it depicts Moses' *first* rather than his *second* ascent of Mount Sinai (Exodus 33–34); but this confusion is immaterial to Freud's subjective identification with Moses, evoked by Stekel in his reference to Korah in the "History".

beam in my brother Freud's eye" (McGuire, 1974, p. 535), he simultaneously demotes Freud from the role of a father to that of a "brother" and invokes Christ's similitude of the mote and the beam in the Sermon on the Mount (Matthew 7: 3–5) to denounce Freud for seeking to analyse Jung's petty slips of the pen when he had not permitted his own grand neurosis to be analysed. By appealing to this New Testament inversion of the Old Testament principle of the *lex talionis*, Jung condemns Freud for adhering to a rigid and ultimately hypocritical Jewish ethos of judgement that should be supplanted by the Christian principle of mercy.[26]

By the same token, when Jung in this same letter rues that no one has yet had the temerity "to pluck the prophet by the beard", he is now using Freud's self-identification with Moses to define him as Jewish in a negative sense. That Jung singles out the beard as a metonymy of Jewishness renders it doubly significant that Freud, in *The Moses of Michelangelo*, proceeds to highlight Moses' clutching of his *beard* as the linchpin of his interpretation of Michelangelo's monumental tomb statue. At least on a subliminal level, Freud appears to have been goaded into responding to Jung's taunt by reaffirming his identification with Moses in this deeply personal essay written in the aftermath of their split.[27]

Freud's insistence on designating Jung as his heir apparent in large measure because he was *not* Jewish had a collateral impact on Freud's relationship with Stekel. When, during the 1910 Nuremberg Congress, Freud burst in on the conclave of his Viennese followers who opposed his plan to appoint Jung as permanent president of

---

[26] The crucial preceding verses, "Judge not, lest ye be judged. For with what judgment ye judge, ye shall be judged: and with what measure ye mete, it shall be measured unto you again" (Matthew 7: 1–2), dialectically at once fulfil, abrogate, and raise to a higher level the Old Testament law of talion. The point is that if one extends mercy to others, one will in turn be forgiven. Thus, what is crucial in Christianity is no longer a fixed and externally imposed rule of tit for tat, but, rather, a sliding scale according to which how a person responds to others determines his or her fate. This principle of *Aufhebung* governs the entire relation of grace to sin, spirit to letter, Christ to Adam, in the New Testament (see especially Romans 5–7).

[27] On Freud's attention to the beard of Michelangelo's *Moses* in the context of contemporaneous norms in both photography and the study of art history, see the excellent essay by Mary Bergstein (2006).

the International Psychoanalytic Association, it was above all Jung's Christianity that Freud emphasized in tearfully pleading that he be allowed to keep the clothes on his back by prevailing in this matter. As Stekel paraphrases Freud's oration in the "History", "Anti-Semitic calumnies were being staged against analysis. It was being degraded to a Jewish science. A 'Christ' had to stand at the forefront of the movement" (1926, p. 556; 2005, p. 114). A quarter of a century later, Stekel, in his *Autobiography*, states that Freud "foresaw a growing anti-Semitism", and quotes him as having said, "'An official psychiatrist and a Gentile must lead the movement'" (1950, p. 129).

From these two slightly different accounts, it is impossible to ascertain whether Freud actually called Jung "a 'Christ'", or whether this is the construction that Stekel placed on his remarks. In either case, the epithet captures the essence of Freud's sentiments about Jung at that time. As Bos (2005) points out, the passage in Stekel's "History" provides a "context" (p. 88) for his own famous exclamation in the *Autobiography*, "I was the apostle of Freud who was my Christ!" (1950, p. 88), though this observation again contradicts Bos's own devaluation of the "History" as a text that "does not record anything that we do not already know" about the psychoanalytic movement. By calling Freud "*my* Christ" in the *Autobiography*, Stekel implies that he continued to pay homage to Freud, who was (like Christ) a Jew, whereas Freud himself had been deluded into trying to make "a 'Christ'" out of the Gentile Jung.[28]

In the "History", Stekel's tacit pairing of Freud with Moses is a corollary of his explicit likening of Freud to "the furious Jehovah" who not only smote Korah, but also "plunged his best child Job into deepest misery in order to test his trustworthiness and his faith". This judgement, as we have seen, is echoed by Ferenczi's description of Freud as a "castrating god". But Stekel's verdict finds its most striking counterpart in the writings of Jung.[29] In *Memories*,

---

[28] On the wider implications of the comparison of Freud to Christ, and of psychoanalysis to a religion, see Chapter One, as well as my discussion of the uses of this analogy by Max Graf, Hilda Doolittle, and Groddeck in *Reading Psychoanalysis* (Rudnytsky, 2002, pp. 193–200).

[29] In light of the analogy drawn independently by Stekel, Ferenczi, and Jung between Freud and God, it is tempting to read Jones's 1913 paper, "The god

Dreams, Reflections, Jung explains Freud's antipathy to religion by arguing that "in the place of a jealous God that had been lost to him, he had inserted another compelling image, that of sexuality" (1963, p. 156). Even more profoundly, as Harry Slochower (1981) was the first to suggest, albeit from a one-sided Freudian point of view, Jung's *Answer to Job* (1952) is, on one fundamental level, a retrospective meditation on the trauma of his relationship with Freud, in which Jung casts himself as the suffering Job and Freud as the implacable Jehovah or Yahweh.

Jung, for example, writes near the beginning of his work that

> it is Yahweh himself who darkens his own counsel and who has no insight. He turns the tables on Job and blames him for what he himself does: man is not permitted to have an opinion about him, and, in particular, is to have no insight which he himself does not possess. [1952, par. 587][30]

This indictment of Yahweh for using Job as a scapegoat for his own spiritual blindness extends to Jung's attack on Freud, in his letter of 18 December 1912, for his habit of "sniffing out all the symptomatic actions in your vicinity", while himself remaining "on top as the father, sitting pretty". Similarly, Jung describes how Yahweh's "jealous and irritable nature, prying mistrustfully into the faithless hearts of men and exploring their secret thoughts, compelled a personal relationship between himself and man, who could not help but feel personally called by him" (par. 568). This passage reflects Jung's own sense of having been "personally called" by Freud, while condemning Freud's "jealous and irritable nature" along with his proclivity to "pry mistrustfully" into the "secret thoughts" of other people.

---

complex", as an allegorical commentary not solely on Jung—as Jones depicted it to Freud in a letter of 29 December 1912—but also, if only on an unconscious level, on Freud himself. Among the traits that Jones ascribes to "god-men" are a "colossal *narcissism*" (p. 247), a tendency to wrap themselves "in an impenetrable cloud of mystery and privacy" (p. 251), and the "*disinclination toward the acceptance of new knowledge*" (p. 256), all of which can fairly be imputed to Freud.

[30] As is customary in citations from Jung, I give paragraph numbers for all references to *Answer to Job*.

In what is perhaps the deepest ethical lesson of *Answer to Job*, Jung begins the work by confessing that the man tormented by an *"amoral"* deity will be goaded into "an equally unconsidered outburst of affect, and a smouldering resentment that may be compared to a slowly healing wound" (1952, pars. 560–561). Thus, Job becomes no less guilty than Yahweh, the only differences between them being, first, that Job is responding to Yahweh's provocation, and, second, that he is at least prepared to accept his own share of the blame: "Although, by giving way to the affect, one imitates all the bad qualities of the outrageous act that provoked it and thus makes oneself guilty of the same fault, that is precisely the point of the whole procedure" (par. 562). Here, after forty years, Jung repents for his own "unconsidered outburst of affect" in his final blow-up with Freud, when he was consumed by the irrational anger that Freud's "divine savagery and ruthlessness" (par. 561) had aroused in him. Ultimately, by his greater degree of self-awareness, Job proves his superiority to Yahweh: "Job, by his insistence on bringing his case before God, even without hope of a hearing, had stood his ground and thus created the very obstacle that forced God to reveal his nature" (par. 584).[31]

Stekel, unlike Jung, does not seem to have identified personally with Job, the "best child" whom Yahweh tormented solely for the perverse pleasure of making a wager with Satan to see whether Job was worthy of being singled out for divine favour. But, long before

---

[31] Several passages of *Answer to Job* hint at Jung's awareness of Freud's affair with Minna Bernays. In addition to being morally superior to Yahweh, Job is privy to the deity's secrets: "Without Yahweh's knowledge and contrary to his intentions, the tormented though guiltless Job had secretly been lifted up to a superior knowledge of God which God himself did not possess" (1952, par. 583). In his interview with Billinsky (1969), Jung affirms, "Freud had no idea that I knew about the triangle and his intimate relationship with his sister-in-law" (p. 42). In Jung's (1952) gnostic theology, moreover, Yahweh possesses two wives—the people of Israel and his "intimate playmate" (par. 619) Sophia, or Wisdom. Adam, too, according to legend, was married first to the demonic Lilith before the creation of Eve. As Jung notes, "the original man who was created in the image of God had, according to tradition, two wives, just like his heavenly prototype". If Jung is not only Job but also Adam, he seems to have taken comfort in the fact that his own polygamous tendencies—given free rein in his forty-year *ménage à trois* with his wife, Emma, and Toni Wolff—had found a "heavenly prototype" in Freud.

Jung wrote *Answer to Job* and in advance also of Ferenczi's rumina-
tions in his *Clinical Diary*, Stekel, in his "History of the analytic
movement", trenchantly diagnosed the tragic flaws in Freud's character that were the underlying "personal causes for the erroneous
development of psychoanalysis".[32] Each of these men, by "bringing
his case" before Freud, "even without hope of a hearing", has
"stood his ground and thus created the very obstacle" that con-
strained Freud to "reveal his nature". Having arrived by independent paths at a collective diagnosis, all three of these stalwart
figures then faced the challenge of a common project—rescuing
psychoanalysis from Freud.

4

In recounting the stories of their relationships to Freud, Stekel,
Jung, and Ferenczi all recall one or more searing moments in which
their hitherto unbounded affection and admiration suffered a grievous injury. However transitory they might have seemed initially,
these experiences of disenchantment became for them, in hindsight,
harbingers of the more serious conflicts to come.

For Stekel, "the discovery that threw the first shadow on my
relation to Freud" (1926, p. 546; 2005, p. 106) occurred when, still in
the days of the Psychological Wednesday Society, he delivered a
lecture on "The psychology of anxiety neurosis". Freud, convinced
that anxiety neurosis belonged to the category of present-day
neurosis and, thus, could not have a psychological root, dealt with

---

[32] To this honour roll of dissidents should be added the name of Otto Rank,
who, from his Parisian exile, commented in *Modern Education* (1932) that
psychoanalysis

is as conservative as it appeared revolutionary; for its founder is a rebellious
son who defends the paternal authority, a revolutionary who, from fear of
his own rebellious son–ego, took refuge in the security of the father position, which, however, was already ideologically disintegrated. [pp. 191–192]

For a lucid dissection of Rank's "compulsive need to address and redress the
story of Oedipus", see Armstrong (2005, p. 60).

Stekel's evidence that the female patient about whom he was speaking indeed suffered from a psychological conflict by insisting, "That is not anxiety neurosis, that's hysteria!" After Stekel, who had initially referred this woman to Freud, produced a calling card on which Freud had written his own diagnosis of "anxiety neurosis", Freud "looked mutely at the card and said later, 'Do not publish the case until we have discussed it'". Upon visiting Freud the following Sunday, Stekel was informed that Freud intended to solve his self-imposed conundrum by bestowing upon Stekel "a royal present" in the form of an entirely new category of "anxiety hysteria" to cover those patients whose anxiety was rooted in psychological factors rather than in what Freud believed to be inferior and even noxious forms of sexual gratification.

Disturbed as he was by this manifestation of intransigence, Stekel places even greater weight on a subsequent incident that he calls his "first bitter disappointment" (1926, p. 553; 2005, p. 111) with Freud. In the afterglow of the first international gathering of psychoanalysts at the 1908 Salzburg Congress, Stekel showed Freud the completed manuscript of his book, *Nervous Anxiety States and Their Treatment*, for which Freud had promised to write a preface "under the condition that I would present the work to him for inspection and correction" (1926, p. 550; 2005, p. 109). At this time, as Stekel admits, he not only "loved" Freud but stood in a position of "material dependence" on him, as did "all the other members of the circle" (1926, p. 551; 2005, p. 110). In a prefiguration of his response to Jung's *Transformations and Symbols of the Libido* (1912), Freud was "very enthusiastic" about the first part of Stekel's book but not the second, in which Stekel challenged his assumption that anxiety was simply "converted libido", and he urged Stekel to postpone publishing it for an unspecified number of years (1926, pp. 550–551; 2005, p. 110).

The upshot came when Freud first sent Stekel a version of his long-awaited preface that proved to be "more a disparagement than a recommendation" (1926, p. 553; 2005, p. 112), and then a second draft that Stekel also could not bear to see printed. Finally, Freud cobbled together something that coolly referred to "Herr Dr. W. Stekel" and alleged that his own influence on the book had been "very limited" even though he had met on at least twenty occasions to discuss it with Stekel, who had read him every sentence and made many changes at Freud's instigation. The only share that Freud acknowledged in the book was to have proposed using the term "anxiety hysteria", thereby reclaiming his ostensibly munificent, but, in actuality, inhibiting, "royal gift".

Ferenczi's equivalent initial moment of disillusionment was the notorious "Palermo incident" in September 1910, during a trip that he took with Freud to Sicily. As Ferenczi sums up the matter in his entry of 4 August 1932 to the *Clinical Diary*, Freud could "tolerate my being a son only until the moment when I contradicted him for the first time (Palermo)" (1985, p. 185). Like that of Stekel, Ferenczi's crisis was instigated by a failed attempt at a literary partnership when Freud sought to induce him to play the role of an amanuensis on the Schreber case, instead of proposing that they work together in a genuinely collaborative manner. Significantly, Ferenczi's only detailed account of this painful experience is to be found in a letter written on Christmas Day 1921, not to Freud, but to Groddeck, whose friendship filled the void left by Ferenczi's increasing emotional withdrawal from Freud, though Ferenczi did bring himself to voice his resentment concerning "the strictness with which you punished my obstinate behavior in the matter of the Schreber book" (Falzeder & Brabant, 2000, p. 383) in a heartfelt letter to Freud on 17 January 1930.[33]

With Jung, as we have seen, the event that he singled out as having dealt "a severe blow to the whole relationship" with Freud was the latter's refusal to continue with the analysis of his dream in New York, thereby placing "personal authority over truth" (1963, p. 158). Like Ferenczi, Jung states that "under the impress of Freud's personality, I had, as far as possible, cast aside my own judgments and repressed my criticisms", and this "was the precondition for collaborating with him" (p. 164). Clearly, however, as is true for both Stekel and Ferenczi, whose grounds for animosity towards Freud extended beyond the Palermo incident to include Freud's interventions in his love life that led him to renounce the nubile Elma Pálos in favour of her mother Gizella, as well as what

---

[33] I have commented on the Palermo incident as it pertains to Ferenczi's relationships with both Freud and Groddeck in greater detail in *Reading Psychoanalysis* (Rudnytsky, 2002, pp. 120, 173).

he believed was Freud's failure to analyse his negative transference, this incident during the September 1909 trip to America was but one in a series of jolts to Jung's idealization of Freud. Freud's first fainting spell, after all, took place in Bremen before the voyage, and Jung, in *Memories, Dreams, Reflections*, also mentions an episode during his second visit to Vienna, in March 1909, when he gave rise to Freud's consternation by correctly predicting that a loud noise both men had heard emanating from a bookcase would be repeated. As Jung recollects, "this incident aroused his mistrust of me", and "I never afterward discussed" (p. 156) it with Freud.[34]

What these remarkably similar narratives show us is that Freud, whom Adler described to Stekel as a "soul-catcher" (1926, p. 560; 2005, p. 118), repeatedly enacted a pattern whereby, after an initial period in which the prospective male follower was avidly courted, he then turned on the "friend" and made him into an "enemy", or at least made it clear to the disciple that he had fallen in his master's esteem.[35] For Stekel, Freud's "trick of soul-catching" took the form

---

[34] If, moreover, we believe Jung's disclosure to Billinsky (1969) about the "agony" (p. 42) he felt upon learning from Minna Bernays of her intimacy with Freud during his first visit to Vienna, in March 1907, then the seeds of his ensuing conflicts with Freud must have been planted at that time. If so, then Jung took Freud's behaviour as a licence to revise his own attitudes towards marriage and sexual morality, while he came increasingly to resent the stubbornness with which Freud refused "to understand consciously the triangle" and "to deal with problems that were closely connected with his theories".

[35] Also citing Adler's expression, of which he may well have been reminded by Stekel's text, Sadger concurs: "for the recruit, the newcomer", even during the meetings of Freud's circle,

> the sky was mostly filled with violins. As a rule, Freud was full of captivating amiability on these occasions, a veritable "soul-catcher," as Adler once called him. ... Then the honeymoon would be over, and one day, perhaps at a lecture when the newcomer had done his best, he had to submit to the experience of the Professor, so to speak, "shredding him into air". [1930, pp. 29–30; 2005, p. 35]

In Sadger's considered opinion, "Freud in his heart of hearts was a terrible sadist, for which his enemies had to pay less than his pupils and most loyal followers".

of playing him off against Adler. As Stekel reports, "Freud for some time overwhelmed me with signs of affection", regaling him with "his pet diagnosis" that Adler was "a paranoiac", a pronouncement in which Freud was "enthusiastically confirmed" by his "chorus of slave natures" (1926, p. 563; 2005, p. 119). Indeed, Freud even made it seem that his decision to appoint Adler as chairman of the Vienna Psychoanalytic Society in his stead was actually a way of paying tribute to Stekel: "He knew that Stekel was not as sensitive or as ambitious. Stekel wouldn't make anything out of being second".

Having been seduced and then abandoned by Freud, Stekel, Jung, and Ferenczi in the end all found themselves ostracized as far as the psychoanalytic movement was concerned. As Ferenczi puts it in the final entry to his *Clinical Diary*, dated 2 October 1932:

> I did indeed also feel abandoned by colleagues (Radó, etc.) who are all too afraid of Freud to be able to behave objectively or even sympathetically toward me, in the event of a dispute between Freud and me. [1985, p. 212]

Stekel, as we have seen, in addition to bearing the brunt of Freud's "irreconcilable hate", found his works literally anathematized, subjected to a prohibition against being quoted by other analysts. And Jung, of course, became the victim of the greatest sacrifice of them all, served up by Freud in *Totem and Taboo* and "On the history of the psychoanalytic movement", and periodically roasted anew by later keepers of the flame such as Eissler and Blum.

In *Beyond the Pleasure Principle* (1920g), Freud comments on certain "normal people" whose lives give the impression of "being pursued by a malignant fate or possessed by some 'daemonic' power":

> Thus we have come across people all of whose human relationships have the same outcome: such as the benefactor who is abandoned in anger after a time by each of his *protégés*, however much they may otherwise differ from one another, and who thus seem doomed to taste all the bitterness of ingratitude; or the man whose friendships all end in betrayal by his friend; or the man who time after time in the course of his life raises someone else into a position of great private or public authority and then, after a certain

interval, himself upsets that authority and replaces him by a new one.[36] [pp. 21–22]

It is impossible to determine whether Freud wrote this passage with an awareness of its autobiographical import or whether this is an irony of which he remained unconscious. In either case, there could be no better description of the compulsion to repeat on whose wheel of fire Freud was himself bound, the consequences of which were so destructive not only in his private life, but also for the entire history of the psychoanalytic movement.

Faced with a man of Freud's undeniable genius, to whom they were incalculably indebted both professionally and personally but whom they came, with increasing clarity, to see, in the words of Ferenczi's valedictory 2 October 1932 entry to his *Clinical Diary*, as an "indifferent power" by whom they would be "trampled under foot" as soon as they decided to go their "own way and not his" (1985, p. 212), Stekel, Jung, and Ferenczi were caught on the horns of the same dilemma: how to preserve what is of permanent value in psychoanalysis, and thus to remain loyal to Freud in the highest sense, while not capitulating to his attempts to subjugate them to intellectual tyranny?

The leitmotif of resistance to Freud in the name of his own teaching is struck by Jung in his letter of 3 March 1912, in which he tells Freud, "I would never have sided with you in the first place had heresy not run in my blood", and proceeds to quote from Nietzsche's *Thus Spoke Zarathustra*:

One repays a teacher badly, if one remains only a pupil.
And why, then, should you not pluck at my laurels?
You respect me; but how if your respect should tumble?
Take care that a falling statue does not strike you dead!
You had not yet sought yourselves when you found me.
Thus do all believers—.
Now I bid you lose me and find yourselves;
and only then, when you have all denied me, will I return to you.
[McGuire, 1974, p. 491]

---

[36] I have quoted this passage in a similar connection in *Freud and Oedipus* (Rudnytsky, 1987, p. 32).

It is another poignant irony that, in his reply two days later, Freud assured Jung that his invocation of Nietzsche on the "need for intellectual independence" had his "full agreement", but went on to wonder: "if a third party were to read this passage, he would ask me *why* I had tried to tyrannize you intellectually, and I should have to say: I don't know" (p. 492).[37] Consciously, Freud seeks to deny that he had ever "tried to tyrannize" Jung, and, hence, he evidently intended to write "when" and not "why"; but Jung's more cynical interpretation of his behaviour is borne out by Freud's consummately revealing slip.

Of all the uncanny coincidences between Stekel's response to Freud and those of Jung and Ferenczi, including his comparison of Freud to "the furious Jehovah" who "plunged his best child Job into deepest misery in order to test his trustworthiness and his faith", none is more extraordinary than the fact that, without any way of knowing what Jung had written in his letter of 3 March 1912 to Freud, Stekel, too, in "On the history of the analytic movement" quotes the "exquisite word" of Nietzsche: "'One serves a teacher badly if one does not grow beyond him'" (1926, p. 572; 2005, p. 127).[38]

Continuing with his well-known similitude that "a dwarf on the shoulders of a giant sees further than the giant", Stekel adds, "based on my experiences, I cannot advise any man to have dealings with giants. They are cannibals not only in fairy tales" (1926, p. 572; 2005, p. 127). Here the most relevant gloss is supplied by a letter from Emma Jung to Freud on 6 November 1911, in which she bravely wonders whether his children might not benefit from analysis and suggests that a broken leg suffered by his son Martin in a skiing accident might have had a psychic determinant:

---

[37] I have restored and italicized Freud's "why" (*warum*), which is emended to "when" (*wann*) in McGuire's English edition.

[38] In reprinting Stekel's "History" in his book with Groenendijk (2007), Bos adds a footnote (p. 159) mentioning that this extract from *Thus Spoke Zarathustra* is also quoted by Jung in his letter to Freud on 3 March 1912, but he fails to credit me with having first made this connection in the original version of this chapter. See also my discussion in *Freud and Oedipus* (Rudnytsky, 1987, pp. 221–223) of Jung's use of this passage from *Thus Spoke Zarathustra* as a rebuke to Freud.

One certainly cannot be the child of a great man with impunity, considering the trouble one has in getting away from ordinary fathers. And when this distinguished father also has a streak of paternalism in him, as you yourself said! [McGuire, 1974, p. 456]

Her letter concludes: "And do not think of Carl with a father's feeling, 'He will grow, but I must dwindle,' but rather as one human being thinks of another who like you has his own law to fulfill" (p. 457).

For Stekel, a particular bone of contention with Freud was the issue of lay analysis, to which Stekel was resolutely opposed but Freud increasingly came to favour. From a contemporary standpoint, virtually everyone would agree that Freud was on the progressive side of this question, though Stekel usefully reminds the reader that, prior to the First World War, "Freud was absolutely against lay analysis", a stance that impelled Tausk to study medicine, and "Rank and Reik were allowed to work only theoretically" (1926, p. 559; 2005, p. 117). Stekel may also be justified in his insinuation that Freud's change of heart had less to do with intellectual principles than with a self-interested desire to "give his best students, the laity—Rank, Reich, Sachs, Aichhorn, Andreas-Salomé, Bernfeld, and perhaps his daughter, Anna Freud—the *venia Analysandi* [permission to analyse] as a testament" (1926, p. 573; 2005, p. 128).[39]

---

[39] Against Stekel's narrative, it might be argued that Emma Eckstein, who, as Freud wrote to Fliess on 12 December 1897, after having been his patient, had herself begun to practise analysis, was not a medical doctor. But as a woman and someone who did not participate in the formation of psychoanalysis as an organized movement, Eckstein was a person to whom the normal rules did not apply. Sadger, who—like Freud, Abraham, and Rank—was never analysed, appears to have commenced work as an analyst "at the beginning of 1898" (May, 2003, p. 137), which would, thus, place him second only to Eckstein (and possibly also to Reitler) in following Freud behind the couch. Sadger, who shared Stekel's opposition to lay analysis, endorses the latter's depiction of the evolution of Freud's outlook on this question. Citing Freud's paper, "'Wild' psychoanalysis" (1910k), and likewise instancing both Rank and Reik as examples, Sadger underscores that "Freud at that time, as well as for all the preceding years and even for a considerable time afterwards, wanted nothing to do with lay analysis", and his "promotion of lay analysis for patients began much later" (1930, p. 77; 2005, pp. 102–103). Stekel, writing in June 1925, appears to have had no inkling of the storm between Freud and Rank that had been gathering for more than a year.

Although Stekel adopted a retrograde position on the issue of lay analysis, he was, in a more profound sense, a harbinger of emancipation when he wrote, "I flatter myself that I am the only real Freudian. I now represent Freud much better than he does himself. That is what I hope posterity will say about me one day" (1926, p. 573; 2005, p. 127). This is also the essence of Jung's plea to Freud when, immediately following his quotation from *Thus Spoke Zarathustra*, he added: "This is what you have taught me through ΨA [psychoanalysis]. As one who is truly your follower, I must be stout-hearted, not least towards you" (McGuire, 1974, p. 492).

Without quoting from *Thus Spoke Zarathstra*, Ferenczi, too, like Stekel and Jung, incarnates Nietzsche's ideal of a pupil who goes beyond his teacher and, thus, may be said to "represent Freud much better than he does himself". Writing to Freud on 3 October 1910, in the aftermath of their strained trip to Sicily, he declares, "Whether you want to be or not, you are one of the great master teachers of mankind, and must permit your readers to approach you, at least intellectually, in a personal relationship as well". Having been "occupied for years with nothing but the products of your intellect", Ferenczi continues, and "always felt the man behind every sentence of your works, and made him my confidant", he himself has become "much, much more intimately acquainted and conversant" with Freud than Freud "could have imagined" (Brabant, Falzeder, & Giampieri-Deutsch, 1993, p. 219).

Of these three pioneers, who arrived by independent routes at a collective diagnosis of "the personal causes of the erroneous development of psychoanalysis" and then embarked through their intellectual and personal odysseys on the common project of rescuing psychoanalysis from Freud, Jung has always been given his due as a major figure in twentieth-century thought and the founder of his own school of analytical psychology, while Ferenczi has, in recent decades, been rediscovered and hailed as a seminal progenitor of contemporary relational and independent thinking. Only Stekel, for whom I confess a special fondness, not least because his first language was Ukrainian, can be said to have been treated as harshly by posterity as he was by Freud himself. Let us, therefore, be grateful to Jaap Bos for bringing his "On the history of the analytic movement" to the attention of a new generation of readers. As a belated act of reparation to Stekel's memory, I think it would be fitting if the psychoanalytic community were to begin using his cherished term "bipolarity", which Freud, for political reasons, caused to be suppressed and superseded by Eugen Bleuler's later coinage "ambivalence".

CHAPTER FOUR

"I'm just being horrid": D. W. Winnicott and the strains of psychoanalysis

"In their precise tracings-out and subtle causations, the strongest and fieriest emotions of life defy all analytical insight. We see the cloud, and feel its bolt; but meteorology only idly essays a critical scrutiny as to how that cloud became charged, and how this bolt so stuns".

(Herman Melville, *Pierre, or The Ambiguities*, 1852)

1

I f you are like me, you think of psychoanalysis as unfolding on two asymptotically converging planes. There is the plane of psychoanalysis as an essentially impersonal scientific theory, many of whose hypotheses have been confirmed over the past one hundred years, while others have not withstood the test of time and should be superseded in light of our better knowledge. And then there is the plane of psychoanalysis as an array of deeply personal artistic visions, in which the value of a given theorist's work depends not on how accurately it represents an objectively existing reality, but, rather, on the imaginative power with which it allows us to apprehend the world in a new way. From this standpoint, it makes no more sense to say of Freud, Klein, Winnicott, or Lacan that the sensibility of one is any more or less "true" than that of the rest than it would to make such a statement of Michelangelo, Goya, Vermeer, or Cézanne, though each of us will inevitably feel a greater affinity with certain artists or psychoanalysts than with others.

In what follows, I shall be considering Winnicott almost entirely from the perspective of his artistic vision, with only a few caveats about his limitations on the scientific side. The focus of my reflections will be on Winnicott and his two wives. In particular, I shall be wondering what impact Winnicott's initially clandestine love affair with Clare Britton, which culminated in his decision to abandon his first wife, Alice Taylor, in 1949, and to marry Clare two years later, may have had on his psychoanalytic theories. At the most general level, I shall be examining the relations between Winnicott's life and his work. This line of inquiry has been opened up by the two superlative biographies of Winnicott—Brett Kahr's *Biographical Portrait* of 1996, and F. Robert Rodman's *Life and Work* of 2003—that have appeared since my own book, *The Psychoanalytic Vocation: Rank, Winnicott, and the Legacy of Freud*, was published in 1991.

2

In a letter written on 30 October 1950 to Hannah ("Queen") Henry, a close friend of both his and Alice's, Winnicott informs her that he has recently left his wife: "I had meant to write & tell you the sad news that I've abandoned Alice. The Winnicott firm has dissolved. It came to that. I'm not trying to get out of the fact that I'm just being horrid" (Rodman, 2003, p. 67).

Acknowledging how awful it is "when one remembers how much Alice & I have experienced together, and have as common memories", Winnicott continues:

> Nevertheless, when two people live together, either the body warms or cools when there is contact, and for me there had come a feeling of strain that is indescribable. For Alice too I'm sure there should eventually be relief. [Rodman, 2003, p. 67]

Winnicott proceeds to inform Queen, who seems to be unaware of the affair that he had been conducting with Clare for the past six years, "there is a third person, someone who has a different effect on me", but claims, "I don't really believe I'd have allowed this to mark things up if I had not been bothered by certain dominating trains of thought $\overset{Alice}{\underset{\wedge}{in}}$ that wrecked my relation to Alice".

These extracts from Winnicott's letter to Hannah Henry already provide ample grist for the analytic mill. When he says, "I'm just being horrid", Winnicott is conceding that his decision to abandon his wife of twenty-eight years—however eccentric or even mentally disturbed she may have been, and however physically and emotionally unfulfilling he may have found the marriage—was, from one point of view, an act of monstrous selfishness with catastrophic effects on Alice. Although Winnicott voices the hope that the impending divorce will turn out to be better for both of them, this sentiment is belied not only by the "floods of tears" (Rodman, 2003, p. 66) that Winnicott's secretary, Joyce Coles, reports were shed by Alice when she informed Coles in 1949 that she had been left by Donald, but also by the few surviving letters from Alice to Donald after the dissolution of their marriage, which Kahr has justly described as "heartbreaking in the extreme" (1996, p. 87).[1]

That Winnicott should refer to his marriage to Alice as the "Winnicott firm", which is now "dissolved", becomes extremely poignant when one recalls that his father and uncle were partners in Winnicott Brothers, a highly successful purveyor of wholesale merchandise in Plymouth. Although this family background suggests that Winnicott would have had great affection for the idea of a "firm", and the metaphor thus conveys his feeling of loss at parting from Alice, Winnicott as a young man had disappointed his father by refusing to follow him into the business world, choosing instead to study medicine at Cambridge. Seen in this light, the notion of belonging to a "firm" would have carried for Winnicott the overtones of compliance on the part of his False Self, and the decision to leave Alice for Clare—which he was able to put into

---

[1] As Kahr informs us, Alice Winnicott lived out her life on a Welsh farm with only her palsied sister as a companion, and at the time of her death in 1969, she was "completely forlorn, and practically unremembered" (p. 88).

effect only after his father's death on 31 December 1948, at the age of ninety-four—was thus a rebellious expression of his True Self analogous to his earlier defiance of his father in setting out on the path that would lead him to become a psychoanalyst.

Two other points in Winnicott's letter to Hannah Henry deserve to be noted. First, as Rodman has observed (2003, pp. 143–144; p. 389, n. 27), Winnicott's statement that "either the body warms or cools when there is contact" between two people evokes his 1957 paper, "Excitement in the aetiology of coronary thrombosis", which implicitly comments on his own initial sequence of coronaries from the late 1940s through 1950.[2] According to Winnicott in this paper, "coronary thrombosis is a disorder of the apparatus of excitement" (1957, p. 35), and to understand this psychosomatic disorder we "need to know what happens when a body 'goes cold', that is to say, does not reach a climax" (p. 36). A juxtaposition of the 1950 letter with the 1957 paper makes it clear that Winnicott regarded his early coronaries as a reaction to his having "gone cold" in his marriage to Alice, which (as is by now common knowledge) was never consummated.[3]

Finally, I am struck by Winnicott's declaration to Hannah Henry that he has been afflicted by a "feeling of strain that is indescribable" in living with Alice. Once one begins to notice it, the word

---

[2] Winnicott's first clearly documented coronary occurred in February 1949, though Rodman (2003, p. 65) reports that Marion Milner recollected an earlier heart attack in 1947. In the letter to Henry, Winnicott refers to a "second attack" (p. 67) in August 1950, but Rodman considers this to have been "at least his third and possibly his fourth" (p. 68). It is possible that he suffered one or two further coronaries in 1954, but this is not certain, and he appears to have had no others until 1968 (p. 186). Thus, Winnicott's 1957 paper refers predominantly or exclusively to his experiences during the final years of his marriage to Alice, from whom he was divorced on 11 December 1951 (Kanter, 2004, p. 32). His marriage to Clare Britton ensued on 28 December 1951.

[3] Under the rubric "Disaster", Winnicott lists the potential consequences of the "tremendous mental and physical distress caused by a failure to reach climax", including "depersonalization, disintegration, sense of unreality" (1957, pp. 36–37), and there is again every reason to think that he is speaking from personal experience in arriving at this formulation. Also of possible autobiographical interest is Winnicott's comment that, in cases of impotence or frigidity, "probably there is an incapacity to masturbate, or masturbation is only possible by the dragging in of pervert and regression mechanisms" (p. 37).

"strain" turns up in all sorts of Winnicottian contexts.[4] Joyce Coles, for instance, echoed Winnicott's own words when she told Rodman in 1988 that "he knew he couldn't stand the strain of Alice anymore" (Rodman, 2003, p. 66).[5] As Rodman remarks, the strain under which Winnicott was labouring at the time he wrote his letter is manifested by two parapraxes: he addresses it not to Queen's home in Suffolk but to Alice's ancestral village of Claverdon; and in seeking to justify his conduct, he inserts the words "in Alice" above the line after "certain dominating trains of thought", as if to foreclose the possibility that his relationship to Alice had been "wrecked" by forces originating in himself rather than in her.

3

Of the many appearances of the word "strain" in Winnicott's own writings, the most resonant for my purposes occurs in "Transitional objects and transitional phenomena", presented to the British Psychoanalytical Society on 31 May 1951, though not published until 1953. In introducing the theory of illusion and disillusionment, Winnicott writes:

> It is assumed here that the task of reality-acceptance is never completed, that no human being is free from the strain of relating inner and outer reality, and that relief from this strain is provided by an intermediate area of experience . . . which is not challenged. [1953, p. 13]

---

[4] Of both historical and theoretical relevance is the fact that in "The concept of cumulative trauma" (1963), Masud Khan aligns his own influential formulation with the distinction previously proposed by Ernst Kris between one-time, massive "shock trauma" and steadily repeated "strain trauma". Citing Kris's definition (1956) of the latter as the "effect of long-lasting situations, which may cause traumatic effects by accumulation of frustrating tensions" (p. 73), Khan (1963) concludes that such "strain traumas" and their attendant screen memories "are derivatives of the partial breakdown of the protective-shield function of the mother and an attempt to symbolize its effects" (p. 52).

[5] Hannah Henry likewise wrote to Rodman in 1993, "the strain must have been enormous" (2003, p. 59), while as early as 1944 Melanie Klein commiserated with Winnicott, "you must have had a very strenuous time" with Alice (p. 124).

The question arises: is there a connection between Winnicott's use of "strain" in the letter to Hannah Henry and in this classic paper one year later? And why should he assume that the task of "relating inner and outer reality" necessarily involves a "strain"?[6]

In setting out to answer these questions, I am guided by two heuristic principles. The first is that the patterns exhibited in Winnicott's adult relationships constitute transferences of their infantile prototypes, and, by extension, that it is possible to reconstruct the infantile antecedents by seeing how they are re-enacted in later life. Since my concern is with Winnicott and his wives, my assumption will be that Winnicott's relationships with Alice and Clare must be seen, both severally and conjointly, as repetitions of

---

[6] That there is no inevitable strain between inner and outer worlds is eloquently attested by Milner (1969):

> I began to consider what may be the exact connection between a state of reverie in which inside and outside are not clearly differentiated, and what could be talked about as a fantasy of being in the womb. I began to consider *whether in full psychic health and effective thinking there is not an easy transition between these two states,* comparable to that between sleep and waking, *whereas in mental illness there could be felt to be an impassable barrier between them.* [pp. 40–41; italics added]

See also Clare Winnicott's early paper, "Children who cannot play" (1945):

> Satisfactory human activity, whether it be called work or play, aims, consciously or unconsciously, at the achievement of harmony between the individual and his environment. Unfortunately, this state of equilibrium is not something which is established once and for all. It has to be constantly maintained and is won and lost over and over again at each stage of development. [p. 112]

This formulation strikingly foreshadows Winnicott's in "Transitional objects and transitional phenomena" (1953), but without the proviso that the ongoing maintenance of an equilibrium between the individual and the environment entails a "strain". Similarly, in "True and false self" (1960a), Winnicott observes that when "the mother's adaptation is *good enough*", the infant "begins to believe in external reality which appears and behaves as if by magic. . . . On this basis the infant can gradually abrogate omnipotence" (p. 146). In contrast to the paper on "Transitional objects", the interplay between illusion and disillusionment is here depicted as gentle rather than arduous.

his early relationship to his mother. The second principle is that Winnicott's writings are, on one level, always autobiographical and can (like Freud's) be read as fragments of his interminable self-analysis.

To be sure, we do not have Winnicott on the couch; nor do we have direct access to his infancy. But, just as Winnicott insists that "it is not from direct observation of infants as much as it is from the study of transference in the analytic setting that it is possible to gain a clear view of what takes place in infancy itself" (1960b, p. 54), so, too, I would submit that Winnicott's writings have the status of analytic communications that allow us to gain an insight into his infancy comparable to that to be derived from a study of the manifestations of transference in the clinical setting. This argument gains credence from Winnicott's dissatisfaction with his analyses with both James Strachey and Joan Riviere, which he came to regard as prolonged collusions with his False Self. This led him to make his writings into the creative gestures that become, through our own responses as his readers, Winnicott's most truly therapeutic acts.[7]

---

[7] I am alluding here to Winnicott's letter of 17 November 1952 to Melanie Klein, in which he chastises her for failing to meet his "creative gesture", adding that such a response "is really in the nature of a therapeutic act, something which I could not get in either of my two long analyses", and "it was just exactly here that [Mrs. Riviere's] analysis failed me" (Rodman, 1987, p. 34). That Winnicott regarded his analyses with both Strachey and Riviere as collusions with his False Self emerges from implicitly autobiographical passages in key papers, from "Communicating and not communicating" (1963a) to "The use of an object" (1969). He writes in the former: "it is only too easy for an analysis (where there is a hidden schizoid element in the patient's personality) to become an infinitely prolonged *collusion* of the analyst with the patient's nega-tion of non-communication" (1963a, p. 189; italics added). In the latter, "In such [borderline] cases the psychoanalyst may *collude* for years with the patient's need to be psychoneurotic (as opposed to mad) and to be treated as psychoneu-rotic. . . . The only drawback is that the analysis never ends" (1969, p. 87; italics added). I believe that Winnicott regarded himself as possessing a "hidden schizoid element" in his own personality, just as his description of "deperson-alization, disintegration, sense of unreality" in the lecture on coronary throm-bosis stemmed from his own experience. For further veiled comments on his own analyses, see "Aggression in relation to emotional development" (1950–1955, p. 212), "Classification" (1959–1964, p. 133), "True and false self" (1960a, p. 152), and "Fear of breakdown" (1974, p. 91).

One of the most valuable services performed by Winnicott's biographers has been to rescue the figure of Alice Winnicott from the shadows, thereby inducing us to re-evaluate his relationship to Clare, and the image of Winnicott so assiduously promoted by Clare in the years of her widowhood, against this tragic backdrop. In speaking of Clare, one should pay tribute also to the labours of Joel Kanter, whose edition (2004) of Clare Winnicott's papers has revealed her to be a person of rare character and intellect in her own right. Kanter shows as well the extent to which Donald's immersion in Clare's world of social work complemented her assimilation into his world of psychoanalysis.

Still, when one reads Clare Winnicott's writings, particularly her accounts of her work with Winnicott on behalf of evacuated children in Oxfordshire during the Second World War—in the course of which they fell in love and began their clandestine affair—and compares these to what was going on in Winnicott's life with Alice at the same time, the discord is jarring. In their jointly authored paper of 1944, "The problem of homeless children", for example, Donald Winnicott and Clare Britton write: "we could perhaps say that a good home is one in which father and mother live together in a stable relationship into which the child can be accepted and welcomed" (p. 103). In their view, the process of building up trust requires that every child put his or her parents through a series of gruelling tests to see whether they "do in fact stand the strain". (Here is that word "strain" again.) But when the parents either "do not exist", Winnicott and Britton continue, "or if they do not stand the strain that belongs to the building up of a stable family life, the child must surely always remain unconvinced, and uncertain of himself and of others". Clare remarks forty years later in her introduction (1984) to Winnicott's posthumous collection, *Deprivation and Delinquency*:

> The evacuation experience had a profound effect on Winnicott because he had to meet in a concentrated way the confusion brought about by the wholesale break-up of family life, and he had to experience the effect of separation and loss, and of destruction and death. [p. 123]

There is considerable irony in Clare and Donald's reference to a good home as one "in which father and mother live together in a stable relationship" at the very time that his marriage to Alice was falling apart. This irony becomes even more acute when one realizes that Donald and Alice, though childless themselves, took at least two extremely troubled younger people—one a boy of nine, the other a woman of twenty-three—into their home in the mid-1940s, even as he was commencing his affair with Clare.[8] Thus, when Clare writes that Winnicott had to deal with "the confusion brought about by the wholesale break-up of family life", including "the effect of separation and loss, and of destruction and death", she neglects to mention that he did not need to travel every Friday to Oxfordshire to experience these same calamities in his own domestic life in London.

The two texts in which one is afforded what Kahr (1996) has called "a painful glimpse of moments from the last phase" (p. 87) of Winnicott's marriage to Alice are Winnicott's own paper, "Hate in the countertransference" (1947), which details the havoc wreaked on their lives by the nine-year-old boy, whom they could tolerate for only three months, and Marion Milner's *The Hands of the Living God* (1969), the incomparable narrative of her fifteen-year psychoanalytic treatment of "Susan", the twenty-three-year-old whom Donald and Alice took into their home in 1943 after she had twice undergone electroconvulsive therapy in a mental hospital. Although Milner disguises the identity of Susan's foster parents as "Mr. X" and "Mrs. X", they were, in reality, the Winnicotts. On the opening page, we learn not only that Winnicott had offered to subsidize Susan's analysis but also that he had assured Milner that "the main treatment would be the fact that he and his wife were providing her with a home" (p. 3). Like Clare and Donald's definition of a good home as one in which a father and mother "live together in a stable relationship", Winnicott's statement to Milner becomes ironic in view of the fact that, by 1949, Susan, who was still living with Donald and Alice, noticed "increasing signs that the X's

---

[8] Kahr (1996) documents that the boy was not the only evacuated child "to have lived residentially with Donald and Alice in their home" (p. 86). That the lad was nine years of age makes his attempted rehabilitation seem to be an act of projective identification in light of the fact that it was at the age of nine that Winnicott looked at himself in the mirror and said, "I'm too nice", and began engaging in various forms of antisocial behaviour (C. Winnicott, 1982, p. 258; 1983, p. 186).

marriage was not going to last very long" (p. 59). What is more, Susan, who was already tormented by a sense of having lost her soul as a result of the shock treatments, which Winnicott had culpably failed to prevent (p. 134), told Milner that she felt "the break-up of the X's marriage was her fault" (p. 87). She likewise became "very paranoid about Mr. X", insisting that "he broke up the marriage deliberately in order to 'bitch her up'" (p. 113). Thus, Donald and Alice Winnicott are themselves parents who "do not stand the strain that belongs to the building up of a stable family life", while it is Susan who bears out the truth of the statement in his paper with Clare that, under such circumstances, "the child must surely always remain unconvinced, and uncertain of himself and of others".

In a series of reversals of figure and ground, the knowledge of his secret affair with Clare forces us to re-evaluate our sense of Winnicott the man and his marriage to Alice, while the knowledge of what Winnicott, in "Hate in the countertransference", has termed "the assault on the inside" (1947, p. 200) taking place in his marriage with Alice forces us to re-evaluate Clare's depiction of her work with Winnicott in Oxfordshire and of their subsequent happiness together. It is the *strain* of reconciling these two seemingly incompatible images of Winnicott as someone who found a marriage of true minds with Clare while in the process destroying the thing he loved with Alice—if I may combine allusions to Shakespeare and Oscar Wilde in a single sentence—that can no longer be evaded in attempting to understand him in his full complexity and that I am seeking to explore psychoanalytically in this chapter.

4

As I have indicated, the two heuristic hypotheses by which I am guided are, first, that Winnicott's relationships to Alice and Clare constitute transferences of his early relationship to his mother and, second, that his writings can be viewed as analytic communications enabling us to reconstruct what must have gone on in his infancy. To be sure, we also possess valuable external clues that show us where to dig deeper in his writings. One of the memorable details about Winnicott's analysis with Strachey, which can be gleaned from the latter's deplorable violations of confidentiality in his letters to his wife Alix in Berlin, is that, as Strachey wrote on 11 November 1924, "poor little Winnie seriously suggested to-day that perhaps he'd pumped over his ma at the moment of his birth" (Meisel & Kendrick, 1985, p. 115).[9] Strachey further informs Alix that "the conversation arose from the enormous pleasure it gave [Winnicott] to pump while he was bathing in the sea", and that he had gone so far as to offer Winnicott the interpretation "that he may even have done it inside her".

Despite Strachey's jocular tone, which continues in his witticism that he fancies Winnicott to have been "cut out to be a Rank-schüler", Winnicott's own reconstruction in the course of his analysis that he may have urinated over his mother at the moment of his birth was ventured in all seriousness. Let us, therefore, see what Winnicott says in his writings about both enuresis and the birth experience. Concerning bed-wetting, Winnicott observes in "The antisocial tendency" (1956) that the accent falls either "on regression at the moment of the dream, or on the antisocial compulsion to claim the right to the mother's body" (p. 313). As is well known, Winnicott understands the antisocial tendency to be a sign of hope on the part of a child who seeks to compel the environment to restore a good object or experience that has been withdrawn after he or she enjoyed it for a period of time. If we apply this formulation to Winnicott himself, and interpret his "pumping" on his mother at his birth as a claiming of the right to her body, it follows that Winnicott must have felt himself to have been deprived while still in his mother's womb, though only after having first been provided with a certain amount of "good-enough" gestation.

That Winnicott would have no objection on theoretical grounds to my drawing this conclusion is corroborated by his paper, "Birth memories, birth trauma, and anxiety" (1949a), where he puts forward the view that "there is certainly before birth the beginning of an emotional development, and it is likely that there is before birth a capacity for false and unhealthy emotional development" (p. 182),

---

[9] This letter, which provided the point of departure for my coupling of Rank and Winnicott in *The Psychoanalytic Vocation*, was written at the height of the turmoil generated by the publication of Rank's *The Trauma of Birth*.

such as might provoke a newborn baby to urinate over the body of its mother as a primordial act of antisocial rebellion. Indeed, as early as his 1919 letter to his sister Violet, in which Winnicott first announces his intention to take up the study of psychoanalysis, he states that "we will take it for granted that there is a division of the Mind into the conscious and a subconscious, and that in the latter are stored all impressions received since birth (and possibly before)" (Rodman, 1987, p. 2); and the effects of prenatal experiences remained one of Winnicott's abiding preoccupations.[10]

If the evidence strongly suggests that Winnicott regarded himself as having suffered impingement while still inside his mother's womb, it is even clearer that he regarded himself as having been traumatized by a premature weaning. According to Rodman (2003), Winnicott told Milner that "he was weaned early because his mother could not stand her own excitement during breast feeding" (p. 14). Once again, this external source helps us to know where to sink our shafts in his writings. In his crucial 1945 paper, "Primitive emotional development", Winnicott discusses "the most primitive state" of mental life, in which "the object behaves according to magical laws, i.e. it exists when desired, it approaches when approached, it hurts when hurt. Lastly," he adds, "it vanishes when not wanted" (p. 153). After having introduced this typology of responses on the part of what he will later term subjective objects, Winnicott expands upon vanishing, which he describes as "most terrifying" and "the only true annihilation". "To

---

[10] In her account (1985) of her analysis with Winnicott, which was prompted in part by hearing him read his paper on the birth trauma (p. 19), Margaret Little reports that during a session in which she felt recurring "spasms of terror" she would cling to Winnicott's hands until the attacks subsided. According to Little, who experienced some fallout from Winnicott's divorce and remarriage from a patient's perspective (p. 29), he "said at the end that he thought I was reliving the experience of being born; he held my head for a few minutes, saying that immediately after birth an infant's head could ache and feel heavy for a time" (p. 20). See also "Primitive emotional development" (1945, p. 148); "Mind and its relation to the psyche–soma" (1949b, p. 249), where Winnicott brings prenatal experience into conjunction with the opposition between a "true self" and a "false self"; "Fear of breakdown" (1974), in which he discusses a patient in whom "there was a premature awareness awakened before birth because of maternal panic" (p. 93); and the posthumously published *Human Nature* (1988, pp. 143–151).

not want, as a result of satisfaction," Winnicott explains, "is to anni-
hilate the object. This is one reason why infants are not happy and
contented after a satisfactory feed". As a clinical example, Winnicott
appeals to an otherwise unspecified "patient of mine", whom I
believe to have been none other than Winnicott himself. This
supposed patient "carried this fear right on to adult life and only
grew up from it in analysis, a man who had an extremely good
early experience with his mother and in his home. His chief fear
was of satisfaction" (pp. 153–154).

If this individual had "an extremely good experience with his
mother", it seems odd that he should have feared having annihilated her. But this duality is the very essence of Winnicott. On the
one hand, Clare Winnicott promulgated the view that "from his
earliest years Donald did not doubt that he was loved, and he experienced a security which he could take for granted" (1978, p. 242),
but, on the other, Winnicott's potency problems render it incontrovertible that "his chief fear was of satisfaction".[11] To the previously
quoted passage from "Primitive emotional development", Winnicott appends a footnote:

> I will just mention another reason why the infant is not satisfied
> with satisfaction. He feels fobbed off. He intended, one might say,
> to make a cannibalistic attack and he has been put off by an opiate,
> the feed. At best he can postpone the attack. [1945, p. 154]

In "Communicating and not communicating" (1963a), Winnicott
refers back to this earlier discussion, saying that when "the infant
feels 'fobbed off' by a satisfactory feed", it will often be found that
"a nursing mother's anxiety" is "based on the fear that if the infant
is not satisfied then the mother will be attacked and destroyed"
(p. 181).

In these passages from two of Winnicott's most important
papers, I think we have a transcription of his own experience as an

---

[11] Compare the comment by Klein (1930):

> The earliest defense set up by the ego is directed against the subject's own
> sadism and the object attacked. . . . In boys this violent defense is also
> directed against his penis as the executive organ of his sadism and it is one
> of the deepest sources of all disturbances of potency. [p. 232]

infant at his mother's breast: he did receive adequate nourishment in the earliest months, but was left feeling "not satisfied with satisfaction" when he was repeatedly prevented from unleashing his sensual "cannibalistic attack" for the reason he spelled out to Milner—"because his mother could not stand her own excitement during breast feeding". This led to his premature weaning. In my reconstruction, moreover, Winnicott's traumatic experiences at his mother's breast supervene on still earlier traumatic experiences while he was inside her womb, for which there is likewise compelling evidence in Winnicott's texts as well as in his analysis with Strachey.

This line of argument perforce alters our response to Clare Winnicott's depiction of Winnicott's childhood, just as a reading of "Hate in the countertransference" and *The Hands of the Living God* provides a counterpoint to her narratives of their work with evacuated children during the Second World War. It is not that Clare's versions of Winnicott's life are wrong—they are, in large measure, Winnicott's own versions of his life—but that there is, both in his childhood and in his adulthood, a competing counternarrative, the truth of which is equally undeniable. After a 1982 talk to the Squiggle Foundation, when a member of the audience objected that his or her impression of Winnicott "didn't quite chime in with what you told us about his own mother" (C. Winnicott, 1982, p. 269), Clare was flustered, asserting on the one hand that Winnicott "would always say to me when he was talking about his mother, 'You know, I had a lovely mother'", while conceding on the other that "I suppose she was so fond of him she was frightened", and "but do you feel he's making up for something his mother didn't give him? . . . I can see what you mean" (pp. 269–270).[12]

---

[12] A comment by Klein (1935) is again apposite:

In some patients who had turned away from their mother in dislike or hate, or used other mechanisms to get away from her, I have found that there existed in their minds nevertheless a beautiful picture of the mother, but one which was felt to be a *picture* only, not her real self. The real object was felt to be unattractive—really an injured, incurable and therefore dreaded person. [p. 270]

In terms of my heuristic principles in this chapter, Clare Winnicott's slant on Winnicott's life can be compared to the "direct observation of infants" as an extra-analytic source of information, while
the inferences to be drawn from Winnicott's writings are analogous
to "the study of transference in the analytic setting", from which, as
Winnicott maintained, "it is possible to gain a clear view of what
takes place in infancy itself". Again, however, I do not mean to
imply that one perspective is true and the other false; rather, it is
necessary to accept the paradox that Winnicott was both the infant
who internalized his mother's "fear of satisfaction" and the child
who "had an extremely good early experience with his mother and
in his home", just as he was the man who was married first to Alice
and then to Clare.

If we continue to focus on the traumatic aspect of Winnicott's
development, the conclusion that I think must be drawn is that his
mother, Elizabeth ("Bessie"), did not survive his very early "cannibalistic attacks", and that this deep fear of the annihilating effects
of his aggression and sexuality was reactivated in his relationship
with Alice. Already in "Primitive emotional development" (1945),
as we have seen, Winnicott explores the "most primitive state" in
which "the object behaves according to magical laws", and he does
so in the context of a discussion of those cases that are deemed
unsuitable for analysis "if we cannot deal with the transference
difficulties that belong to an essential lack of a true relation to external reality" (p. 152).

When Winnicott uses the pronoun "we", he is speaking as a
member of the community of analysts, but he also belongs among
those patients who cannot be reached by classical analysis because
they exhibit "an essential lack of a true relation to external reality".
Indeed, in the letter to Klein in November 1952 that marks his repudiation of his identity as a Kleinian, Winnicott acknowledges that
the issues he has brought forward "can always be dismissed as
Winnicott's illness", but concludes by insisting that his illness "is
not far away from being the inherent difficulty in regard to human
contact with external reality" (Rodman, 1987, p. 37). Winnicott's
nearly verbatim echo of "Primitive emotional development" con-
firms the extent to which the concerns of that landmark paper are
rooted in autobiography. The question remains, however, whether
the "difficulty" to which he refers is indeed "inherent" in the

human condition, or whether it ought not to be conceptualized instead as the result of the traumatic breakdowns in Winnicott's own—or in any infant's—earliest experience.

5

In the introduction to his last great paper, "The use of an object" (1969), Winnicott states that it "is in the direct line of development that is peculiarly mine" (p. 86). When one retraces the major milestones of that development, from "Primitive emotional development" (1945) through "Transitional objects and transitional phenomena" (1953) to "Ego distortion in terms of true and false self" (1960a) and "Communicating and not communicating leading to a study of certain opposites" (1963a), and culminating in "The use of an object" (1969), it is impossible to deny that the relation between internal and external reality is indeed the central theme of his work. What I hope is becoming clear from my analysis is that this development is "peculiarly" Winnicott's not only in a theoretical sense, but also because it arises out of his most urgent personal concerns.

I would augment my reconstruction of Winnicott's infancy with the aid of "The use of an object" (1969) as follows: because his mother failed to survive his destructive attacks during breast-feeding, he was unable to place her "outside the area of the subject's omnipotent control" (p. 90). As a consequence, there remained a bedrock of Winnicott's psyche that never discovered external reality and in which his internal objects (to revert to "Primitive emotional development") continued to behave "according to magical laws". It was this psychotic core of Winnicott's personality that initially drew him to Alice Taylor, and which he reactivated by deserting her for Clare Britton, making Alice into a *revenant* of the mother whom he believed he had annihilated with his instinctual urges and who thereby impeded his transition from object-relating to object-use.

In the larger context of the history of psychoanalysis, the phenomenon understood by Winnicott as a failure of object-use is closely akin to what Freud meant by being "wrecked by success". As Freud (1916d) explains, when a "deeply rooted and long-cherished wish has come to fulfilment" (p. 316), an individual will be

overcome with guilt if the wish was a forbidden one, and its fulfilment is, thus, thought to have been brought about by the power of
one's own fantasy, even though this is not true in reality.[13] For both
Freud and Winnicott, the phenomenon to be elucidated is the
omnipotence of thoughts, and the subject's psychic murder of the
object lies at the origin of magical thinking. The historical link
between the conceptualizations of Freud and Winnicott is Joan
Riviere's paper, "A contribution to the analysis of the negative therapeutic reaction" (1936), which begins by taking up Freud's concept
of "the unconscious sense of guilt" (p. 135) before turning to "the
ego's relation to its internalized objects" (p. 138), particularly in
those "refractory cases" in which "the underlying unconscious reality is more unbearable and more horrible" (p. 146) than in others.
Strikingly, Riviere's essay is actually printed under the running
head, "Those wrecked by success", in Athol Hughes's edition of her
collected papers.

According to Clare Winnicott (1982), Donald recounted the
following story of what prompted him to begin his analysis with
James Strachey: "He told me that he was with a friend in a taxi and
said, 'You know, I never dream. I wonder why I never dream.' And
this friend said, 'You want an analysis'" (p. 262). Even if one questions the historical accuracy of this anecdote, it possesses a mythic
truth. Alice, whom he married in 1923, one year before he entered
analysis with Strachey, was correlated in Winnicott's mind with not
dreaming, just as she was with sexual abstinence. Clare, on the
other hand, with whom he achieved genital potency, was equated
not only with the restoration of the capacity to dream but also with
the lifting of his amnesia for his transitional object in childhood. She
quotes (1978) from a letter he wrote to her in 1950:

> Last night I got something quite unexpected, *through dreaming*. . . .
> Suddenly you joined up with the nearest thing I can get to my

---

[13] In *Freud and Oedipus* (1987), I have argued that the death of Freud's baby
brother Julius, when he himself was not yet two years of age, was experienced
by Freud in just such a fashion and that it left him "with an uncanny dread of
the omnipotence of his own wishes" (p. 20). This in turn caused him to react
with such intensity to the death of his father nearly forty years later that he was
led to discover the Oedipus complex.

transition object: it was something I have always known about but I lost the memory of it. [p. 252; italics added]

The object in question was a doll, which Winnicott describes as "a kind of other me, and a not-me female". He goes on to tell Clare, "If I love you as I loved this (must I say?) doll, I love you all out. And I believe I do", and announces that he has resumed work on his paper on transitional objects.

As this letter movingly testifies, through his love affair with Clare Britton, with whom, as she wrote later, "the question of hurting each other did not arise because we were operating in the play area where everything is permissible" (1978, p. 250), Winnicott "joined up" his sundered psyche. This suturing allowed him to bridge the gap between internal and external reality, a process symbolized by his recovery of the memory of his transitional object, the "kind of other me, and a not-me female" who was reincarnated by Clare herself.[14] To turn yet another of Winnicott's pivotal ideas, set forth in his paper on classification (1959–1964), back on himself, the illness he experienced in his marriage to Alice was "a system of defenses organized relative to past breakdown", but he was able to "remember the breakdown only in the special circumstances of a therapeutic setting, and because of ego-growth" (p. 139) made possible by Clare's being there for him to destroy, and to love, and to destroy yet again.

To be sure, Winnicott's marriage of true minds with Clare Britton began as an adulterous liaison, and one that had to be kept secret from the world. In seeking to account for the feeling of strain in "relating inner and outer reality" that Winnicott seems to take for granted not only in his paper on transitional objects but throughout

---

[14] As Kahr (1996) has recognized, the psychological healing that took place in Winnicott through his turn from Alice to Clare was accompanied by an extraordinary upsurge in his productivity:

During his marriage to Alice Taylor, Winnicott published only one book—a textbook on paediatrics. In the course of his marriage to Clare Britton, on the other hand, he produced six more books before his death, and he wrote enough papers, lectures, and correspondence to fill another twelve volumes published after his death. [p. 94]

his writings, it would be natural to suppose that a man who harboured a secret he was fearful of spilling might find it more difficult than one with a clear conscience to bare his innermost thoughts. But, as Winnicott intriguingly suggests in his review (1964) of Jung's *Memories, Dreams, Reflections*, this is actually a superficial view of the matter. Reflecting on Jung's avowal that he had told Freud a lie concerning one of his own dreams, Winnicott comments: "When Jung deliberately lied to Freud he became a unit with a capacity to hide secrets instead of a split personality with no place for hiding anything" (p. 487).[15] As Rodman (2003) has emphasized, Jung, who likewise had a depressed mother and had to cope with psychotic dissociation, was looked upon by Winnicott as his psychoanalytic "twin" (p. 287), and what Winnicott has to say about Jung is, therefore, profoundly self-referential.[16] If we then apply what Winnicott says about Jung's "capacity to hide secrets" to Winnicott himself, it follows that he too "became a unit" thanks to his affair with Clare, whereas in his relationship with Alice he was simply "a split personality with no place for hiding anything".

In the final analysis, it was not the fact that he lived what Rodman (2003) has called "a secret, parallel life with a professional colleague, unknown to Alice, for at least five years" (p. 208) that caused Winnicott's permanent sense of strain between inner and outer worlds. It was, rather, the irony of fate whereby the same freedom that allowed him to unleash, in Clare's (1978) words, "his unconscious ruthless and destructive drives" (p. 250) in his newfound love with her meant that he subjected Alice to a devas-

---

[15] On Jung's dissimulation concerning his dream of the "two skulls" and its connection to his awareness of Freud's affair with Minna Bernays, see Chapter Two, n. 9, and Chapter Three, n. 13, above.

[16] Rodman draws on Winnicott's (1963b) account of a dream he had in connection with writing his review of Jung, about which Winnicott states that it helped to explain his feeling "that I would be all right if someone would split my head open" (p. 228). Winnicott observes that Jung "seems to have no contact with his primitive destructive impulses" and highlights the "difficulty Jung may have had in being cared for by a depressed mother" (p. 229). Although the recipient of the letter in which Winnicott reported this dream is not specified in *Psycho-Analytic Explorations*, Rodman discloses that it was Jung's distinguished English follower, Michael Fordham.

tating attack from which she could not recover—though she did not die physically for another two decades—and that this catastrophe re-enacted his mother's failure to survive his attempts to gratify his instinctual urges, first in her womb and then at her breast.

Seen from this standpoint, Winnicott's history of coronaries can be understood as psychosomatic expressions of the magical thinking in which whatever is done unto the other is also visited upon the self. In addition to the irreparable harm he inflicted on both Alice and "Susan", Winnicott from the beginning to the end of his career was haunted by the deaths of patients, whether due to his own negligence or because they committed suicide (Kahr, 1996, pp. 39, 89; Rodman, 2003, pp. 162, 333–337). What is more, Clare Winnicott (1982) reports that he "always blamed himself" (p. 270) for his mother's death of a heart attack in 1925.[17] The best-known manifestation of Winnicott's survivor guilt centres on his friends and schoolmates who were killed in the First World War, about whom Clare (1982) quotes him as having written: "'I always felt I had to live for them all because I survived and they didn't'" (p. 259; see also Reeves, 2004).

6

Having set forth the essential dynamics that I believe underlie Winnicott's deeply personal artistic vision of psychoanalysis, I cannot conclude without briefly touching on what I take to be his scientific limitations. The key text is his 1963 paper on communication, and my critique—as I have already intimated in questioning his assertion concerning "the *inherent* difficulty in regard to human contact with external reality"—is that he goes astray by confusing normal and pathological phenomena. Winnicott, in other words, is always drawing on the wellspring of his own experience, and, while he often recognizes the severity of his illness, with its roots in

---

[17] Clare Winnicott (1982) guesses that Elizabeth Winnicott "was forty-seven or something" (p. 270) when she died, whereas she was, in fact, sixty-three. This exaggeration of the prematurity of Elizabeth's death accords with Winnicott's subjective perception of his responsibility for the event.

his early relationship to his mother, at other times he fails to allow for the distortions of his own perception and mistakes what are, in actuality, the consequences of potentially avoidable traumatic breakdowns for inevitable and even desirable manifestations of the human condition.

Winnicott begins "Communicating and not communicating" (1963a) by announcing that, to his own "surprise", the paper he has written has turned out to be a claim "to the right not to communicate" (p. 179). The negative corollary is that the paper represents "a protest from the core of me to the frightening fantasy of being infinitely exploited", which Winnicott paraphrases as "the fantasy of being found". These declarations frankly acknowledge the subjective affect informing Winnicott's argument, and this language continues to resonate in his central theoretical statements. Winnicott writes: "I suggest that in health there is a core to the personality that corresponds to the true self of the split personality; I suggest that this core never communicates with the world of perceived objects" (p. 187). Then, in a sentence the last portion of which is italicized, he elaborates: "Although healthy persons communicate and enjoy communicating, the other fact is equally true, that each individual is an isolate, permanently non-communicating, permanently unknown, in fact unfound". He poses what he takes to be the most important question that follows from his foregoing assertions: "The question is: how to be isolated without having to be insulated?"

What I find most striking here is that Winnicott depicts being "an isolate" and "permanently non-communicating" as the condition of "healthy persons". I regard this position as untenable, and, indeed, it is contradicted by Winnicott himself in his moments of greater lucidity. "When the mother's adaptation is not good enough at the start," he writes in "Ego distortion in terms of true and false self" (1960a), "the infant remains isolated" and "lives falsely" (p. 146). Given this premise, it becomes possible for Winnicott "to trace the point of origin of the False Self, which can now be seen as a defense, a defense against that which is unthinkable, the exploitation of the True Self" (p. 147). In this more cogent presentation, Winnicott sees being "isolated", as well as the fear of "exploitation", not as signs of health but as forms of "defense" employed by an infant traumatized by the failure of his "mother's adaptation". In similar fashion, the state of being "unfound", which

Winnicott celebrates in "Communicating and not communicating", is portrayed much more sombrely in "Aggression in relation to emotional development" (1950–1955). Tracing the earliest roots of aggression to the "motility that dates from intra-uterine life" (p. 211), during which, as I have argued, he himself is likely to have suffered impingements, Winnicott describes a worst-case scenario in which "what there is left of a core is hidden away and is difficult to find even in the most far-reaching analysis. The individual then *exists by not being found*" (p. 212).

No less influential a commentator than Adam Phillips (1988) has pronounced "Communicating and not communicating" to be Winnicott's "greatest paper" (p. 141), but, despite its pivotal place in that "line of development that is peculiarly" Winnicott's, its contention that it is "healthy" to be an "isolate" makes it, in my view, one of his least satisfactory performances, in which his frequently scintillating paradoxes turn into an intellectual muddle. As long ago as 1968, Harry Guntrip branded the idea that it was possible "to be isolated without being insulated" a "dubious proposition", and he diagnosed Winnicott's thesis of an "incommunicado" true self as "a primitive fear reaction, such as we could envisage in an infant who is not adequately protected and ego-supported by his mother and thus exposed to a fear of annihilation because of his own extreme weakness" (pp. 236–237). Guntrip reformulates Winnicott's question as it should properly be stated: "how to have *privacy and self-possession without isolation or insulation?*" (p. 236).[18]

---

[18] Much of my argument in this paragraph recapitulates that already proffered in *The Psychoanalytic Vocation* (Rudnytsky, 1991, pp. 140–141). In a similar vein, Rodman (2003) has observed that Winnicott, who is otherwise renowned for his "attentiveness to external reality", here resorts to "a *shutting out of the external*", an "extreme position" that is "the strange twin to Klein's exclusion of the mother" (p. 266) in her theories. Concerning Winnicott's 1952 paper, "Psychoses and child care", Rodman (2003) has pointed out that it, too, contradicts his paper on communicating by upholding the view that "the secret inner life is incommunicable as a result of pathogenic circumstances and not a normal condition" (p. 169). Like all the other papers prior to Winnicott's breakthrough in 1969 with "The use of an object", the paper on communicating lacks an adequate account of how "*a subjective phenomenon becomes an object objectively perceived*" (1963a, p. 180). He is able to say only that this transition "gradually develops" when "the facilitating environment can be taken for granted in . . . the earliest and most formative stages of human growth".

Far more than the oft-repeated charges that Winnicott ignores the father or slights sexuality, his confusion in the paper on communication about what is normal and what is pathological, and his attempt to glorify a retreat into schizoid isolation, exposes a fault-line in his thought, though what I deplore as a scientific weakness I cherish as an astigmatism that is integral to the distinctiveness of his artistic vision.

7

If one scours Winnicott's writings for traces of the psychic price he paid for his desertion of Alice, with its revival of his mother's failure to survive his destructive attacks, one is bound to alight on his November 1963 poem "The Tree", the complete text of which is now available in Rodman's biography (2003, pp. 289–290).[19] The stanza where Winnicott compares himself to Christ hanging on the cross, which he equates with the lap of the depressed mother of his early childhood, is already well known:

> Once, stretched out on her lap
> as now on a dead tree
> I learned to make her smile
> to stem her tears
> to undo her guilt
> to cure her inward death

But I do not think anyone has observed that the poem also laments Winnicott's decades of abstinence in his marriage to Alice, "I could have loved a woman", as well as his struggle to escape the pressure to comply with the expectation that he would join the "Winnicott firm": "I must be about my father's business". Indeed, even Winnicott's decision to become a child analyst becomes part of the

---

[19] As Rodman (2003, p. 291) discloses, the poem was sent to Jim Taylor, the brother of Alice, whom he had abandoned fifteen years earlier, whereas I, along with other scholars, had previously believed that its recipient was James Britton, the brother of Clare. This clarification of which brother-in-law was the recipient of "The Tree" highlights Winnicott's continuing anguish about the failure of his first marriage.

martyrdom imposed by his imitation of Christ: "Children came and loved and were loved / Suffer little children to come unto me".[20]

A reading of "The Tree" makes it difficult to credit Clare Winnicott's (1982) statement that his mother "was the lively one in the family" (p. 270). Yet, it was Winnicott himself who repeatedly told her, "You know, I'm a deeply happy person, deeply happy", and as a child his cup of love must have been filled to overflowing, not simply by his mother, but also by his two older sisters and all the other doting aunts and domestic servants who appertained to the Winnicott household. Whereas "The Tree" is Winnicott's most eloquent testament to his legacy of maternal deprivation, his childhood bounty is harvested in the undated poem "Sleep":

> Let down your tap root
> to the center of your soul
> Suck up the sap
> from the infinite source
> of your unconscious
> And
> Be evergreen.
> [quoted in C. Winnicott, 1978, p. 253]

I find it exquisite that Winnicott resorts to the same metaphor of a tree to convey both the "inward death" he relived with Alice and

---

[20] Winnicott's identification with Christ goes back to his 1919 letter to his sister Violet, in which he refers to Christ as "a leading psychotherapist" (Rodman, 1987, p. 3). Rodman (2003) has connected "The Tree" to a crucifix that he made out of matches during an analytic session with Marion Milner in the 1940s, through which he sought to communicate his "personal agony" as a "marital sufferer" (p. 137). Intriguingly, in *The Hands of the Living God* (1969), Milner comes to understand Susan's first dream, "about Christ being taken down from the cross by five men", as "envisaging the analysis as a process of becoming freed from being nailed to the torturing internal mother-tree", with the five men representing the weekly "five days of analysis" (p. 230). They arrive at the realization that Milner had been experienced by Susan in fantasy as "a dead tree inside her" (p. 407). In *Reading Psychoanalysis* (Rudnytsky, 2002, pp. 192–199), I have compared Winnicott's deployment of the cross as a metaphor for the depressed mother to that of Groddeck. See now also Roger Willoughby's (2005, p. 7) quotation of Khan's poem, "I Cannot Hear", addressed to his "mad, inconsolable mother", against whose "shriek" his ears are "stuffed" with "dead leaves". Like "The Tree", Khan's poem was composed in November 1963, and was almost certainly inspired by it.

the "evergreen" love he rediscovered with Clare. Can it be a coincidence that, as Clare Winnicott (1978) has recalled, "there was a special tree, in the branches of which Donald would do his homework in the days before he went to boarding school" (p. 241)? Or that one of her final memories (1983) of him should have been of him at his home in Devon, where she was startled to discover him "up at the top of a tree, in the last year of his life" (p. 192), lopping off the branches because they blocked the view from their window? Was this tree of his old age the same tree he climbed as a youth? Or do we have simply a symbol of the circle that contains both sides of his divided self?

8

In this chapter, I have sought to draw on the new information that is now available about Winnicott's life, and specifically about his relationship to his two wives, to touch up my earlier portrait of the man and his work. In particular, I have attributed Winnicott's puzzling insistence that there must be a "strain" in the intercourse between inner and outer reality to the tragedy that his finding of true love with Clare could only come at the price of his abandonment of Alice, which revived his sense of guilt and belief in the omnipotence of his wishes as a result of having destroyed his mother in fantasy in infancy.

Doubtless, there is much that is partial and even distorted in my own vision. But, in choosing to approach him from one particular angle, I take comfort in Winnicott's own reminder, in his paper on birth memories (1949a), that "in a discussion of any one subject one should not be afraid *temporarily* to seem to overestimate the importance of the subject under discussion" (p. 177). My purpose has been to show Winnicott in all his human frailty so that we can better appreciate the enduring majesty of his contributions to psychoanalysis. To quote for the last time from "Mind and its relation to the psyche–soma", also written in the fateful year of 1949, "what releases the mother from the need to be perfect is the infant's understanding", and "if she is *good enough* the infant becomes able to allow for her deficiencies by mental activity" (p. 245). I have tried to use my understanding to release Winnicott from the need to be perfect—or, rather, to release *us* from our need to have a perfect Winnicott—and, in the process, to show that he is indeed good enough.

CHAPTER FIVE

In praise of Nina Coltart

"It is of the essence of our impossible profession that in a very singular way we do not know what we are doing".

(Nina Coltart, "Slouching towards Bethlehem", 1986)

1

In reading the work of a psychoanalytic author, there is one question that I think we should ask ourselves above all others: would I want to be in analysis with this person? Is this someone I would trust to probe the innermost recesses of my psyche and with whom I would be likely to have a genuinely therapeutic experience?

To be sure, we also hope to profit intellectually from reading a psychoanalytic paper. But a brilliant theorist may not be the man or woman to whom one would turn for emotional healing. Even today, the figure of Freud casts by far the longest shadow over the psychoanalytic field, while both Klein and Lacan have indubitably expanded the universe of analytic discourse; but I suspect I may not be alone in feeling that I would rather have gone for treatment to

Ferenczi or Winnicott—or, indeed, to any number of lesser mortals, provided they were possessed of genuine humility and compassion.

In proposing that we assess every analytic writer by our readiness to see him or her for therapy, I am asking us to reflect on the image of the human being that we form from reading a given author's work. Indeed, with those of past generations whom we will never have the privilege of meeting in the flesh, the only way we *can* get to know them is through their texts, as well as through the memoirs of others and ancillary historical sources. (This, in turn, is how we will be remembered—if at all—by those who come after us.) Even with our contemporaries, I think we are likely to arrive at a deeper understanding of them by paying close attention to their writings than through ordinary social interactions, though the most intimate communion comes through such privileged relationships as those between teacher and student or analyst and analysand.

As with our teachers and analysts, moreover, it is not by explicit self-disclosures that we develop an inwardness with an author. Rather, it is through the experience of reading itself, the quality of pleasure and illumination it brings us—as well as our sense of the writer's tact, insight, empathy, and skill—that we come to know him or her and make up our minds about whether we would be comfortable lying on that person's couch. Out of this transferential investment in an author, however, there naturally arises a desire for closer acquaintance, a curiosity about what he or she was really like as a person . . .

2

Although she has been largely forgotten, even by mental health professionals, outside of her native England a little more than a decade after her death on 24 June 1997, and I myself regret never having met her during her lifetime, there is no one whom I would rather have had as my analyst than Nina Coltart. My purpose in this chapter is to try to put into words something of the love and admiration inspired by my reading of Coltart, in hopes that others may be induced to discover—or rediscover—her work for themselves.

There are several facts about Coltart that need to be brought out immediately. The first is that, besides being a psychoanalyst, she became for most of her adult life (after having lost the Christian faith of her youth), a Theravadin Buddhist, the practice of which centres on daily meditation; and her writing is informed by a profound synthesis between these two modalities of spiritual healing. The second is that, as far as her analytic allegiances are concerned, Coltart was a leading member of the Independent Group in the British Psychoanalytical Society; indeed, she described herself, in a magnificent late interview with Anthony Molino (1997), as "the most independent representative of the Independent Group" (p. 177). After retiring from clinical practice in December 1994, at the age of sixty-seven, and relocating from Hampstead in northwest London to a rural seat in Leighton Buzzard, moreover, Coltart formally resigned from the British Society, becoming only the third person—after Charles Rycroft and Peter Lomas—to have taken this step in the contemporary era.[1]

In the third place, no study of Coltart can fail to confront the fact that she died by her own hand, from an overdose of sleeping pills. To anticipate my subsequent argument, Coltart's suicide may be seen as either an act of freedom or an act of despair—or as both simultaneously—and how we come to terms with this painful circumstance will be inseparable from our view of Coltart's career as a whole.

Underlying everything else, there is the overwhelming trauma of Coltart's childhood: the train accident in which both of her parents were killed. Along with her sister, Gill, four years her junior, and their devoted nanny, Nina had been evacuated from London to Cornwall during the Second World War. In 1940, Gill contracted a mysterious illness, probably glandular fever; the girls' father, a respected general practitioner, was summoned by the local doctor. Father and mother boarded a night train to the southwest of England. The train jack-knifed, crushing several cars, and Nina,

---

[1] Fifty years earlier, in 1944, Edward Glover resigned from the British Society in protest against the outcome of the Controversial Discussions. In her interview with Molino (1997, p. 170), Coltart cites the precedents of Rycroft and Lomas, both of whom I interviewed for my book *Psychoanalytic Conversations* (Rudnytsky, 2000).

having taken a taxi to meet her parents at the station, was brought home four hours later, having been shielded from the news by the compassionate driver. Only on the following day, after an agonizing delay, was she informed that her parents had died.

Coltart's destiny was indelibly marked by this catastrophe of double parental loss. It largely explains the fact that she "always lived alone" and became known as "quite a recluse" (Molino, 1997, p. 180). She did, to be sure, have a gift for friendships—mainly with women—but she renounced lasting intimacy with a partner of either sex. Coltart was not an ascetic. She was an inveterate smoker, enjoyed a good meal, and, as she told Molino, she developed an "active sex life" in her late twenties, a breakthrough she correlated with having ceased to believe in God "almost overnight" (p. 200). For what it is worth, her sexual orientation appears to have been heterosexual. But it is not only in the professional domain that Coltart cultivated an extreme independence.

To the extent that Coltart's name continues to be remembered today, it is above all as the author of "Slouching towards Bethlehem", a paper she first presented at a conference of English-speaking psychoanalysts in 1982, then published in expanded form in Gregorio Kohon's 1986 volume, *The British School of Psychoanalysis: The Independent Tradition*, before reprinting it in 1993 as the lead essay in the first of her three books. Coltart did not bequeath to psychoanalysis any original theoretical concepts. But "Slouching towards Bethlehem"—the title of which comes from Yeats's poem "The Second Coming"—teaches analysts an invaluable lesson: the necessity of retaining a faith in the analytic process, the outcome of which can never be foreseen, which in turn depends on the capacity to wait without closing down by premature interpretation for the "rough beast" that is struggling to be born in the patient.[2]

As is evident from the sentence I have taken as my epigraph— the most famous that Coltart ever wrote—her stress on faith in experience (as opposed to "Faith" in a transcendental sense)[3] is

---

[2] Coltart quotes "The Second Coming" in full in her paper, and my references to Yeats's poem throughout this chapter are taken from her transcription.

[3] On the distinction between faith with a small and a capital letter, see Coltart (1993a, pp. 110, 113).

allied to a respect for mystery and the readiness to "tolerate not knowing" (1986, p. 3); and in "Slouching towards Bethlehem" Coltart pays tribute to Bion as her precursor in setting forth these principles that are far less recommendations concerning analytic technique than they are compass points for the mind and heart of the analyst. And if, as I have suggested, the true test of an analytic author is whether one would want to be in treatment with him or her, then Coltart bestowed the highest compliment imaginable when she told Molino (1997), "I've always wanted to have my second analysis with Bion" (p. 175).

Coltart left behind a comparatively small body of writing—just three books in all, the first and third of which are collections of papers, *Slouching towards Bethlehem* (1993b) and *The Baby and the Bathwater* (1996c), while only the second, *How to Survive as a Psychotherapist* (1993a), was conceived as a unified work.[4] Almost all of Coltart's writings can be divided into two categories, the first being a gallery of riveting case studies that make her the Jane Austen of psychoanalysis, and the second being her immensely valuable cogitations on practical matters, while a smaller third category comprises her essays on psychoanalysis and Buddhism (1985, 1996e), although the philosophy she spells out here, and in the final pages of *How to Survive as a Psychotherapist*, implicitly informs her exclusively psychoanalytic texts.

Paradoxically enough for a Buddhist, what Coltart has to offer her readers is nothing more or nothing less than her self. But is this not the most important quality one looks for in a healer? Coltart wrote in the same way as she practised. Having been trained first at public school and then at Oxford in the art of essay writing, she always strove "to achieve the greatest simplicity of expression" and to leave out, "as far as possible, technical language or specialized language, so that lay people can read the stuff with some enjoyment" (Molino, 1997, p. 168). What Coltart says of the Enlightened One can with equal justice be applied to her own prose:

> The Buddha had a memorable style, he told a lot of stories that show what an astute psychologist he was, and he also had a knack

---

[4] For an outstanding study of Coltart's life and work, see the as yet unpublished monograph by Sara Boffito (2008).

of grouping things so that they hung together; one could rapidly grasp the essentials of what he taught, and then take them away and start absorbing them. [1996e, p. 125]

In what follows, I first undertake a closer scrutiny of Coltart's life, for which the indispensable source is the interview she gave in two instalments to Molino less than a year before her death. Having retired from clinical practice and extricated herself from the trammels of institutional affiliation, secure in the knowledge that she had nothing left to write and very likely already planning to shuffle off this mortal coil, Coltart laid herself bare in this colloquy to a degree that renders my task as an expositor little more than one of recapitulation and synthesis. Besides the interview, I shall also be mining what I believe to be Coltart's most autobiographically revealing paper, "Two's company, three's a crowd" (1996g), about her experience in 1989 as a participant in a course offered by the Institute of Group Analysis.[5] Then, after having placed Coltart's life under the microscope, my endeavour will be to demonstrate how an awareness of their subjective origins enhances our appreciation of her contributions to psychoanalysis. I shall close with some brief reflections on the enigma of her suicide.

3

The inevitable starting point is the death of Coltart's parents. A curious detail, symptomatic of the upheaval resulting from such a blow, is that Coltart refers to the accident as having taken place "when I was eleven", reiterating that "you can't be in analysis for very long without realizing that it's not as if an idyllic, blissfully happy childhood of eleven years was suddenly fractured by a nasty trauma" (Molino, 1997, p. 194). But, since Coltart was born on 21 November 1927, and the train crash occurred on 4 November 1940, she was, in actuality, almost thirteen, not eleven. Psychically, Coltart must have experienced herself as still a child when the tragedy occurred. In any

---

[5] This paper was delivered in 1991 at a conference sponsored by the same institute, though not published until *The Baby and the Bathwater*.

event, as Coltart acknowledges in *How to Survive as a Psychotherapist*, "a certain element of psychopathology, induced by a fracture in my own story, contributed to the vocational sense" that led her to become a psychoanalyst (1993a, p. 101).[6]

As I have already intimated, the sudden loss of her parents is connected quite directly to what she describes in "Two's company, three's a crowd" as "an extreme degree of need of separateness", a quality that Coltart conceded might also be "called critically a sort of stand-offishness" (1996g, p. 50). Even more unwelcome to her than a romantic commitment, which always carries with it the risk of heartbreak through death or infidelity, was the prospect of having children; for, as Coltart told Molino (1997), the "neurosis" induced by her parents' death meant that she "always had an anxiety about having children, and possibly leaving them with such an affliction as being orphaned" (p. 179).

Like many abused or traumatized children, Coltart emerged from the catastrophe of her parents' death with a sense of specialness. Reverting in the interview with Molino (1997) to her metaphor of a "fracture", she expatiates, "a tragedy like that fractures your life completely, and from then on you're a different person, you lead a different life. You've got a secret life. . . . I used to feel secretly that I knew a great deal more than other people" (pp. 191–192). Even after decades as both a psychoanalyst and a Buddhist, Coltart owns up to having preserved "a sort of superiority from such a prolonged struggle with survival" (p. 192). If one were to affix a diagnostic label to Coltart's "psychopathology", it would be difficult to avoid resorting to the term "narcissism", though its outward manifestations are a secondary formation covering over her underlying insecurity and emotional fragility. With characteristic irony, Coltart relished skewering her own vanity. She writes of her "immediate reaction" to an attack unleashed by an elderly male patient that it "was almost entirely governed by my narcissism" (1991b, p. 88), and she confesses that a conversation with one of her "normal"

---

[6] Elsewhere in this book, Coltart describes herself as someone with "a long-past experience of double parental loss at a vulnerable stage in life (early adolescence)" (1993a, p. 11), which comports better with an age closer to thirteen than to eleven.

friends outside the psychoanalytic bubble prompted her to "sigh as I realized yet again that I must inspect my narcissism and the possibility that I was idealizing, making special my new-found knowledge" (1993a, p. 57).

Pivotal though the death of her parents undoubtedly was, Coltart's analytically fostered recognition that her childhood had not been "blissfully happy" even before this disaster opens far-reaching vistas. As she elaborates, "I used to get very anxious and cry easily as a child", while her mother was likewise in all probability "anxious and somewhat depressed" because she was "by no means" the "favourite child" of her own mother, who "had a fearful temper and was very jealous" (Molino, 1997, p. 194).

In the trauma that was transmitted through the generations in Coltart's family, the child favoured by Coltart's grandmother was her firstborn son, the elder brother of Coltart's mother. By a tragic irony, however, this son had "fought in and survived the First World War, only to come home and be killed in a motorbike accident just up the road from where the family lived" (Molino, 1997, p. 194). The bereavement of Coltart's grandmother was compounded when, "ten years later", her "relatively young husband—a handsome, dashing general practitioner—dropped dead beside her in a theatre queue". Finally, Coltart explains, "ten years after that, her only other child, my mother, died in a train crash".

Given that Coltart's parents died in 1940, and that Coltart's uncle died in the immediate aftermath of the First World War, we can date his death and that of Coltart's grandfather to 1920 and 1930, respectively. Since Coltart's mother had been predeceased by both her brother and father, Coltart infers, she must have been left with "her own increasingly difficult mother to cope with" (Molino, 1997, p. 194) in the years that she and her husband were raising their two young daughters. After their parents' death, Coltart and her sister themselves became wards of this "rather demonic old lady", a "wicked grandmother" who "didn't look after us" as a caretaker should. Coltart's insecurity and proclivity to tears even as a young child, therefore, constituted the refracted expressions of her mother's anxiety and depression, which were in turn introjections of the emotional hole left in *her* mother, Coltart's grandmother, by the series of tragic losses that blighted that grim matriarch's life.[7]

Coltart's crucial insight is that the devastating "fracture" resulting from her parents' death was superimposed on earlier experiences that were themselves cumulatively traumatic—to borrow once again Masud Khan's (1963) useful concept—and that her tendency as a survivor to be consumed by the massive event had the further deleterious consequence of causing her to idealize the period that had preceded it, impeding access to the grief and anger that lay buried beneath the rubble of the obvious calamity.[8] Coltart cites Winnicott's aphorism that "the dreadful has already happened",[9] which she glosses in illuminating fashion by explaining that the death of her parents "had to be preceded by what the Buddhists call 'preconditioning'", and she recognizes in hindsight that she "was in many ways an anxious child, ready for depression" (Molino, 1997, p. 194).

As I noted earlier, Coltart and her sister Gill were accompanied on their evacuation to Cornwall by their nanny, who had also been their mother's nanny in her youth, and Coltart attests that this "salt of the earth" woman was "always my primary love object" and the "saviour of both my and my sister's sanity" (Molino, 1997, p. 195). Although Coltart's nanny gave her the unstinting devotion that she sought in vain from her mother, the nanny was also a midwife who worked in Coltart's father's medical practice; this meant that, during Coltart's formative years, she would periodically vanish

---

[7] In a personal communication, Coltart's sister, Gillian Preston, has given a different picture of her and Nina's grandmother, describing her as "a highly intelligent and cultured woman, who had run a highly successful Red Cross Unit in World War I, and had been decorated for it". In later years, she adds, the girls and their grandmother "became good friends. She had a killing sense of humour, and as we grew up, she introduced us to much, especially in literature. We all became closer, with both parties benefiting by it".

[8] In his paper on cumulative trauma, Khan attributes this phenomenon to a "partial breakdown of the protective-shield function of the mother" (1963, p. 52). See also Chapter Four, n. 4, above.

[9] Coltart's allusion seems to be to Winnicott's paper, "Fear of breakdown", probably written in 1963 though not published until after his death. In this influential text, Winnicott elucidates the complex dynamics whereby the breakdown feared by certain patients *"has already been"*, although it is *"not yet experienced"* (1974, pp. 90–91) because it could not be assimilated by the immature ego.

from the family home for weeks at a time to live with a newborn baby and its mother.[10] As Coltart recalls, "I don't think I ever quite got the hang of her disappearances; certainly, I never knew when she was coming back, or if she was ever coming back" (p. 195). Thus, it was above all in relation to this indispensable person that Coltart became accustomed to "the comings-and-goings of someone so loved, who'd disappear and often fail to return"; and this *fort/da* rhythm formed the "preconditioning" for the shattering trauma of her parents' death. "So in a way", Coltart concludes, "my parents never getting to Cornwall on the night they died was the culmination, an apex of sorts, of a dynamic that had always been for me a source of great anxiety".

Luckily, her sister recovered from her illness; had Gill also perished, Coltart had no doubt that she herself would have turned into a "lunatic" (Molino, 1997, p. 191). But the cumulative agonies of separation and loss that preceded the fatal train crash were exacerbated by the ordeals to which the girls were subjected subsequently. As John Bowlby (1980) has pointed out, in order for a child to be able to mourn the death of a parent in a healthy fashion, it is indispensable that he have "the comforting presence of his surviving parent, or if that is not possible of a known and trusted substitute, and an assurance that that relationship will continue" (p. 276). But not only were the sisters given over to their "demonic" grandmother, but first Nina and then Gill were speedily dispatched by this same unreliable caretaker to Sherborne School, a prestigious boarding establishment where Nina cultivated a love of English

---

[10] In a personal communication, Gillian Preston has again placed things in a different light, stressing that "'Nan' only left the family home, in Kent, on the rare occasion for a midwifery job *prior* to November 1940, i.e., when we would still be in the care of our mother", and recalling "two or three times, as a small girl, visiting her when on a 'case', and seeing the new baby", adding that Nina "obviously blocked this out". After their parents' death, however, Gillian Preston continues, "Nan kept her promise to our mother always to look after us and make a home for us. *Only during term time*, while we were at boarding school, did she take the very occasional midwifery job (in order to earn a little, as she had no salary from our estate)". But even when one allows for the inevitable divergences between the recollections of two siblings, since Nina Coltart's account of her nanny's disappearances pertains to the period *prior* to their parents' death, there does not appear to be any basis to question the accuracy of her version of these events.

literature but predictably became "very depressed and disturbed" (Molino, 1997, p. 191). From the standpoint of attachment theory, one could not have scripted a more devastating sequence of events, and although Nina Coltart went on to achieve great things in her life, any prospect of genuinely recovering from the tragedy of the stunningly sudden loss of both parents may well have been doomed by the inability of her grandmother to provide the "comforting presence" and assurance of continuity that the barely adolescent Nina desperately needed.

Upon graduation from Sherborne, Coltart went on to read Modern Languages at Somerville College, Oxford, although she had already determined to become a doctor. Overcoming her constitutional ineptitude for mathematics and her lack of preparation in the natural sciences, Coltart won an Arts Scholarship to take a second degree in medicine at St. Bartholomew's Hospital. No sooner had she achieved this goal, however, than Coltart discovered that it was not what she had wanted since (as she fathomed years later during her analysis) by becoming a doctor she had accomplished her unconscious project of identifying with her father: "I'd restored him to life" (Molino, 1997, pp. 197–198). Looking back on her journey, Coltart depreciated both her Oxford degree and her medical training as "so much bathwater" (1996d, p. 156), unavoidable detours that were not without their dividends, but not to be confused with the baby that remains when everything inessential has been jettisoned.

Coltart came to psychoanalysis through serendipity. While working for three years at a psychiatric hospital in Essex, she met a congenial woman doctor from New Zealand who was in the midst of analytic training and who encouraged Coltart to try it for herself. At the time she applied, Coltart had never read any Freud and was "absolutely, deeply ignorant" about psychoanalysis in general; she presumes that she must have been accepted by the British Society because she was "such a *tabula rasa* that they felt they could imprint me with anything" (1993a, p. 100).

Like Coltart's family history, her experience in analysis warrants detailed examination. Her analyst was Eva Rosenfeld, who was nearing seventy and induced to come out of retirement to take on Coltart as her final training case. Coltart was matched up with Rosenfeld because of the remarkable similarities between their personal histories. Just as Coltart had suffered the deaths of her parents, so also had Rosenfeld—who had the distinction of having been analysed first by Freud and then by Klein—been wounded by losses, though for Rosenfeld it was the deaths of her children that had been traumatic. Of her four children, three boys and a girl, two of the boys died of dysentery at the end of the First World War, while the girl, "whom she adored . . . died as a result of a mountain climbing accident" (Molino, 1997, p. 176). Rosenfeld eventually separated from her husband and emigrated from Vienna by way of Berlin to London, where she was "left with only one son". What is more, the death of Rosenfeld's daughter finds an uncanny parallel in the fact that Melanie Klein's eldest son also died in a mountain climbing accident. In her interview with Molino, Coltart even wonders whether Rosenfeld's daughter and Klein's son might have perished in the same accident, though she quickly allows, "I may be making this up"; and since Klein's son died in 1934, seven years after Rosenfeld's daughter, the two incidents cannot have been connected in reality.

As in her family of origin, therefore, when Coltart entered analysis with Rosenfeld she once again found herself enmeshed in an intergenerational history of trauma that had been transmitted through the female line from Melanie Klein through Eva Rosenfeld to her. The "preconditioning" for the train crash had been laid down not simply in Coltart's own childhood, but in the lives of her mother and grandmother, and this dynamic was replicated in her analytic genealogy. Like Coltart's mother, Rosenfeld "had a tragic life", which left her "depressed"; not surprisingly, Coltart came to the conclusion that Rosenfeld's sorrows "considerably influenced her countertransference to me" (Molino, 1997, p. 176).

Although Coltart acknowledges the benefits of her analysis with Rosenfeld, telling Molino (1997) that "so far as it went it helped me a lot", her emphasis falls on its limitations and her conviction that "it didn't go far enough" (p. 196). Just as Coltart says of her own anxiety, "I never got near this core in my analysis" (p. 195), so, too, she surmises of Rosenfeld, "I don't suppose Freud had got anywhere near the core of her experience" (p. 176). She rues that her analysis was "extremely classical, old Freudian stuff", and though Rosenfeld "would often say that I was angry with my parents or that I felt guilty about my parents", the words "never clicked with me. They did not become real" (p. 196). Emblematic of Coltart's frustrations is a comment in *How to Survive as a Psychotherapist* on the subject of consulting-room decor:

> I might have survived my own analysis with a little less distraction if there had *not* been an evocative picture that hung as I faced it directly from the couch. I think a bare wall allows for freer fantasy in the patient; and I would certainly always choose to have white walls as my personal preference. [1993a, p. 30]

As always, Coltart's advice to the prospective therapist is eminently practical, but it grows out of an awareness that she had not received what she needed from her analysis with Rosenfeld. In Coltart's own terms, the "evocative picture" on her analyst's wall, like Rosenfeld's classical Freudianism, impeded the regression that would have made it possible for her to give birth to the "rough beast" that was languishing inchoately in the womb of her psyche.

Coltart is far from being the only patient to have been let down by her first experience of analysis, especially one undertaken for training purposes. It is, doubtless, the sense that Bion could have guided her into the terrain that she was unable to explore with Rosenfeld that prompted Coltart to fantasize about re-entering analysis with him. Coltart conceptualizes her psychopathology as a compound of anxiety and depression, with the anxiety brought to its "apex" by her parents' non-arrival on that night in Cornwall being "psychotic" (Molino, 1997, p. 196) in its intensity; and her mixed verdict on the analysis with Rosenfeld is that, "although it helped with my depression", it "didn't do much for my anxiety" (p. 201).

Following her renunciation of Christianity, Coltart turned to Buddhist meditation as a means of coping with the suffering that continued to afflict her even after completing her analysis. She was also able to confide in "one or two friends" (Molino, 1997, p. 195), and she continued to engage in the introspection that forms a vital undercurrent in her writings. Beyond these private and spiritual resources, however, Coltart did have one experience in a therapeutic setting that led to a breakthrough with respect to her childhood trauma. It is recorded in "Two's company, three's a crowd" (1996g), which I have identified as her most autobiographically revealing paper, even though she refrains in this context from going into specifics about the event that had taken place nearly fifty years earlier and that she found herself reliving most unexpectedly.

As a congenital outsider, Coltart regularly aligned herself with individuals and organizations from which most psychoanalysts were at pains to steer clear. She had good things to say, for instance, about both Karen Horney and R. D. Laing, and she was a long-time supporter of the Arbours Association, a residential therapeutic community in London, which currently sponsors an annual lecture in her memory. Even before resigning from the British Psycho-analytical Society, she had become disenchanted with its "authori-tarianism" and resolved that she would "henceforth only take on for supervision experienced psychotherapists" with whom Coltart "thought there would be a far greater chance of an egalitarian rela-tionship" (1996a, p. 110).

Coltart's decision in 1989 to enrol in the introductory course offered by the Institute of Group Analysis, being something that "very few, if any, practising senior psychoanalysts" had ever done (1996g, p. 43), was of a piece with her iconoclastic temperament. In addition to a weekly lecture followed by a discussion, the course consisted of "a weekly experiential group of one-and-a-half hours" (p. 41). In her paper, Coltart goes on amusingly about her efforts to conceal her identity as an analyst from the other members of the group as well as about how she came to realize that her "running stream of inner commentary on people tended towards the critical, with intolerance at the extreme" (p. 52), leading her to give "private names" (p. 51) to her fellow participants.[11]

Beyond its grace notes, however, at the heart of "Two's company, three's a crowd" there lies Coltart's account of how, while participating in this year of group therapy, she "abreacted some buried feelings" (1996g, p. 54) about the trauma of her youth. For a considerable period, Coltart reports, she "did not detect any partic-ular signs of transference" in herself towards the group conductor, an "attentive and containing" woman in her early forties. One day,

---

[11] Nor were Coltart's patients exempt from her penchant for bestowing nick-names. As she remarks about a depressed woman whom she dubbed in the second week of her analysis the "Little Hedgehog", the "nickname thrown up by the analyst's unconscious invariably carries an apt cogency about the patient's psychopathology" (1991b, p. 84).

however, Coltart "noticed that I was pleased and rather relieved for her when she said something shrewd". Coltart connected this assuaging of her anxiety about the conductor to "an ancient feeling about my younger sister, who was a worry in her teens, doing something grown-up and admirable".

Initially, therefore, Coltart's transference to the group conductor was sororal, though it became maternal several months later. The decisive episode was triggered, in Gestalt fashion, "because there were some empty chairs, and quite intensive group talk about people who were absent or missing" (1996g, p. 94). Under the stress induced by these circumstances, Coltart "developed an anxiety attack" in which she "for a while felt very helpless and overcome, but also violently angry with our group conductor, wanting her to help and feeling she, too, was 'missing' this and failing me". The evocation of "people who were absent or missing" in a physical sense, symbolized by the "empty chairs", in other words, was augmented by Coltart's conviction that the group leader, though physically present, was "missing" emotionally by failing, first, to recognize Coltart's feeling of abandonment and, second, to rescue her from it. Fortunately, however, "the group, as it was capable of doing at times, rallied to what felt like a crisis and worked superbly to contain me and put me together again".

As a result of her breakdown, which was also a breakthrough, Coltart became aware that, beneath her "apparently rather neutral response to the group leader", she had unconsciously "been building up a primitive and strong transference to a mother, who then suddenly disappeared—or seemed to". She continues:

> After I was able to let the anxiety attack happen, then be angry, and then rescued, I gained some valuable insight into something that had never before been accessible to me, in all these years—namely, the anger towards my mother, which had been locked inside the anxiety. [1996g, p. 55]

In this unlikely setting, Coltart was able to discover the emotional reality of the transference, and, hence, of her anger towards her mother, that had remained inaccessible throughout her training analysis with Rosenfeld. This emergence of her "rough beast" from its psychic lair at least approximates the experience that she would have wanted to have with Bion, but that Coltart was wise enough to ensure she extracted from life even though she did not achieve it in the formal context of a psychoanalysis.

Pondering this anxiety attack set off by the empty chairs, Coltart stresses that what it brought to light was not a response to her parents' death, but the realization that "I had been all those years stewing away a sort of fury at my mother, from long before she died" (Molino, 1997, p. 196). She was, that is, able to get in touch with the "preconditioning" of the cumulative experiences of abandonment that had lain buried beneath the rubble of the catastrophe of the train wreck. Because Coltart as a girl had been so "furious with her for letting me down, for being so absent", it was paradoxically only "through her death that I later discovered she'd been an absent mother in life". Initially, however, when Coltart's mother died, and thereby became "totally absent", any awareness that Coltart may have had "of her shortcomings first needed to go into profound repression". There it lay dormant for decades, until the dynamic of anxiety and anger at the failed reappearances of her loved objects could be reactivated by her transference to the group conductor and the containment afforded by the other participants when they rallied to her side at the critical moment.

Everything that I have set forth about Coltart's life is indebted to Coltart's own hard-won insights, as imparted in her valedictory interview with Anthony Molino and in "Two's company, three's a crowd". With extraordinary lucidity, Coltart has shown how her destiny was shaped not only by the "fracture" induced by the trauma of her parents' accidental death but, even more profoundly, by the "preconditioning" both of the history of losses going back three generations in her family and of the repeated disappearances of her two mothers—her biological mother and her beloved nanny—during her childhood. She likewise allows us to see how her family history was recreated when she entered analysis with Rosenfeld, and how Rosenfeld, for a combination of personal and theoretical reasons, was not able to help her very much. It is quintessentially psychoanalytic that Coltart achieved the most profound self-knowledge by re-enacting her early experiences in a transference neurosis, albeit one that she developed in the course at the Institute of Group Analysis. It remains for me now to reflect on Coltart's work in light of what we have learned about her life and then to close by touching on the delicate topic of her suicide.

4

Nina Coltart was under no illusions about her place in the history of psychoanalysis. "I don't think I should be remembered", she told Molino (1997), "not in the way that Winnicott and Bion and others are remembered" (p. 179). As I have noted, she did not originate any theoretical concepts. It is, rather, for "Slouching towards Bethlehem", the paper that first made her reputation, that she continues to live on, however tenuously, in psychoanalytic memory. This paper struck a chord by its evocative use of Yeats's poem, with its metaphor of the "rough beast", to talk "about breakdown and the possibility of healing" (1986, p. 1), as well as by the eloquence with which Coltart propounded her radical view that "the essence of our impossible profession" (p. 2) is an acceptance of ignorance or even incompetence, since only by evincing the capacity to tolerate not knowing can the analyst aspire "to be continually open to the emergence of the unexpected" (p. 6), which is how healing takes place through the psychoanalytic process.[12]

As a Buddhist, Coltart was as reconciled as it is possible for a human being to be to impermanence, including the ephemerality of her own fame. She did admit to Molino (1997) that she was "proud" to have written her books, which "say pretty well everything I want to say. So people needn't really miss me. 'Me' is in my books" (p. 179). "Then again", she hastens to add, "everything is transient anyway!"

Although Coltart is doubtless right about transience, and even Freud's cloud-capped towers will melt into air one day, there is no need for us to hasten her passage to oblivion. On the contrary, Coltart's efflorescence of creativity during her final fifteen years is, in my estimation, one of the greatest glories in the psychoanalytic literature, and the three books in which she has distilled herself for posterity deserve to be much more widely known and cherished than they are.

---

[12] Coltart emphasizes that there is always a "delicate balance" between the need for faith and "our reliance on our theories and on our knowledge of human nature in many of its dimensions" (1986, p. 6), but it is the mystical dimension of her respect for the unknown for which Coltart is inevitably—and justly—celebrated or castigated in "Slouching towards Bethlehem".

When one examines Coltart's work through the lens of her life, the humpbacked shape of her career immediately solicits commentary. For after the paper she was required to present in 1967 to attain full membership in the British Psychoanalytical Society, "The man with two mothers" (1996f), which remained unpublished until it was included in *The Baby and the Bathwater*, Coltart wrote nothing for fifteen years until "Slouching towards Bethlehem" was delivered at the conference of English-speaking analysts in 1982. Then, firing on all cylinders, Coltart propelled herself into the orbit of her later period, which conspicuously mirrors the first half of her career in extending for fifteen years.

Even more uncanny than this temporal symmetry, however, is how Coltart's second birth as a writer in "Slouching towards Bethlehem" exemplifies the description of the treatment process that she proffers in the very paper in which she achieved her breakthrough. The theme of the 1982 conference was "Beyond Words", and Coltart writes that "profound silence itself, as well as what it conceals, can be a rough beast which is slouching along in the depths of a communicative, articulate patient and whose time may need to come round and be *endured* in the analysis" (1986, p. 9). No less pertinently, she observes that often, after a period of preliminary work, there comes a time in an analysis "when darkness begins to close in, but it is a darkness having that special quality of the unknown which is moving towards being known" (p. 7).

As her prime clinical example in "Slouching towards Bethlehem", Coltart instances an elderly male patient to whom she later devoted an entire paper (1991a), and who returns for a cameo appearance also in "The silent patient" (1991b).[13] Clearly, silence was a topic dear to Coltart's heart, and it must have possessed for

---

[13] This example became notorious because of Coltart's revelation that she one day "simply and suddenly became furious and bawled [the patient] out for his prolonged lethal attack on me and on the analysis" (1986, p. 10). In her subsequent case history, Coltart stood by her conduct, asserting that "we can do no harm to a patient by showing authentic affect, within the limits of scrupulous self-observation" (1991a, p. 161). As Franco Borgogno has concurred, even expressions of hate and anger by the analyst can be justified if these emotions "are, in a moment of the treatment, the sentiments in play that urgently call for their recognition" (2007, p. 54).

her a personal as well as a theoretical significance. Coltart herself, after all, had had to endure fifteen years of silence in her analytic career in order for the darkness within her soul to move from the unknown towards beginning to be known in "Slouching towards Bethlehem".

On a still deeper level, not only does Coltart's prolonged gestation as a writer exemplify the intertwined dynamics of emotional breakdown and healing set forth in her classic paper, but her understanding of the treatment process constitutes a supremely creative response to her own most agonizing traumatic experiences. Describing the dynamic of disappearance and failed return of the caretakers in her childhood as "a wound from which one never recovers", though her ego "has had to grow various defences or skins around it", Coltart confides to Molino (1997) that "the pure anxiety of waiting for someone whom I love and depend upon to come to me is still, at times, unbearable" (pp. 195–196).

Now, the essence of Coltart's plea in "Slouching towards Bethlehem" is that the analyst should make each hour into an "act of faith" both in himself and in the analytic process, and this—following Bion—Coltart construes as "the capacity to sit it out with a patient, often for long periods, without any real precision as to where we are" (1986, p. 3). The greatest temptation, accordingly, is to try "to take possession of our patients too soon", with the forceps of intellect, but though such precipitate displays of cleverness may "appeal to quite conscious layers of the patient", they inadvertently reinforce the resistance and thereby prevent "the true unknown reality" (p. 6) that lies hidden within the womb of the psyche from being born when (in Yeats's words) its hour comes round at last.

Like those of any thinker, the value of Coltart's ideas is independent of their autobiographical roots. "Slouching towards Bethlehem" would be a sublime paper with much to teach us even if we knew nothing about its resonance on multiple levels with its author's personal experience. But, in my view, it only enhances our appreciation of Coltart's achievement when we are able to grasp that, through the metaphor of the "rough beast", she has been able to transform "the pure anxiety of waiting" that was her acutest dread in life into the source of her most generative contribution to psychoanalysis.

Similarly, when Coltart chose to call her second book *How to Survive as a Psychotherapist*, she highlighted the centrality of the theme of survival not only to her conception of psychotherapy, but also to her entire outlook. As the title of her opening chapter specifies, by survival she means "Survival-with-Enjoyment", and not, as she puts it elsewhere, "grimly hanging on" (1996a, p. 120). Coltart frequently voiced her delight that, in becoming a psychoanalyst, she had found her true calling in life and that this serendipity allowed her to feel herself "a round peg in a round hole" (1993a, p. 8). The title of her book sums up Coltart's lesson that would-be therapists or analysts must be able to take unalloyed pleasure in their often gruelling work, including the arduous training process, and that this capacity to "survive-with-enjoyment" is an indispensable concomitant to sustaining a vocation in the field of mental health.[14]

Yet, on an existential plane, the question of survival was fraught with peril for Coltart. As we know, she diagnosed a "fracture" in her being, as well as the compensatory sense of "superiority", resulting from her "prolonged struggle with survival" after the deaths of her parents. Thus, although Coltart did find her work to be a source of fulfilment that enabled her to "survive" for decades according to the unique definition she gave to this word—while always insisting that psychoanalysis did not fill the void left by her abandonment of Christianity, and that this spiritual hunger was appeased only when she discovered Buddhism—we can see once again how this contribution to our understanding of what it means to be a psychotherapist possessed a dimension of subjective significance for Coltart. Indeed, Coltart's insight into what it means to "survive-with-enjoyment" was a further inspired transformation of her "unbearable" anxiety that someone who, at the age of twelve, had suffered an incurable wound might, beneath the surface, in fact have been "grimly hanging on" all along, and thus not have survived at all.

---

[14] Coltart specifies the "five features that, together, characterize a vocation" as "giftedness, belief in the power of the unconscious (indeed, in the unconscious itself), strength of purpose, reparativeness, and curiosity" (1996h, p. 34).

5

There can be no more painful topic for friends and family members than the suicide of a beloved person. Yet, I think it is incumbent on those of us who have come to love Nina Coltart, if only through her writings, to grasp this nettle as firmly as possible, trusting that she herself would have wanted the truth to be known and secure in our conviction that the best way to pay tribute to her memory is by walking the tightrope of an infinite compassion and an unsparing honesty.

It is worth recalling in this connection that the death of Freud was a physician-assisted suicide.[15] No one, to my knowledge, feels it necessary to reproach Freud because he could no longer live with the pain of his cancer, and why should we imagine that Coltart's agony was any less excruciating or presume to deny her the same right of self-determination over her own existence?

I do not think we can do better than to try to adumbrate the mystery of Coltart's suicide by using her own most luminous metaphor. Whereas her long-delayed burst of creativity, beginning in "Slouching towards Bethlehem", represented an epiphany of the "rough beast" in the positive guise of her deepest wisdom about the meaning of analysis, fired in the crucible of a struggle with anxiety and depression stemming from her childhood traumas, when she took her own life fifteen years later this "shape with lion's body and the head of a man"—Yeats's line identifies the menacing creature with the Egyptian Sphinx—finally turned its "stare blank and piti-less" on its human antagonist and claimed her life.

When Coltart left the analytic world and ensconced herself in Leighton Buzzard—a place, as she noted to Molino (1997), that brought her life "full circle" by being "just up the road" from the birthplace of the nanny who was her "primary love object" (p. 195)—she was already in declining health and increasingly dependent on

---

[15] For an authoritative review of the actual circumstances and untrustwor-thy narratives concerning Freud's death, see Lacoursiere (2008). Like Coltart, Stekel committed suicide, in Bos and Groenendijk's (2007) words, "after pro-longed suffering from a severe disease", but these authors blur an important distinction in asserting that Freud "also ended his life by his own hand" (p. 18, n. 2).

the care of others. Coltart suffered from osteoporosis, as well as heart and thyroid problems, and she underwent major abdominal surgery in the autumn of 1996. Thus, just as she had been forced as a child to hang on, as it were, for what seemed an eternity before being informed of the deaths of her parents, a cataclysmic blow that seared her forever with "the pure anxiety of waiting for someone whom I love and depend upon to come to me", to which she had already been subjected repeatedly during her prior years of "preconditioning", so, once again, at the end of her life Coltart unconsciously recreated the situation that she found most "unbearable"—one that she had symbolically reenacted in the transference when she felt abandoned by the group conductor during the "empty chair" episode—in which she would have to wait for a mother or sister who might or might not show up when Coltart needed her most.

But, like an anamorphic image, Coltart's suicide, which seen from one perspective is an act of despair, is from another vantage point also an act of existential freedom. Coltart was for four decades a member of the Voluntary Euthanasia Society, and, in addition to notes addressed to her family and doctor, she left in her kitchen an article about suicide from the newsletter of the Society under which she had written, "I agree with this" (*Hampstead and Highgate*, 1997). With characteristic pungency and practicality, she posted a sign on her front door, "Please do not disturb—having an extra lie-in".

The shadow of Coltart's impending death looms over her encounter with Molino. Praising his perspicacity in questioning her about this theme in her writing, she observes that "quite a lot of my patients die", including two by suicide and several others "relatively young" (Molino, 1997, p. 192), such as the subject of "The man with two mothers".[16] It was, she says at the very close of the

---

[16] There are many striking parallels between this sexually perverse patient and Coltart. Each of the following statements about him could also be taken autobiographically: (a) "he has known about the strangeness of his inner world for years, and often had a conscious dread of breakdown" (1996f, p. 9); (b) "if he chooses one mother, he is guilty of having betrayed the other" (p. 1); (c) "he abandoned his belief in God, though, I suppose inevitably, he sometimes looked back to it regretfully" (p. 12); and (d), in the patient's own words: "'I was just feeling so good last week, and as if you were a real good person I could rely on. Now you're not even bad, don't flatter yourself—you've *gone*, don't you see?'" (p. 15).

interview, "to keep the memory of a patient alive" that she wrote the chapter, "Paradoxes", in *How to Survive as a Psychotherapist*, and she describes this woman who, in a fit of rage, had swept the objects off Coltart's mantlepiece and had even brought a knife to one of her sessions as "a great, great character" (Molino, 1997, p. 208). In "Paradoxes", Coltart remarks with tragic poignancy that "one cannot escape the stark knowledge that suicide stands for failure" (1993a, p. 45); and it is impossible to read her account of this patient's suicide without being reminded of Coltart's own. Although Coltart had mailed her a postcard after a Friday session, expecting it to arrive on Saturday, it was not delivered until Monday, after the patient had killed herself. In a last letter to Coltart, written on her deathbed, the patient had said she knew the card would come on Monday, but, in Coltart's words, "its non-arrival had been all (all?) that was needed to tip her over the edge" (p. 54). Can it be a coincidence that, just as her life had come "full circle" by returning to the birthplace of her nanny, Coltart's thoughts should have returned, in her final public testament, to this forlorn yet indomitable woman who was likewise undone by "the pure agony of waiting"?

Of her other patient who committed suicide—a voluble and intellectually gifted man who chose to end it all on the anniversary of the day he had terminated his analysis, and whose case is recounted in "A philosopher and his mind"—Coltart pays tribute to his reticence in not leaving a note: "I admired the dignity and forbearance of his silent departure" (1995, p. 90).

CHAPTER SIX

Rethinking *King Lear*: from incestuous fantasy to primitive anxieties

"I realize that I can't count on the virtuous regard of other adults. But what can I do about the fact that, as far as I can tell, nothing, *nothing*, is put to rest, however old a man may be?"

(Philip Roth, *The Dying Animal*, 2001)

Near the end of Plato's *Phaedrus* (Hamilton & Cairns, 1973), Socrates famously argues for the superiority of speech to writing. "Written words", he says to his young friend, "go on telling you just the same thing forever", whereas "living speech" is "the sort that goes together with knowledge, and is written in the soul of the learner" (275e–276b).

Socrates' distinction bears on the question of the relation between psychoanalysis as a mode of literary criticism and as a mode of therapeutic practice. There is, to be sure, a profound ethical difference between treating a live patient and interpreting a text—one is unlikely to be sued for one's crimes against Shakespeare—but I cannot agree with those who draw a sharp distinction between clinical work and what is often referred to as "applied" analysis. In the view of such "purists", because only a live patient can respond to the therapist's interventions, the clinician can refine and even test his interpretations in a way the literary critic cannot; and these analysts would, therefore, agree with Socrates on the superiority of speech to writing.

But, as anyone who has ever reread a classic work of literature can attest, its meaning does indeed change as one comes to see it differently as a result not only of one's own personal development, but also of shifting intellectual currents in the culture at large as well as in the field of literary studies. Socrates, therefore, is wrong. Speech and writing are not as inimical as he would have us believe, and the uses of psychoanalysis in the interpretation of literature have far more in common with its deployment as a form of therapy than is frequently recognized. Both place a premium on sustained attention, and the skills of close reading are closely akin to those of empathic listening.

As a test case for this thesis of the affinity between the clinical and the critical dimensions of psychoanalysis, I shall take *King Lear*, about which I published a feminist psychoanalytic article, "'The darke and vicious place': the dread of the vagina in *King Lear*" (Rudnytsky, 1999a), twelve years ago. In the present chapter, I try to articulate how my views of the play have evolved in the intervening period. I begin by recapitulating the key points in my earlier paper and teasing out some of their implications. Then, I survey the paradigm shifts that have taken place recently in literary studies, and over a longer period in psychoanalysis, and contend that they combine to make possible an enhanced appreciation of Shakespeare's tragedy. My exhibits are Stephen Greenblatt's controversial but influential book, *Will in the World* (2004), and Arnold M. Cooper's exemplary paper, "Infant research and adult psychoanalysis" (1989). Greenblatt's approach to Shakespeare, I go on to argue, has much in common with that of Ella Freeman Sharpe in her 1946 paper, "From *King Lear* to *The Tempest*".

As it happens, one of Sharpe's patients during the time she wrote her paper was Margaret Little, who, after Sharpe's death in 1947, sought treatment with Winnicott. In my third section, I take off from Little's memoir (1985) of her experiences with both analysts to compare Sharpe as an interpreter of *King Lear* with her work as a clinician. Sharpe emerges as a representative of classical analysis, skilled at detecting incestuous fantasies but at a loss when it comes to the primitive anxieties displayed by Little as a patient in real life and by Lear in Shakespeare's play. Little's own insights into transference psychosis will turn out to lead us further into Shakespeare's masterpiece than do Sharpe's formulations. In conclusion, I examine Lear through the prism of Cooper's concept (1988) of the narcissistic–masochistic character. By juxtaposing Little's work with Cooper's, I propose to reconstruct the hypothetical infantile origins of Lear's pathology and to show the convergence of the paradigm shifts in British and American psychoanalysis. Placed against this backdrop, Freud's seminal essay, "The theme of the three caskets" (1913f), despite its focus on the mother, can be seen to reinscribe Lear's tragedy within an Oedipal framework, and, thus, to be in need of emendation from a contemporary perspective, no less than is my 1999 article.

1

Despite the justified perception on the part of many clinicians that academic uses of psychoanalysis have for too long been dominated by postmodernist trends with little relevance to their own work with patients, there is a distinguished counter-tradition, which has had its greatest impact on Shakespeare studies, that seeks to synthesize object relations psychoanalysis with feminist theory.[1] Launched by the anthology *Representing Shakespeare* (Schwartz & Kahn, 1980) and reaching its zenith in Janet Adelman's *Suffocating Mothers* (1992), this more clinically and experientially grounded mode of reading includes Coppélia Kahn's essay, "The absent mother in *King Lear*" (1986), among innumerable other outstanding contributions.

My 1999 article took as its point of entry into *King Lear* Edgar's report in the final scene of how, while in disguise as Poor Tom, he

---

[1] For my own efforts in this direction, see my edited volumes, *Transitional Objects and Potential Spaces: Literary Uses of D. W. Winnicott* (Rudnytsky, 1993) and *Psychoanalyses/Feminisms* (Rudnytsky & Gordon, 2000).

became the guide of his eyeless father: "and in this habit / Met I my father with his bleeding rings, / Their precious stones new lost" (5.3: 189–191).[2] Shakespeare's comparison of eyeballs to "stones" and sockets to "rings", I noted, carries a secondary reference to male and female genitalia, so that Gloucester is left with a bleeding vagina in place of a testicle in each eye, thereby lending credence to the psychoanalytic interpretation of blindness as a symbolic castration.

The title of my paper came from a second speech by Edgar in the final scene, addressed to the dying Edmund, his illegitimate half-brother, "The dark and vicious place where thee he got / Cost him his eyes" (5.3: 173–174). Since the Bastard's machinations precipitate Gloucester's suffering, Edgar pitilessly opines that his father's copulation with a whore has returned to haunt him, and Shakespeare's language again emblazons the "dark and vicious place" of the vagina on the blind man's face.

Having delineated this pattern of imagery, I sought to link it to a thesis about the structure of the play. The "fairy-tale" quality of *King Lear*, with its "vertical" split between the "good" and "evil" children of both Lear and Gloucester, I argued, can be correlated with the "horizontal" split in the representation of the female body in Lear's misogynistic diatribe: "But to the girdle do the gods inherit, / Beneath is all the fiends" (4.6: 126–127). I went on to claim that it is a fantasy about gender that explains the moral polarities of the Lear universe, not the other way around. The supporting characters who turn out to be "good" are either uncontaminated by femininity and sexuality (Kent, Edgar, the Fool) or else they purge themselves of these taints (Albany). The "evil" characters (Edmund, Oswald), conversely, are aligned with Lear's elder daughters and their sexuality. Cordelia, though a woman, embodies the patriarchal ideal of a femininity that is chaste, silent, and obedient. When he enters with her dead body in his arms, Lear recalls that "Her voice was ever soft, / Gentle, and low" (5.3: 273–274), and there is no indication that her marriage to France, whom she abandons to return to England and lead his armies into battle on Lear's behalf, was ever consummated.

---

[2] All quotations from *King Lear* are from *The Riverside Shakespeare* (Evans, 1974), with act, scene, and line numbers given parenthetically in the text.

With respect to the two protagonists, Lear and Gloucester, my proposal was that they comprise two halves of a single masculine psyche. Just as Gloucester's eye sockets are equated with vaginas, Lear expostulates when he beholds Kent in the stocks: "Oh how this Mother swels up toward my heart! / *Hysterica passio*, down, thou climbing sorrow, / Thy element's below" (2.4: 56–58). In Edward Jorden's 1603 treatise, *A Brief Discourse of a Disease Called the Suffocation of the Mother*, the "Mother" is a synonym for the womb, which was held to cause constriction in the throat when it rose from its appointed place. Gloucester mirrors Lear in fantasizing that he harbours the female organs within his own body. Indeed, as Adelman (1992) notes, Lear's belief that he has a uterus "makes Shakespeare the first person to describe hysteria in a man" (p. 300) in the annals of Western culture.

I come now to a point only implicit in my earlier paper—the conjunction between Shakespeare and Freud in their attitudes toward gender and female sexuality. Luce Irigaray, in my view the most brilliant of the French feminists, begins *Speculum of the Other Woman* (1974) by dissecting Freud's lecture on "Femininity" in the *New Introductory Lectures* (1933a), and his assumption that sexual difference should be understood according to a masculine norm. Although Freud never questions his "phallocentric" ideology, Irigaray demonstrates that his texts mark a rupture in the history of Western thought in which its latent conflicts come to the surface: "By exhibiting this 'symptom', this crisis point in metaphysics where we find exposed that sexual 'indifference' that had assured metaphysical coherence and 'closure', Freud offers it up for our analysis" (1974, p. 28).

What Irigaray says of Freud is no less true of Shakespeare. As Shakespeare anticipates Freud's discoveries in so many other ways, so, too, do his works four centuries earlier expose the "crisis point" of a patriarchal tradition of which he is simultaneously a consummate representative. Although it can be debated how much weight should be given to Freud's blind spot with respect to gender in assessing the totality of his thought, just as it can be asked how deeply Shakespeare as a playwright is invested in the fantasies of his protagonists, from a feminist standpoint the answer is clear. Freud's misogyny is far from being a marginal element in his life and work, and Shakespeare is deeply implicated in the destructive fantasies of his male heroes.

A reconsideration of two examples from my earlier article serves to illustrate this contention. First, it is striking how the storm in *King Lear* breaks out just as Lear exclaims, "I shall go mad" (2.4: 284), and he severs all ties with Regan, having already parted irrevocably from Goneril. Although a natural phenomenon, the storm is inevitably experienced not only by Lear himself, but also by the reader or spectator as an "objective correlative" of Lear's breakdown; and in this crucial respect the external reality of the play is indistinguishable from Lear's inner world. Second, Cordelia's return from France without her husband is mandated by the emotional logic of the play, which requires that she reunite with Lear, though under normal circumstances one would expect the king to be at the head of his armies. Whereas in the Quarto version of the tragedy, *The History of King Lear*, printed in 1608, Shakespeare tried to paper over the contrivance by ascribing to a Gentleman the excuse that France had to attend to unspecified matters in his own kingdom, in the revised Folio text of 1623, *The Tragedy of King Lear*, Shakespeare eliminated this awkward scene (4.3) entirely and allowed Cordelia to reappear in England without offering so much as the semblance of a narrative justification.

My argument in 1999 concluded by interpreting Lear's longing for fusion with Cordelia, which reaches its apotheosis in his "birds i' th' cage" (5.3: 9) speech in the final scene, as the expression of the incestuous fantasy that motivated his "darker purpose" (1.1: 36) of dividing his kingdom at the outset. It was, I suggested, the impending marriage of Cordelia that prompted Lear's scheme of abdicating the throne in the first place, and when he imposed the love contest on his daughters, he did so with the unconscious foreknowledge that Cordelia would not join her sisters in flattering him, and was, thus, destined to fail his test. Consequently, Lear's anger, and his decision to disinherit her, masked his secret satisfaction that she would, in all likelihood, now be spurned by both her suitors, France and Burgundy, making it possible for him to keep her as his daughter forever. Lear's true surprise in the opening scene, therefore, came not in Cordelia's disobedience but when France agreed to marry her even without a dowry, thereby frustrating—at least temporarily—the "darker purpose" that would doubtless have been repudiated by Lear himself had it been brought prematurely to his attention by an early modern psychoanalyst.

2

A clear statement of the paradigm shift that has occurred in American psychoanalysis since the appearance of the self psychology of Heinz Kohut in the 1970s, but took place considerably earlier with the consolidation of object relations theory in British psychoanalysis, is offered by Arnold Cooper in "Infant research and adult psychoanalysis". Cooper writes:

> I think the case can be made that the growth of object-relations theory in this country and our increased focus on preoedipal constellations have been enormously reinforced by what we have learned from infant and child development. Not only has that work led many people away from instinctual motivational theories toward object-relational ones but, more importantly, the work has altered the narrative possibilities, the plot paradigms of growth and development, that the analyst is inevitably creating with his patient as he hears his or her own story. [1989, p. 97]

Beyond drawing attention to the turn from drive to relational theories of motivation that has reshaped psychoanalysis, Cooper makes two salient points. The first is that, by speaking of "narrative possibilities" and the "plot paradigms" that are jointly created by analyst and patient, he underscores the similarities between literary and clinical deployments of psychoanalysis. Second, Cooper reminds us of the extent to which the alterations in how analysts work clinically have been propelled by scientific advances in fields—including not only developmental psychology but also neurobiology—that derive their data from research conducted outside the psychoanalytic situation.[3]

Taken together, these two principles underpin Cooper's thesis that analysts inevitably operate "with a limited array of mental templates that predetermine the shape we give to the communications we receive from the patient" (1989, p. 95). For progress to take

---

[3] See also Chapter One, above, where I invoke Cooper's work to make the point that the greatest controversy in psychoanalysis today is between those who recognize that psychoanalysis must seek to integrate the contributions of other disciplines and those who insist that only material gathered in the clinical setting can provide a foundation for psychoanalytic theory.

place in clinical work, analysts must be prepared to modify their "templates" in light of the new knowledge emanating from extra-clinical domains. If they are able to do so, analysts will be far more likely to listen to their patients keenly and empathically.

As an example, Cooper cites the case of an anxious thirty-five-year-old woman whom, in previous decades, one might have viewed in terms of "her obvious oedipal attachment to her father, and her guilty self-denigration and avoidance of self-assertion as penance for her oedipal desires" (1989, p. 101), but who would now be understood to be coping also with deficits originating in the pre-Oedipal period. The Oedipal account, Cooper emphasizes, "is not a false story". Indeed, the patient herself "thrusts it forward at the first session, but it fails to deal with the recoverable earlier origins of her difficulties" (pp. 101–102). Thus, Cooper continues, "development has occurred, and the persistence of early patterns has undergone numerous epigenetic alterations of form and meaning in different developmental stages" (p. 102). The analyst, accordingly, needs to attend not only to the primitive roots of the patient's pathology, but to as many "different developmental stages" as possible that can be uncovered in the course of the treatment.

Arising independently from the paradigm shift delineated by Cooper in psychoanalysis, there has, in recent years, been a broad trend in literary studies away from both linguistic and cultural versions of postmodernism and back to more traditional concerns of character and psychology. Within Shakespeare studies, this tendency is exemplified by Harold Bloom's book, *Shakespeare: The Invention of the Human* (1998), and, more surprisingly, by Stephen Greenblatt's *Will in the World* (2004). As the founder of new historicism, which undertakes to map the "social energies" that flow through texts of the early modern period, Greenblatt has been castigated by many of his erstwhile disciples for his turn to biography in the Shakespeare book, as well as for the avowedly speculative nature of many of its reconstructions and imagined scenes.

Greenblatt's metamorphosis, however, should be welcomed by those in the psychoanalytic camp. His outlook in *Will in the World* is not psychoanalytic, but it is compatible with psychoanalysis. He writes, "The whole impulse to explore Shakespeare's life arises from the powerful conviction that his plays and poems spring not only from other plays and poems but from things he knew firsthand, in his body and soul" (2004, pp. 119–120). Greenblatt's mention of the body is noteworthy in a psychoanalytic context, and the same "powerful conviction" that Shakespeare's works are grounded in "things he knew firsthand" animates Sharpe's effusions in "From *King Lear* to *The Tempest*":

> In *King Lear* I found revealed a child's massive feelings and fantasies,[4] evoked by conflict of emotions associated with actual traumatic events in childhood. The poet in childhood did not express himself as King Lear does, but he felt as King Lear feels. . . . At the end of the play the poet gives Lear a fourfold "Howl," by which the child once expressed what was then inexpressible in language. The play is the fourfold "howl" put into words. [1946, p. 21]

The "impulse to explore Shakespeare's life" that Greenblatt shares with Sharpe follows naturally from the psychological study of his characters, and a central question in *Will in the World* is how to account for Shakespeare's radically new depiction of human subjectivity in *Hamlet* and the other major tragedies. As Greenblatt observes, by the turn of the seventeenth century Shakespeare "had perfected the means to represent inwardness" (2004, p. 229). He did so, Greenblatt argues, through the simple yet far-reaching expedient of creating a "strategic opacity" (p. 324) in his characters by eliminating a "key explanatory element" (p. 323) in their motivations. By refusing to provide adequate explanations for their actions, that is, Shakespeare imparts an illusion of depth that makes his characters seem uncannily real.

I have already discussed one example of Shakespeare's "strategic opacity" in *King Lear* in my analysis of the unconscious motivations behind Lear's "darker purpose" at the outset of the play. But I would like to take this line of argument one step further by using Greenblatt's idea to comment on the relation of Shakespeare's tragedy to its principal source.

An anonymous play, *The True Chronicle History of King Leir* was first published in 1594, but was probably written some years earlier, and then reprinted in 1605 to capitalize on the success of

---

[4] As I consider it to be a distinction without a difference, I have normalized both Sharpe's and Little's spelling of "phantasy" to "fantasy".

Shakespeare's reworking of this Elizabethan antecedent. The older play begins with a speech in which Leir declaims to his assembled nobles:

> Thus to our griefe the obsequies performd
> Of our (too late) deceast and dearest Queen,
> Whose soule I hope, possest of heavenly joyes,
> Doth ride in triumph 'mongst the Cherubins;
> Let us request your grave advice, my Lords,
> For the disposing of our princely daughters . . .
>   [Bullough, 1973, p. 337]

Leir goes on to say that, "wanting now their mothers good advice", his daughters are bereft of their primary parent, and, therefore, it behooves him to safeguard their future by marrying them off to the prospective husbands among whom he will divide his kingdom.

Shakespeare's source, that is, thrusts the death of Leir's wife into the foreground as a motive for his actions. It also bears noting that all three daughters are unmarried and each has at the outset only one suitor—Cordella subsequently meets and falls in love with the disguised Gallian king—whereas Shakespeare alters this design so that the two elder daughters are already married and the conflict hinges on Cordelia, who is alone still single and is courted by not one but two competing suitors. Shakespeare's use of "strategic opacity" thus functions not only to "represent inwardness" in individual characters but to transform his entire conception of the play, homing in on the bond between the father and youngest daughter. As Adelman has written, "*Leir* starts with the fact of maternal loss; *Lear* excises this loss, giving us the uncanny sense of a world created by fathers alone" (1992, p. 104).

The suppression of any allusion to the deceased mother in Shakespeare's opening scene—what I would call the "loss of loss"—persists throughout the play.[5] The only time Lear, or anyone

---

[5] In a wide-ranging discussion, Bennett Simon (1988) has called attention to the importance of the "refusal to mourn" (p. 109) in the tragedy. Simon connects this theme to Lear's "narcissistic character structure" (p. 108), and he anticipates my opening argument in noting that one's "reactions and sympathies" to the play "may change considerably in different life stages and situations" (p. 133).

else, mentions his wife is when he responds to Regan's feigned expression of pleasure at seeing him after he has been stripped of half his retinue of knights by Goneril: "If thou shouldst not be glad, / I would divorce me from thy mother's tomb, / Sepulchring an adult'ress" (2.4: 131–133). Lear summons the memory of his wife only to fantasize that she has cuckolded him as a way of blaming her, rather than himself, for his daughters' treachery. Gloucester's wife, moreover, is not mentioned even once in the play, while the concubine who was Edmund's mother is acknowledged by Gloucester only in the opening scene in the form of a joke to Kent on the word "conceive" (1.1: 12) intended to deflect his embarrassment at having begotten a child out of wedlock.

The world of *King Lear*, like that of Freudian theory, is, thus, one manifestly governed by Oedipal dynamics, but in which what Madelon Sprengnether (1990) has aptly termed "the spectral mother" hovers on the margins, casting her shadow so hauntingly over the psyches of her sons that they bear her inner organs inscribed symbolically in their flesh.

3

As indicated by its title, "Winnicott working in areas where psychotic anxieties predominate", the principal historical interest of Margaret Little's memoir lies in its record of her experience of analysis with Winnicott. But, as I have noted, Little was in analysis with Sharpe prior to her treatment with Winnicott, and it is this portion of her narrative that provides the impetus for my further reflections on *King Lear*.

Little makes no bones about the fact that she was a severely disturbed woman, and her analysis with Sharpe, which lasted from 1940 to 1947, unfortunately qualifies as a failure. She initially consulted Sharpe on a single occasion in 1938, at the behest of her first therapist, a male Jungian, though the analysis proper did not begin until two years later. Little reports that, in her 1938 encounter with Sharpe, she "'saw' her in a kind of grey mist, like a spider in a web which was her hair. I knew it at the time to be delusional—a spider 'of the mind'", and Little "literally *ran* from the house in panic" (1985, p. 14).

The allusion to *Macbeth*, Shakespeare's most harrowing journey into madness, provides a fitting omen for what was to come when Little returned to Sharpe in 1940: "In the first session I lay rigid on the couch, again unable to speak or move. Then, as she remained silent I began to scream, 'This *can't* be real,' recalling my earlier near-hallucinatory vision of her and my flight" (1985, p. 14). Little continues:

> She interpreted my fear as "castration anxiety" and related it to my having met her through Dr. X, which was, of course, the obvious thing, for the problem I had taken to her was clearly oedipal. But this did not fit the *intensity* of my panic, which was far more than any mortal terror, or fear of death. [p. 14]

Little's self-portrait closely resembles Cooper's vignette of the woman who displayed an "obvious oedipal attachment to her father", but whose problems had "earlier origins", and whose narrative accordingly needed to be comprehended using more up-to-date "templates". As Little came to realize, her terror in that first session was the manifestation not of a "transference neurosis", but of a "transference psychosis", and the analysis became a "constant struggle", with Sharpe "insisting on interpreting what I said as due to intrapsychic conflict to do with infantile sexuality, and I trying to convey that my real problems were matters of existence and identity" (1985, p. 15). Paradoxically, therefore, although Sharpe's approach to *King Lear* as the repository of "a child's massive feelings and fantasies", which achieve expression through the characters but originate in Shakespeare's own experience, articulates a point of view that is only now regaining wider currency in literary studies, in psychoanalytic terms Sharpe's outlook remains old-fashioned and needs to be superseded by the more contemporary views advanced by such theorists as Winnicott and, indeed, Little herself.

In an interview with Robert Langs prior to the publication of her autobiographical paper, Little links her disappointment in Sharpe for failing to recognize the severity of her illness to the latter's interpretation of *King Lear*: "She wrote about King Lear as an obsessional neurotic, with no reference to his paranoia" (Little & Langs, 1981, p. 273). Sharpe's insistence on viewing Little's difficulties solely in terms of "intrapsychic conflict to do with infantile sexuality" had damaging effects not only on her understanding of Little's past but also on their relationship in the present. Although Sharpe—an English teacher prior to her training as an analyst—was a smoker and in obvious ill health by the 1940s, these perceptions by the medically qualified Little could not be brought into the treatment: "Always on the couch reality had to be set aside, including observations of her age and her health, and specifically of her heart condition" (1985, p. 16). Most astonishingly, Sharpe "dragged a heavy couch from one end to the other of a long room, at every session", while Little "had to stand by useless" (p. 17). This denial of reality re-enacted the way that "my own and my mother's psychosis was dismissed as fantasy" by Sharpe, who, thereby, echoed the mother's accusation that it was only Little who was "the crazy one", while she herself was "the one who 'knew'" (p. 16).

Sharpe's commentary on *King Lear* is, to borrow Edgar's words, "matter and impertinency mix't" (4.6: 174). That Shakespeare's mother "lost two babies in earliest infancy before William was born" (1946, p. 24) is a salient fact, and the unlikely suggestion that "mother–Goneril's pregnancy is the cause of child Lear's 'storm' in the play" (p. 23) at least has the merit of inviting the reader to consider that Goneril may be already be pregnant when Lear prays that nature "Dry up in her the organs of increase" (1.4: 279). Sharpe, however, goes overboard in claiming that "the 'Goneril' aspect of the mother is the dominating one of the play" (1946, p. 23). She also makes serious errors. It is not true that, in the opening dialogue with Kent, Gloucester recalls "the happy intercourse with his wife" (p. 22). He is referring to his fornication with the mother of Edmund, a whore, and the phrase "good sport" (1.1: 23) suggests satiated lust rather than emotional happiness. Nor is it Shakespeare "who has made the younger son into an illegitimate one" (1946, p. 22). Had Sharpe been less eager to leave "the question of the sources of the plots to the academic student" (p. 20), she would have discovered that in Sir Philip Sidney's *Arcadia*, published in 1590, Shakespeare's source for the Gloucester plot of *King Lear*, the Paphlagonian king likewise has two sons, and is induced by his younger "bastard sonne" to try to undo his lawful older son, who is "undeserving destruction" (Bullough, 1973, p. 405).

Such lapses are not designed to give psychoanalytic criticism a good name among traditional scholars, but the gravest limitation of Sharpe's essay lies elsewhere. As Adelman has summed it up,

Sharpe maintains that "Lear's regression to oral fantasies of merger represents a defense against genital/oedipal desire", instead of seeing his "oedipal rage as a potential defense against a more primitive vulnerability" (1992, p. 310). In Sharpe's own words, "Lear's compulsive hate against the mother with which this play starts and which is undisguised is only explicable when taken in relationship to the subtly disguised feelings to the father" (1946, p. 26). She reiterates, "to reenter the mother as a whole baby, to emerge from her again, reborn, evades the crucial problem of the Oedipus incestuous desires at the genital level" (p. 29).

Precisely as in her clinical analysis of Little, therefore, Sharpe, in her literary analysis of *King Lear*, mistakenly construes what is essentially a problem of "primitive vulnerability" as one of "incestuous desires at the genital level". While refraining from speculations about the biographical origins of Shakespeare's art, I propose now to draw on Little's own writings to show how, even though they do not concern themselves with Shakespeare, they yield far-reaching insights into his tragedy.

An excellent place to start is by recognizing that Lear, like Little, exhibits not a transference neurosis but a transference *psychosis* in the course of the play. As Little emphasizes, there are "patients whose reality sense is seriously impaired, who cannot distinguish delusion or hallucination from reality, cannot use transference interpretations because the transference itself is of a delusional nature" (1957, p. 75). The recovery of such patients, she extrapolates, can take place only through a "delusion of total identity" (1960, p. 110) with the analyst.

There could scarcely be a better example of a delusional transference than when Lear, Kent, and the Fool seek to enter the hovel where Edgar, disguised as Poor Tom, has taken refuge during the storm, and the mad king insists, "nothing could have subdu'd nature / To such a lowness but his unkind daughters" (3.4: 71–72). In his psychotic state, Lear can see in the apparently mad beggar nothing other than himself.

Little proposes that the severity of a patient's illness can be assessed by his response to transference interpretations:

> If such interpretations are consistently felt by him to be meaningless, even if in fact he shows that they do mean something somewhere, or

if on the contrary they are accepted but no changes in behavior or ways of thinking follow, either of these I would regard as pathognomic of the presence of a deep split and a great deal of paranoid anxiety, the defenses against it being stronger in the second case than in the first. [1957, p. 77]

Here, we have a reference to "paranoid anxiety", a manifestation of the extreme pathology that Little believed had been missed by Sharpe when she characterized Lear as an "obsessional neurotic". In positing that an imperviousness to transference interpretations is indicative of a "deep split", moreover, Little permits us to infer that there must be such a fissure in Lear's psyche, and his decision to set in motion what Gloucester calls "the division of the kingdom" (1.1: 4) constitutes an externalized representation of his mental state.

Where there exists "a 'split' that makes the ego inaccessible to transference interpretations", Little traces it back to "a failure of integration between psyche and soma" (1958, p. 83). In turn, this "failure of integration depends upon very early body experience" (pp. 83–84), and "in those areas where the delusion is operative the patient is to all intents and purposes literally an infant, his ego a body ego" (1960, p. 113). The transference delusion defends against a "fear of annihilation" that "is dynamic and all-pervading" (p. 112), and in this breakdown that the patient "both needs and fears to reach", there is "only a *state of being* or of experiencing and no sense of there being a person. There is only an anger, fear, love, movement, etc., but no person *feeling* anger, fear or love, or moving" (1958, p. 84).

I find all this extremely helpful in sounding the abyss of madness that lies beneath Lear's actions in the opening scene and that becomes increasingly visible as the play unfolds. When Kent intervenes to calm the enraged king after he has disowned Cordelia in response to her perceived rejection of him, Lear retorts:

> Peace, Kent!
> Come not between the dragon and his wrath;
> I lov'd her most, and thought to set my rest
> On her kind nursery. (1.1: 121–124)

Lear here is no longer a person, but a wrathful dragon, and in that condition he "cannot use" Kent's attempt to create a space "between" himself and his unregulated emotion that would allow

Lear to "distinguish delusion or hallucination from reality". His frustrated longing to repose himself on Cordelia's "kind nursery", like his previously voiced desire to "Unburthen'd crawl toward death" (41), registers the infantile substrate of the experience of annihilation that Lear "both needs and fears to reach".

Kent refers to himself as Lear's "physician" (1.1: 163), and if we think of Lear as a patient in analysis, he may be said to move from Kent, who seeks in vain to offer interpretations, to the Fool, whose riddles—"Can you make no use of nothing, nuncle?" (1.4: 130–131)—"do mean something somewhere" to a more deeply regressed Lear even though they "are consistently felt by him to be meaningless", and finally to Edgar as Poor Tom, with whom he reaches full-blown transference psychosis. As Little expounds:

> Interpretation does not make any impression on delusion. The only thing that does so is the presentation of reality in a way that is comparable to waking up out of a dream—that is, finding that something that had been believed to be literally true is untrue, by confrontation with what is true. [1957, p. 78]

Just such a "presentation of reality" occurs during the storm scene in which Lear learns "to feel what wretches feel" (3.4: 34), and it brings him to acknowledge in his epiphanic encounter with the blinded Gloucester, "I am not ague-proof" (4.6: 105).

The psychological significance of the storm scene can, likewise, be understood in Little's terms. As she writes of patients who break through their transference delusion to reach the "state of undifferentiatedness" that underlies it, "The quality of the disturbance is cataclysmic and can be compared to orgasm. It might be described as an 'orgasm of pain,' with tension rising to a climax, discharged in an impulsive movement, and followed by relief" (1958, p. 84). Following the "discharge" of the storm scene, the Gentleman observes, "Our foster-nurse of nature is repose" (4.4: 12), and it is after he awakens from sleep that Lear comes closest to healing what Cordelia terms "this great breach in his abused nature" (4.7: 14). As he recovers consciousness, he wonders aloud, "For (as I am a man) I think this lady / To be my child Cordelia" (67–68). With these words, as Coppélia Kahn has discerned, "Lear comes closer than he ever does later to a mature acceptance of his human dependency. He asserts his manhood, and admits Cordelia's separateness from him at the same time that he confesses his need for her" (1986, p. 48).

Calamitously, however, Lear's recovery is overtaken by events—the defeat of the French armies, the arrest of Lear and Cordelia, and Cordelia's murder on Edmund's orders. Cordelia's death renders Lear oblivious to the final reversal of fortune whereby "good"—personified by Albany, Edgar, and Kent—nominally triumphs over "evil", and Lear's last words are a deluded expression of hope that the breath of life has miraculously returned to his daughter: "Look on her! Look her lips, / Look there, look there!" (5.3: 311–312). As Little has remarked,

> Verbalization has to go back not only to nursery and onomatopo-
> etic words but to very primitive sounds and mouth movements,
> from where other movements and body happenings can be
> reached, so as to make contact between inner and outer reality and
> to help the change over from concrete and magical thinking to the
> acceptance of substitutes and symbolization. [1958, p. 86]

Fittingly, at the end of perhaps the most sublime tragedy in Western literature, Shakespeare takes us back to the "primitive sounds and mouth movements" that lie at the origins of speech, and his expiring hero reverts to the "concrete and magical thinking" with which we all began in infancy.

4

If Lear is in the grip of primitive anxieties, which are indicative of "a failure of integration between psyche and soma", it is natural to wonder what might have led him to develop such an extreme psychopathology. Here, again, Little's ideas provide an excellent point of departure. When these conditions are encountered in clinical work, she writes, they "seem to have arisen out of a situation where the mother herself was infantile, and as incapable of bearing either separateness or fusion as her baby, a mother whose anxiety and inadequacy acted as real persecutions to the child" (1958, p. 82).

The sudden outbreak of Lear's madness in the opening scene, which otherwise seems inexplicable, can be accounted for if one imagines him to be harbouring buried memories of a disruption in his archaic bond with the mother. Paradoxically, however, when Lear imposes the love-test on his daughters, "Which of you shall we say doth love us most" (1.1: 51), he is himself in the position of the mother "whose anxiety and inadequacy" act "as real persecutions to the child". Seen in this light, Lear begins the play by evincing a projective identification with the narcissistic mother by whom he must have been traumatized and undergoes a regression back to his own infancy that leads to the delusional transference with Poor Tom.

As I sought to demonstrate in my 1999 article, that Lear simultaneously plays the roles of not only father but also mother and child is powerfully conveyed through Shakespeare's imagery. Lear castigates the recalcitrant Cordelia as a "barbarous Scythian" (1.1: 116)—a phrase evidently applicable to himself—while in the storm scene he imagines that the "flesh" of Poor Tom has been ravaged by his "pelican daughters" (3.4: 74–75), again a transferred epithet, since the breast-piercing pelican was ordinarily an emblem of maternal devotion, but is here invoked by the deranged king to convey the ruthless destructiveness of Tom's imaginary offspring.

What the reading I am now proposing throws into relief is that the opening scene is transferential in the psychoanalytic sense. It takes place simultaneously in the present, with father and daughter in their appointed roles, and in the past, with Lear as the infant beseeching his omnipotent mother, and it undergoes a further reversal in which Lear becomes the narcissistic mother in the present and his daughters are now facets of himself split off by an extension of the process of projective identification. The dynamic whereby an analysis of Lear's behaviour in the present proceeds in tandem with a reconstruction of its infantile determinants receives definitive exposition in Arnold Cooper's landmark paper, "The narcissistic–masochistic character" (1988).[6] As a historical matter, there is a developmental lag of several decades between psychoanalysis in Britain and in the United States. By the time that

---

[6] Although published in 1988, an embryonic version of Cooper's paper was presented as early as 1963, and it was given again in a more complete form in 1973. The final version of the paper thus represents the culmination of an intellectual and personal odyssey extending across twenty-five years.

Winnicott died in 1971, the Independent tradition in Britain had already consolidated the essential breakthroughs that would be disseminated in America in the 1980s and 1990s, thanks to the combined influence of self psychology and the rise of an indigenous relational movement out of the interpersonal school.[7] Cooper is a representative American analyst in that he acknowledges an indebtedness to Kohut for legitimizing the progressive trends by which he had already been influenced through Sándor Radó and Edmund Bergler, but he alludes very sparingly—if at all—to Fairbairn, Winnicott, Balint, Milner, and the other major figures of British object relations theory, to say nothing of such lesser luminaries as Nina Coltart and Margaret Little.

By an alternative route, Cooper, in his 1988 paper, arrives at almost exactly the same destination that Little had reached by 1960. Recapitulating Little's turn away from Oedipal issues, Cooper begins by announcing that

> a full appreciation of the roles of narcissism and masochism in development and in pathology requires that we relinquish whatever remains of what Freud referred to as the "shibboleth" of the centrality of the Oedipus complex in neurosogenesis. [1988, p. 121]

That Cooper attends to both "development" and "pathology" underscores his binocular focus on the root causes as well as the ongoing manifestations of the narcissistic–masochistic character.

Employing self psychological language, Cooper again challenges Freudian orthodoxy by insisting that "libidinal pleasures and aggressive satisfactions will be sacrificed or distorted if necessary to help prevent the shattering disorganizing anxieties that arise when the self-system is disturbed or the ties to the object disrupted" (1988, p. 130). He instances a range of British and American theorists, including Kohut, Sullivan, and Winnicott, all of whom offer "ways of addressing the crucial issues of the organism's primary needs for self-definition out of an original symbiotic bond". Although Cooper bypasses Little, her most important concept,

---

[7] On Kohut's belatedness *vis-à-vis* Winnicott, and their shared opposition to the postmodernism of Lacan, see my chapter, "Winnicott, Lacan, and Kohut", in *The Psychoanalytic Vocation* (Rudnytsky, 1991).

together with transference psychosis, is basic unity. This she defines as the infant's belief—which is a reality in the intrauterine state—in an "absolute identity with the mother upon which survival depends" (1960, p. 123). As Little explains to Robert Langs, "symbiosis comes later in development, basic unity being the primary state of total undifferentiatedness—a one-body relationship, whereas symbiosis must be a two-body relationship that is apparently denied" (Little & Langs, 1981, p. 305).

Whether one calls it symbiosis or basic unity, however, Cooper aligns himself not only with Little, but also with the emerging consensus in contemporary psychoanalysis that views selfhood as arising out of a relational matrix between infant and mother. When disruptions occur in this primordial bond, the consequence can be understood either, in severe cases, as a transference psychosis, or as belonging to the spectrum of disorders that comprise the narcissistic–masochistic character.

Let us now apply Cooper's concept to *King Lear*. In keeping with Cooper's awareness of the interplay between "development" and "pathology", I begin with his elucidation of "a three-step behavioral sequence that is paradigmatic of masochistic behavior" (1988, p. 126), to which Bergler referred as the "oral triad".

> *Step 1.* Through his own behavior or through the misuse of an available external situation, the masochist unconsciously provokes disappointment, refusal, and humiliation. He identifies the outside world with a disappointing, refusing, preoedipal mother. *Unconsciously*, the rejection provides satisfaction. [Cooper, 1988, p. 126]

One could not ask for a clearer illustration of this first step in the sequence than Lear's behavior in the opening scene. In the division of the kingdom, he indeed "provokes disappointment, refusal, and humiliation", and by involving his daughters the situation is perfectly designed to allow him to identify "the outside world with a disappointing, refusing, preoedipal mother". Cooper's addendum that "*unconsciously*, the rejection provides satisfaction" resonates with my own suggestion that Lear, unbeknown to himself, set up the love test in the expectation that Cordelia would fail, and that he would therefore not be obliged to marry her off to either of her suitors.

There follows

Step 2. Consciously, the masochist has repressed his knowledge of his own provocation and reacts with righteous indignation and *seeming* self-defense to the rejection, which he consciously perceives as externally delivered. He responds, thus, with "pseudoaggression," that is, defensive aggression designed to disclaim his responsibility for, and unconscious pleasure in, the defeat he has experienced. [Cooper, 1988, p. 126]

Again, Lear fits the bill exactly. He lashes out with "righteous indignation" at Cordelia and Kent, having "repressed his knowledge of his own provocation" and remaining blind to any "unconscious pleasure" he might feel in "the defeat he has experienced".
Finally, there is

Step 3. After the subsidence of pseudoaggression, which, because ill-dosed or ill-timed, and not intended for genuine self-defense, may provoke additional unconscious wished-for defeats, the masochist indulges in conscious self-pity, feelings of "this only happens to me." Unconsciously, he enjoys the masochistic rebuff. [Cooper, 1988, p. 126]

After the debacle of the opening scene, Lear proceeds to "provoke additional unconscious wished-for defeats" in his confrontations, first with Goneril and then with Regan. Upon being rejected by both daughters, Lear "indulges in conscious self-pity" epitomized by his lamentation during the storm scene, "I am a man / More sinn'd against than sinning" (3.2: 59–60).
As Cooper outlines the components of masochistic pathology, he also summarizes the developmental processes out of which this constellation is crystalized. He begins with a bedrock principle:

Pain is a necessary and unavoidable concomitant of separation–individuation and the achievement of selfhood. Perhaps *Doleo ergo sum* (I suffer, therefore I am) is a precursor of *Sentio ergo sum* (I feel, therefore I am), and *Cogito ergo sum* (I think, therefore I am). [1988, p. 130]

At the height of his madness, Lear preaches to Gloucester, "When we are born, we cry that we are come / To this great stage of fools"

(4.6: 182–183). Cooper enables us to grasp the psychological power of these lines. The crying of newborn babies is a primordial manifestation of the suffering inherent in existence and supports the claim that "pain is a necessary and unavoidable concomitant of separation–individuation and the achievement of selfhood". When Lear enters bearing the dead Cordelia in his arms at the end of the play, his "Howl, howl, howl!" (5.3: 258),[8] which should be vocalized as a continuous primal scream rather than as discretely enunciated words, is the full visceral realization of the truth that even in his madness Lear is able to articulate only in a discursive form.

Cooper continues by anatomizing the psychological effects of his initial axiom on the organism emerging from symbiosis:

> The frustrations and discomforts of separation–individuation, necessary events in turning us toward the world, are perceived as narcissistic injuries—that is, they damage the sense of magical omnipotent control and threaten intolerable passivity and helplessness in the face of a perceived external danger. This is the prototype of narcissistic humiliation. [1988, p. 130]

According to Cooper, "narcissistic injuries" are byproducts of the "frustrations and discomforts" of normal development. Although I would impute to Lear a history of childhood deprivation that goes beyond ordinary experience, Cooper could be presenting Lear's case when he defines "narcissistic humiliation" as the loss of "magical omnipotent control", and when he attributes the anxiety of the budding self to a sense of "intolerable passivity and helplessness in the face of a perceived external danger".

Compelling evidence for the severity of the traumas that inform Shakespeare's characterizations of both Lear and Gloucester is afforded by the centrality of bodily experience in the play. As Bennett Simon (2006) has observed, tragic drama as a genre can be "conceptualized as telling stories about the transmission of trauma within families or societies, from one generation to the next" (p. 120), and traumatic memories "are much more prone to be encoded in bodily form—sensations, affects, images—and to be less

---

[8] The word "howl" appears four times in the 1608 Quarto and three times in the First Folio.

successfully registered as communicable narratives" (p. 128). Simon's thesis dovetails with Little's contention that the "failure of integration between psyche and soma" that underpins a delusional transference emanates from "very early bodily experience, when awareness is essentially body awareness", and "tension is experienced as something intolerable, threatening life itself" (1958, pp. 83–84).

The somatic substrate of Lear's anxiety is palpable, not only in his fire-breathing anger, but also in his fantasy of being suffocated by his wandering womb. As the expression of a repressed feminine identification, Lear's hysteria finds a counterpart in Gloucester's blindness; and the scene in which Gloucester's eyes are put out on stage by Cornwall, with a hideous interval of more than ten lines (3.7: 70–83) separating the loss of one eye from the other, is the most excruciating in all of Shakespeare. And as Lear sees in Poor Tom a hallucinatory image of his own betrayal by his daughters, so, too, is Tom's "uncover'd body" (3.4: 102) the paradigmatic representation of the "very early bodily experience" to which Lear seeks to return to repair the breach in his basic unity or "absolute identity with the mother upon which survival depends".

Thus, although Lear exemplifies a narcissistic–masochistic character, his symptomatology falls at the most severe end of the spectrum. With this caveat, we may now take up a final crucial point in Cooper's exegesis of the origins of this ubiquitous syndrome. After setting forth the axiom, *Doleo ergo sum*, and the corollary that blows to the infant's sense of omnipotence result in "narcissistic humiliation", Cooper explains what happens next:

> The infant attempts defensively to restore threatened self-esteem by distorting the nature of his experience. Rather than accept the fact of helplessness, the infant reasserts control by making the suffering ego-syntonic. "I am frustrated because I want to be. I force my mother to be cruel." [1988, p. 130]

He elaborates this insight in his discussion of the case of a twenty-six-year-old woman who repeatedly became involved with unsuitable men, became angry because she feared the relationships would not last, precipitated quarrels that led to separations, and ended up feeling depressed after having been abandoned. In Cooper's words:

What she *now* sought in her relationships, disguised as an insatiable demand for attention, was the repetition of the painful abandonment, but with the hidden gratification of narcissistic control and masochistic satisfaction. The demand for love had been given up in favor of the pleasure of rejection. [p. 134]

Just as I have proposed a transferential reading of the opening scene of *King Lear,* in which Lear is simultaneously the Oedipal father, the narcissistic mother, and the infant flooded with anxiety, so, too, a juxtaposition of these two passages from Cooper highlights the homology between the defensive stratagems of the narcissistically injured infant and the man or woman who choreographs a "repetition of the painful abandonment" in his or her adult life. In both instances, the linchpin of the manoeuvre is that the already wounded protagonist "reasserts control by making the suffering ego-syntonic". The subject, that is, transforms pain that had at first been endured passively into pain that is actively chosen, and in the process gratifies not only his masochism but also his injured narcissism.

If this has a familiar ring, it may be because it echoes the most famous psychoanalytic interpretation of *King Lear,* the one propounded by Freud in "The theme of the three caskets". As is well known, Freud argues that the third daughter or sister, represented by Cordelia in this play and by the lead casket in *The Merchant of Venice,* "is the Goddess of Death, Death itself" (1913f, p. 298). In reality, he reminds his readers, "no one chooses death, and it is only by a fatality that one falls victim to it". Yet, in both the casket motif of *The Merchant of Venice* and the plot of *King Lear,* Freud finds that there has been a "wishful reversal", so that "choice stands in the place of necessity". Indeed, he concludes, "no greater triumph of wish-fulfilment is conceivable" (p. 299).

Freud presents his analysis in proto-existential terms, as a confrontation of man with the inevitability of death, and he does not attempt to explain either Lear's behaviour or the theme of the three caskets as a function of individual experience in childhood. The paper is, however, one in which the child's relation to the mother is placed by Freud in the foreground to an unusual degree—in all likelihood, as Sprengnether (1990, pp. 121–24) has recognized, in response to Jung, whose ideas Freud did not hesitate covertly to

appropriate even as he publicly anathematized them in the aftermath of their break. Freud writes, in unmistakably Jungian terms,
"the great Mother-goddesses of the oriental peoples . . . all seem to
have been both creators and destroyers" (1913f, p. 299). Even
Freud's celebrated peroration that the myth shows "the three
inevitable relations that a man has with a woman—the woman
who bears him, the woman who is his mate, and the woman
who destroys him", and that these constitute "the three forms taken
by the figure of the mother in a man's life" (p. 301), uncannily
resembles the following passage from Part 2 of Jung's *Transformations and Symbols of Libido*, published the preceding year: "in the
morning the goddess is the mother, at noon the sister–wife, and in
the evening again the mother, who receives the dying in her lap"
(1912, p. 272).[9]

But, though Freud speaks in Jungian accents, his voice remains
unmistakably his own. By emphasizing the successive incarnations
of the mother rather than the goddess, Freud not only grounds the
astral myth firmly in the realm of human psychology, he also envi-
sions the fate of the masculine subject in quintessentially Oedipal
terms. The wife is chosen in the image of the mother, and the
daughter who signifies death is but the mother in her final guise.

At the conclusion of my earlier article, and reposing on Freud's
"The theme of the three caskets" as a bulwark, I asserted that
"despite its inexhaustible vicissitudes of meaning", the key to deci-
phering the hieroglyphic of Shakespeare's tragedy is "at bottom
simplicity itself. It is that Lear's fantasy of merger with Cordelia,
which goes back to a child's incestuous longing to return to the
body of the mother, is ultimately a death sentence" (Rudnytsky,
1999a, p. 310).

---

[9] Jung's work is known in English by the title of Beatrice Hinkle's 1916
translation, *Psychology of the Unconscious*. He goes on to compare the mother
"who receives the dying in her lap" to "the Pietà of Michelangelo" (1912, p.
272)—a possible provocation to Freud's *The Moses of Michelangelo* (1914b), a text
bearing many traces of the split with Jung. When Lear enters with Cordelia's
body in his arms, the tableau is of a reverse Pietà—the father carrying the
daughter, instead of the mother the son—though Cordelia, who has previously
declared, "O dear father / It is thy business that I go about" (4.4: 23–24), is
implicitly defeminized by being identified with Christ, a final loop to the
arabesque of inversions in the play.

From my present standpoint, however, the reading I proposed in 1999 seems to me to fall short in precisely the same way that Freud's classic essay of 1914 is also inadequate. Yes, the tragedy goes back to the infant's bond with the mother, but what is re-enacted in Lear's "fantasy of merger" with Cordelia is not simply an "incestuous longing", but, more fundamentally, an expression of the primitive anxieties that arise from a traumatic disruption in the experience of basic unity that is the precondition for psychic integration in later life. Although I did not cite Sharpe, and Sharpe does not cite "The theme of the three caskets" in her 1946 paper, the limitation in all three of our readings of *King Lear* is that we confined our analysis of the unconscious dynamics governing the play to "incestuous desires at the genital level" and did not peer deeply enough into the pre-Oedipal and even psychotic fissures that may lurk beneath the complexes of triangulation.[10]

As Cooper has reminded us, however, the Oedipal narrative "is not a false story; it is a later story" (1988, p. 101) that must be augmented by bringing to bear an expanded set of "mental templates" on "the communications we receive from the patient"—or, I would add, the literary text. The words may remain the same, but we hear different melodies. The plot of *King Lear* still drives inexorably towards the apparent fulfilment, and then the absolute crushing, of Lear's fantasies of fusion with Cordelia, but I now understand Lear's "birds i' th' cage" speech to be impelled less by his desire for incestuous consummation with the mother–daughter than by an imperative to restore basic unity that is summed up in the phrase: "We two alone" (5.3: 9). The defensive stratagem that propels Lear's actions remains, as Freud discerned, the reversal of necessity into choice, but instead of seeing this manoeuvre solely as a response to the fear of death, I would now interpret it as a transferential re-enactment of the intricate process by which the narcissistic–masochistic character is consolidated in infancy.

---

[10] I thus concur with Charles Hanly (1986) that Freud "did not do justice to Lear's daughters or to Lear's relations with them" (p. 211). Hanly likewise finds that Sharpe, "for the most part, has missed the psychological significance of the relation between Lear and his daughters" (p. 216), and he acutely highlights Lear's "narcissistic blindness"—manifested in the obvious favoritism he shows to Cordelia at the expense of her sisters—as "the source of his folly which sets the tragedy in motion" (p. 217).

That Shakespeare's "written words" in *King Lear*, like the "living speech" of a patient in analysis, do not, as Socrates believed, "go on telling you just the same thing forever", ensures that the quest to discern their meanings will likewise continue indefinitely. But, rather than being a cause for pessimism, is not the inherent interminability of analysis, whether as a mode of critical or clinical practice, the source of our impossible profession's most abiding joy?

CHAPTER SEVEN

The bridge across Clifton Road: Emory University and the future of psychoanalytic studies

"This is our moment".

(Lynne Moritz, "Turning to Our Work", 2007)

In his introduction to *The Origins of Psychoanalysis*, the original, abridged edition of Freud's letters to Wilhelm Fliess first published in 1950, Steven Marcus (1977) remarks that the process of creative discovery by which psychoanalysis came into being "may be appropriately regarded as a culmination of the particular tradition of introspection which began with the adjuration of the oracle at Delphi to 'Know thyself'". Citing Freud's epochal interpretation of *Oedipus Rex* in October 1897 as revealing "a general phenomenon of early childhood", Marcus goes on to call it "more than a fortunate accident that this most highly developed form of Western secular introspection should have returned at one of its moments of climactic breaking-through to its cultural origins" (p. vii).

I believe Marcus's claims about the cultural significance of Freud's self-analysis to be warranted, and I propose to use them here as the starting point for a twofold narrative not simply about psychoanalysis, but also about my own relation to Freud's instantiation of the Delphic injunction. By reflecting simultaneously on my personal experiences and on the broader history of psychoanalysis, I hope to make the case that the time is now ripe to inaugurate a doctoral programme that would include clinical training and, thereby, to accomplish something truly historic through the Psychoanalytic Studies Program at Emory University.

In order for any young person to find his or her way to an inborn calling, it is necessary to be exposed to the right influences at critical periods in one's formation. In my own case, after having read Norman O. Brown at Germantown Friends School in Philadelphia, I was fortunate enough, as a sophomore at Columbia University, to come upon a new sequence of courses listed in the catalogue under the rubric of Psychiatry–Contemporary Civilization. In the autumn semester, Dr Willard Gaylin taught the Development of Freudian Theory, while in the spring Dr Arnold Cooper lectured on the post-Freudians from Anna Freud through R. D. Laing. In the second year, Dr Cooper taught a seminar on psychoanalysis and literature, and Dr Gaylin taught a seminar on masculinity.

As it turned out, I was the only student to take all four semesters of Psychiatry–CC, so, in my senior year, when the first two lecture courses were repeated, with an enrolment that had quadrupled from twenty to eighty, I was honoured to be asked to serve as the grader first for Dr Gaylin and then for Dr Cooper. At the same time, I was majoring in English, taking both the Romantics and a seminar on Dickens with Steven Marcus and assimilating a tradition that took it for granted, as Lionel Trilling (1940) had argued in a passage I have already quoted in the opening chapter, that

> the Freudian psychology is the only systematic account of the human mind which, in point of subtlety and complexity, of interest and tragic power, deserves to stand beside the chaotic mass of psychological insights which literature has accumulated through the centuries. [p. 32]

Thus, by the time I received my BA in 1973, I was hooked. Although still only in embryonic form, this four-semester sequence taught by

Drs Gaylin and Cooper was, in fact, the first psychoanalytic studies programme at any American university, of which I can proudly call myself the first graduate.

I again found myself in the right place for psychoanalytic studies as a graduate student at Yale, where I arrived in 1975, after having spent two years on a Kellett Fellowship reading English at Clare College, Cambridge. In my first semester, I took a seminar on Lacan with Shoshana Felman, conducted in French, which culminated in Lacan's visit to the Yale campus. Professor Felman graciously invited her students to meet Lacan at her home, and I still recall the question I posed to Lacan, as well as his pungently enigmatic reply: "Que sont les implications politiques de vos récherches psychanalytiques?" "C'est comme une nappe. Ce qu'on gagne d'un côté, on perd de l'autre". ("What are the political implications of your psychoanalytic research?" "It's like a tablecloth. What you gain on one side, you lose on the other".)

After completing my coursework, not only with Shoshana Felman, but also with other luminaries such as Geoffrey Hartman and Harold Bloom, the latter of whom became the director of my doctoral dissertation, I was named a Kanzer Fellow. This innovative venture, then in only its second year, was originally endowed by Mark Kanzer and continues today as the Muriel Gardiner Program in Psychoanalysis and the Humanities at Yale. Under its auspices, I was permitted to take a year of non-clinical courses at the Western New England Institute of Psychoanalysis, as well as to attend the monthly Kanzer Seminars that brought together leading analysts and scholars in the New Haven community to hear a visiting speaker. Among the mainstays were Hans Loewald, Albert Solnit, Samuel Ritvo, and Morton Reiser, all now sadly deceased, and others including Stanley Leavy and Rosemary Balsam, but perhaps my most vivid memory is of having been a student in George Mahl's course on Freud's first phase, and Marshall Edelson's course on *The Interpretation of Dreams*, at the Western New England Institute along with Peter Gay, who was then beginning his research training in psychoanalysis.

My season of academic bliss extended from 1969 to 1979, well before the settlement in 1988 of the lawsuit that opened clinical training at institutes of the American Psychoanalytic Association to anyone other than medical doctors, when it was still unthinkable for a scholar in the humanities or the social sciences to become a psychoanalyst. But, first as an undergraduate and again as a graduate student, I was the beneficiary of the initial incursions of psychoanalysis into the American university, and my experiences exemplify what can happen when a prospective vocation makes itself available to a young person in search of what it has to offer.

If we circle back now to the beginning of the larger story, it is important to bear in mind, as Sarah Winter (1999) has underscored, that, "in his academic career, Freud seems to have positioned himself both culturally and institutionally as an outsider—and also to have used this sense of alienation to rhetorical advantage in his assertions of the autonomy of psychoanalysis" (p. 220). During the same decades that Freud was promoting his cause, by contrast, the equally novel disciplines of anthropology, sociology, and experimental psychology—associated, respectively, with Frazer in England, Durkheim in France, and Wundt in Germany—were becoming institutionalized within an academic setting. In "On the history of the psychoanalytic movement" (1914d), Freud connected the founding of the International Psychoanalytic Association in 1910 to the rejection of psychoanalysis by "official science" (p. 44); and he went on to declare, in "On the teaching of psychoanalysis in universities" (1919j), that while "the inclusion of psychoanalysis would no doubt be regarded with satisfaction by every psychoanalyst . . . it is clear that the psychoanalyst can dispense with the university without any loss to himself" (p. 171). This latter paper was written at the conclusion of the First World War, when it appeared that chairs in psychoanalysis might be established first in Budapest and then in Berlin, although, as Winter (1999) has noted, "neither of these possibilities ever materialized", and "even in America, the country and culture of its greatest success, [psychoanalysis] has never become an independent academic discipline" (p. 220).

As I have argued throughout this book, the central dilemma bequeathed by Freud to succeeding generations is how to preserve what is of imperishable value in his legacy while emancipating ourselves from its baleful aspects. With the benefit of hindsight, I think his assumption that the integration of psychoanalysis into the university would redound to the benefit solely of the latter is one of those instances in which he was clearly mistaken. By setting up psychoanalysis as a movement rather than a discipline—a movement over which he presided with sovereign authority—Freud tragically betrayed his own vision of psychoanalysis as a quest for truth. He paid the price not only in the series of broken friendships with which his career is littered, but also in his stubborn insistence on adhering to his pet ideas long after they had been discredited by the disciplines from which he had originally borrowed them.[1]

Although it has taken nearly three quarters of a century, there is reason to hope that the collective undertaking of "rescuing psychoanalysis from Freud" is reaching a successful conclusion. Whether one looks at the rapprochement between what used to be bitterly divided schools and institutions, or at the emerging consensus concerning the indispensability of subjecting our theoretical allegiances to scientific scrutiny, I believe that psychoanalysis gives every indication of being poised on the brink of an exciting period of growth and renewal.

Among the positive signs to which I would point—all emanating from the increasingly forward-looking American Psychoanalytic Association (APsaA)—are the founding of a new Education Department; the initiative, which I have been privileged to lead, to make APsaA an Affiliate Organization of the Modern Language Association of America; the fellowship programme targeting gifted professionals in the earlier stages of their careers; the University Forum, which affords clinicians the opportunity to hear from, and interact with, prominent scholars; the poster sessions devoted to empirical investigations; the decade-long success of the annual essay prize competition sponsored by the Committee on Research and Special Training; and the recent publication of the *Psychodynamic Diagnostic Manual* (PDM Task Force, 2006), a monumental counterblast to the resolutely neo-Kraepelinian *Diagnostic and Statistical Manual of Mental Disorders*.

For all these reasons, I concur with Lynne Moritz (2007), a former president of the American Psychoanalytic Association, that

---

[1] See Chapter One, above, where I have connected Freud's extreme difficulty in admitting he could be wrong in the personal realm to what Patricia Kitcher (1992) has pinpointed as Freud's refusal to abandon certain theories in which he had a deep investment even when the anticipated discoveries on which these theories were based never materialized.

"this is our moment" (p. 3). It is time for psychoanalysis to dream big dreams again. Now that the psychoanalytic world is actively reaching out to college students, would it not be magnificent to be able to tell them there is a place they can go to get a PhD and also receive clinical training? I know it would have sounded good to me when I was applying to graduate schools from Cambridge, and I am convinced that such an unprecedented opportunity would draw the best and the brightest to Emory today.

For psychoanalysis to flourish, it does not need to cater to the masses. It does need to find ways, if I may put it in Winnicott's terms, to offer its breast to the hungry infant who already has an idea of it in his mind. It is probably enough that there should be one such nursery in the country, just as Austen Riggs, in Stockbridge, Massachusetts, stands as a beacon among psychiatric hospitals. We can see the synergies that are generated when scholars become clinicians from the example set by Claire Nouvet, the current director of the Psychoanalytic Studies Program as well as a research graduate of the Emory University Psychoanalytic Institute, whose reflections on her stay at Riggs were featured by Edward Shapiro, the medical director, in a newsletter article. Speaking of the capacity of the patients at Riggs "to open a space for loss to resonate", Nouvet concludes, "One of the most invaluable 'lessons' that I take from Austen Riggs is that a clinician must be able to speak from that silence and from that loss, and not simply against it" (Shapiro, 2007, p. 1).

Undoubtedly, a series of administrative hurdles will have to be cleared in order for a PhD programme with a clinical dimension to become a reality, but my focus here is not on the problems but on the possibilities. My message is that psychoanalytic studies is, both literally and figuratively, a field of dreams, and "if you build it, they will come". Or, as Wordsworth (1815) has memorably said that the poet has the task of "*creating* the taste by which he is to be enjoyed" (p. 426), so, too, this new PhD in Psychoanalytic Studies, which would redraw the disciplinary map nationally, must create the demand it will supply with its graduates.

In a history of the Psychoanalytic Studies Program at Emory, written more than ten years ago with Edward Gamarra, Robert Paul recounts how he and Dr Ralph Roughton used to speak "part jokingly and part seriously" of the desirability of "building a (metaphorical) bridge across Clifton Road, the street that divides the Psychiatry Department and the institute from the College of Arts and Sciences" (Paul & Gamarra, 1999, p. 448). As I have contended in the previous chapter, it is not to overlook the ethical responsibilities that come with treating patients to say that the skills of close reading and receptivity to a text on which literary scholars place a premium are very similar to the attentive listening and empathic attunement to another human being that should be cultivated by analysts in a clinical setting. As a therapeutic art, analysis is a hermeneutic enterprise in which there is no escaping from ambiguities. But, as an adherent of the theory of evolution, and one committed to the materialist position that there is no soul apart from the body, I also believe that psychoanalysis as a theory of mind must be scientific, and, indeed, that its core tenets hold up robustly under empirical scrutiny, as Drew Westen (1998) has masterfully expounded.

Thus, behind the dream of fully integrating psychoanalysis into the university by building that metaphorical bridge across Clifton Road, there is a second dream—one that I have called the "dream of consilience" (Rudnytsky, 2002)—of psychoanalysis as a resurgent discipline uniquely poised to reconcile the human and the natural sciences. In *Moses and Civilization*, Robert Paul (1996) remarks that Freud's myth of the primal horde "brings together two quite different discourses that are often thought to be incompatible, namely, a Darwinian and a Hegelian" (p. 15). In a broader sense, the enduring value of Freud's legacy lies precisely in such a synthesis of Darwin and Hegel. The paradox that we must strive to preserve through psychoanalysis is the recognition, on the one hand, that everything is biological and, on the other, that the spirit is irreducible and its autonomy must be respected.

My use of the term "consilience" is borrowed from E. O. Wilson (1998), who eloquently argues for a vision of the unity of knowledge in which it is the purpose of the humanities to pose questions about the meaning of life and the purpose of the sciences to guide us in the search for answers by progressively discovering the nature of reality through experimental verification. No frontier poses greater challenges, but also holds greater promise, for this noblest of quests than the human mind itself. In his address on receiving the Nobel Prize in Physiology or Medicine in 2000, Eric Kandel

(2006) began by reminding the assembled dignitaries that "engraved above the entrance to the Temple of Apollo at Delphi was the maxim, Know thyself" (p. 403). Speaking on behalf of his fellow honorees, Arvid Carlsson and Paul Greengard, Kandel continued:

> In looking toward the future, our generation of scientists has come to believe that the biology of mind will be as important to this century as the biology of the gene has been to the twentieth century. In a larger sense, the biological study of mind is more than a scientific inquiry of great promise; it is also an important humanistic endeavor. The biology of mind bridges the sciences—concerned with the natural world—and the humanities—concerned with the meaning of human experience. Insights that come from this new synthesis will not only improve our understanding of psychiatric and neurological disorders, but will also lead to a deeper understanding of ourselves. [p. 404]

Like Steven Marcus in his commentary on Freud's self-analysis, Kandel conceives of neurobiology as a return to, and fulfilment of, the injunction of the Delphic oracle to "know thyself". Indeed, as I have maintained is true of psychoanalysis, according to Kandel "the biology of mind bridges the sciences—concerned with the natural world—and the humanities—concerned with the meaning of human experience". And if psychoanalytic studies requires that one be conversant with ancient tragedy no less than with contemporary neuroscience, because both are indispensable to understanding the human condition, it would surely be helpful to be able to move back and forth between the psychiatry department and the College of Arts and Sciences. That is why the bridge across Clifton Road, which I look forward to seeing become a reality at Emory University, will also be the bridge that beckons psychoanalysis onward into the twenty-first century.

"Nitty-gritty issues": an interview with Eric R. Kandel

Peter L. Rudnytsky (PLR): What is the most important thing that you are trying to tell those in the psychoanalytic community?

Eric R. Kandel (ERK): My overriding concern is to try to bridge the gap between biology and psychoanalysis. Biologists of the brain are interested in understanding how the mind works, and it's difficult for them to do that unless they have a nuanced understanding of mental processes. And psychoanalysis to this day provides the most interesting set of ideas about the functioning of the human mind. From the point of view of the analyst, I feel that analysis has become a hermeneutic discipline. It's not a discipline that is evolving scientifically, and it needs to get over that problem. First of all, it needs to show that psychoanalytically based psychotherapy—or, in the limit, psychoanalysis itself—is empirically useful. People are paying for treatment, and they have every right to know what the chances are of improving. And we as a scientific community have a right to see what types of therapy are effective for what patients. These are nitty-gritty issues, but they're absolutely fundamental.

PLR: Right.

ERK: One of the reasons I admire Aaron Beck so much is that he's shown us what needs to be done. The second issue is that there are wonderful opportunities now to take analytic ideas—for example, the existence of the dynamic and the implicit unconscious, the preconscious, and conscious—and ask: Where are they located in the brain? What do they concern themselves with? We're in a terrific position to do this, and we should get on with the job!

PLR: You have written, "I certainly think that my analytic experience has been useful to me, and there is no question that this positive attitude contributes to my insistence that biology can transform psychoanalysis into a scientifically grounded discipline" (2005, p. xxi). Could you articulate the connection between your own personal experience of analysis and your positive attitude towards the larger project of grounding psychoanalysis scientifically?

ERK: I would say my exposure to psychoanalysis, not just my personal analysis. My personal analysis I've been very grateful for, but even prior to getting involved in an analysis myself, the contact that I had with the Krisses and with Herman Nunberg through their children was extremely influential for me. I would not have gone to medical school if I had not known Anna Kris Wolff and had she not introduced me to her parents. I was thinking of a career in comparative literature, and I went to medical school fully with the idea of becoming an analyst, and it was only by chance, taking an elective in biology of the brain, that I found that I enjoyed this so much. So, even though I ultimately got training in psychiatry and had an analysis, I continued to work on the brain, but in working on the brain I wanted to do things that were relevant to the larger issues in behaviour. The central issue in psychoanalysis in some ways is memory: we are who we are because of what we learn and we remember, and I felt early on—this is not unique to me—that in so far as psychotherapy works, it's because it creates an environment in which people can *relearn*, they can change, so psychoanalysis is a learning process.

PLR: I agree.

ERK: Well, my work showed that learning produces changes in the brain, and that long-term memory produces anatomical changes.

I did this before imaging came along, in the paper "Psychotherapy and the single synapse" (1979). It became clear to me that, in so far as psychotherapy works, it should produce anatomical changes that sooner or later we should detect. I differed dramatically from what is conventionally viewed as a reductionist approach, and I think that most reductionists don't have the radical view of reductionism that some people have. When molecular biology joined with genetics to produce a new discipline, molecular genetics, it wasn't that Mendel was forgotten and wiped out, it was that Mendelian knowledge was used as the basis for creating a richer science that explained genes in terms of the molecule's DNA that gave rise to them.

PLR: So you have a non-reductive view of reductionism.

ERK: This is what I would hope we would imagine here. That the overall view, the *Weltanschauung*, the deep insights, would, of course, come from cognitive psychology and psychoanalysis, and then, together with molecular neurobiology, we would create what I call a new science of mind, which would build on Freud, build on Sherrington, build on Brenda Milner, and *all* of this into a much more powerful science.

PLR: So, in the same way as Mendel's discovery of genetics vindicates the underlying assumptions of Darwin's theory of evolution, so, too, neuroscience could perform a similar function for psychoanalysis.

ERK: Absolutely. Darwin was probably the most important biologist who ever lived, but did he get things wrong? He didn't understand genetics at all. He didn't think of it as discrete units— genes—he saw it as the mixing of substances. Mendel came along and gave us the idea that these were unique things, and then Morgan gave us the idea that they were ranged on the chromosome. So, are things that Freud said going to be wrong? We know that already! His view of female sexuality was completely wrong. He didn't quite understand the bonding between infant and mother, but how could he possibly? If his insights about instincts, about unconscious mental processes, about the superego are correct, those are such enormous contributions. His elaboration of Helmholtz's concept that *most* of mental life is unconscious is a profound idea that is obviously true. So I think that those are beautiful areas to move forward. Freud was a damn good biologist and would have been interested had he been alive today to bring the two together more than anyone.

PLR: How do you see this new direction for psychoanalysis impacting the work that analysts do every day with their patients in the consulting room?

ERK: Immediately, not at all. But this is to be expected in medicine. I'm now involved in developing animal models of schizophrenia in mice. How rapidly is this going to affect the person treating schizophrenia? Not rapidly at all, but we hope that ten or fifteen years from now it will. How will objective ways of measuring mental illness affect the analyst? Number one, we'll have much more accurate diagnoses. With time, we hope to be able to image borderline personality, and we'll see exactly how many different subcategories there might be, what brain regions are involved. Number two, we have three or four or five different ways of approaching it psychotherapeutically, alone or in combinations with drugs. Which of these are more effective? And, for a given patient, not only the mode of treatment, but the therapist: should the patient have a male therapist or a female therapist? I am not sufficiently conversant with the clinical literature, but are there any criteria for selecting a male or female therapist?

PLR: I think that it's really the personal preference of the patient.

ERK: Right, but if we were to let the personal preference of the patient completely determine who her surgeon should be for breast cancer, she is likely to make a mistake. So, we develop criteria for what is outstanding surgery, what is mediocre surgery, and what is poor surgery. Especially in the context of psychotherapy, where the transference is such a powerful aspect of the treatment, the patient's judgement may not be perfect. Now, obviously, if a patient has benefited enormously from a therapeutic experience, one can't deny that, but one would like to have some independent measures. It's conceivable to me—I'm making this up—that there might be some objective indications that with an adolescent girl it might be better to work with a woman, and that with a woman in her thirties to work with a man.

PLR: So one could do studies that would allow not only more accurate diagnoses, but that could also predict the likelihood of better patient–therapist matches?

ERK: Yes.

PLR: I take it that you understand science to proceed by falsification and by progressing through empirical methods towards a discovery of truth. How can this be reconciled with the uncertainty principle in physics and a certain trend in science itself that suggests that there's no objective view of a phenomenon because the phenomenon changes from the perspective of the observer? Is the traditional objectivist view of science in question within the scientific world?

ERK: No. I think the uncertainty principle, which the analysts love, is misguided. Heisenberg said that under certain highly selected conditions, measurement of very rapid, small events is so difficult because the mere fact of measurement interferes with the process. But we measure the phenomenon in different ways, measuring it with and without perturbation, just to control for that. We know every time we do something we're likely to screw up the system, so one of the intrinsic things built into the experiment are controls for the experimental manipulation. Could we be wrong under some circumstances? Of course. Science is a perpetually self-correcting process. If you were to ask, "Do you believe that there is a definitive truth?", then I would answer, "In the limit, no, but after a while the evidence gets to be so strong that it's *als ob*, as if it was the final answer". So, if it's going to be modified more, chances are it's going to be a tweak. The double helix: take my word for it, it's going to be around for a *very*, very long time.

PLR: I expect so.

ERK: Darwinian evolution, the selection of the species, these are profound ideas that, if *anything*, with the development of molecular biology and comparative genomics, have become *overwhelmingly* supported. The only question in my mind is, why do we call it Darwinian theory? This is a Darwinian *principle* that is as solid as any principle in physics. So, it is true that there are certain circumstances in which there is uncertainty, but I wouldn't worry about it. I tell my friends, "Psychoanalysis should have such problems".

PLR: Do you think there's any way that science can help us arrive at an interpretation of a poem?

ERK: No. I'm not in any way suggesting that science is going to replace our sense of spirituality or beauty. But it may give us insight as to why we respond to something that's beautiful. Music is a wonderful example. You can be depressed and listen to Mozart, and you're uplifted. Or a Schubert *Lied*, a Strauss waltz, kitsch stuff. Somehow a Viennese tune moves me dramatically. What *is* it about the rhythm of a waltz that does that? There must be some biological oscillations that are going on. Look, we know that the heart is a pump, we really understand how the heart works in enormous detail. Does that in any way detract from your enjoyment of the fact that the heart is beating in your body? It doesn't, it's another world. I mean, you know it, and it may affect you in some ways, but it doesn't in any way alter it.

PLR: Certainly, even in offering an interpretation, whether it's in an English class or in a clinical session, I would not want to start from a point of view where I knew that what I was saying was based on premises that had been demonstrated to be false. To that extent I absolutely agree with you about the indispensability of sound science in the things that we do that may not be fully explicable or governed by the principles of science as we experience them.

ERK: Also, it may turn out that even though we understand that this table is made of atoms, we pay no attention to the fine structure of it: we use it as a table. And I think that that's going to happen in many areas of life. It doesn't mean that if you want to cut this in pieces, you may not want to know what the nature of the wood is.

PLR: Right.

ERK: So, from a practical point of view, in terms of intervention psychotherapeutically, pharmacologically, or surgically, we want to understand where the mental processes are located, how they function, how they interact with each other, beyond the aesthetics of it, and beyond its relationship to the enjoyment of everyday life.

PLR: So you're recommending a fair dose of pragmatism in how we go about our business?

ERK: Right. I think that this is urgent for psychoanalysis, because it has developed for such a long time as a Talmudic discipline. There is a Hebrew phrase called *dahyenu*. At Passover, you thank God for the fact He took us out of Egypt. If He'd *only* taken us out of Egypt, we would be satisfied (*dahyenu*); if He'd *only* allowed us to cross the Red Sea, we would be satisfied. So, one is satisfied often with very little things. I think if only at this particular point we began to move in an empirical direction, it would be sufficient. When I was a house officer at the Massachusetts Mental Health Center, from 1960 to 1962, psychiatry was so grandiose in its ambition that even though psychiatrists couldn't treat anybody, they thought they should get involved in the discussions that the Soviets were having with the United States. Now, understandably, they've shrunk from that. Psychiatry no longer thinks you can treat schizophrenia with psychotherapy; it no longer thinks it can treat psychosomatic illnesses, as Grete Bibring did, with psychoanalysis. Hypertension probably does not respond to psychoanalysis. It may help, but you need a lot of other physical intervention as well. I think we've got to get to a phase in which we shrink that grandiosity and focus in on a few paradigmatic questions, in which the first one is, "Does it work?" Can we localize different mental functions in the different regions of the brain? And then we need to follow the changes that occur with different psychotherapeutic experiences. And from that as a base we can really develop a new synthesis, much as Freud tried to do in 1895 with the *Project for a Scientific Psychology*, but at a completely new level, a synthesis between biology and psychoanalytic treatment.

PLR: And that's what I've called the dream of consilience.

ERK: I think that's wonderful. I think that's what's necessary. It's a dream, but that's what we live for.

REFERENCES

Abraham, N., & Torok, M. (1987). *The Shell and the Kernel, Volume 1*, N. T. Rand (Ed. & Trans.). Chicago, IL: University of Chicago Press, 1994.

Adelman, J. (1992). *Suffocating Mothers: Fantasies of Maternal Origins in Shakespeare's Plays, "Hamlet" to "The Tempest"*. New York: Routledge.

Adler, J. (2006). Freud in our midst. *Newsweek*, 27 March, pp. 43–51.

Alexander, F., & Selesnick, S. T. (1965). Freud–Bleuler correspondence. *Archives of General Psychiatry, 12*: 1–9.

Alexander, F., Eisenstein, S., & Grotjahn, M. (Eds.) (1966). *Psychoanalytic Pioneers*. New York: Basic Books.

Armstrong, R. H. (2005). *A Compulsion for Antiquity: Freud and the Ancient World*. Ithaca, NY: Cornell University Press.

Bair, D. (2003). *Jung: A Biography*. Boston, MA: Little, Brown.

Bass, A. (2009). An Independent theory of clinical technique viewed through a relational lens: commentary on paper by Michael Parsons. *Psychoanalytic Dialogues, 19*: 237–245.

Bergstein, M. (2006). Freud's "Moses of Michelangelo": Vasari, photography, and art-historical practice. *The Art Bulletin, 88*: 158–176.

Berman, E. (2004). Sándor, Gizella, Elma: a biographical journey. *International Journal of Psychoanalysis, 85*: 489–520.

Berman, E. (2009). Ferenczi and Winnicott: why we need their radical edge: commentary on paper by Michael Parsons. *Psychoanalytic Dialogues, 19*: 246–252.

Billinsky, J. (1969). Jung and Freud (The end of a romance). *Andover Newton Quarterly, 10*(2): 39–43.

Binswanger, L. (1956). *Sigmund Freud: Reminiscences of a Friendship*, N. Guterman (Trans.). New York: Grune and Stratton, 1957.

Bloom, H. (1998). *Shakespeare: The Invention of the Human*. New York: Riverhead Books.

Blum, H. P. (1998). Freud and Jung: the internationalization of psychoanalysis. *Psychoanalysis and History, 1*: 44–55.

Blumenthal, R. (2006). Hotel log hints at illicit desire that Dr. Freud didn't repress. *The New York Times*, 24 December, pp. A1, 4.

Boehlich, W. (Ed.) (1989). *The Letters of Sigmund Freud to Eduard Silberstein, 1871–1881*, A. J. Pomerans (Trans.). Cambridge, MA: Harvard University Press, 1990.

Boffito, S. (2008). La più indipendente degli indipendenti: la psicoanalisi e la vita di Nina Coltart. Tesi di Laurea. Università Cattolica del Sacro Cuore, Milan [unpublished manuscript].

Bonomi, C. (1997). Mute correspondence. In: P. Mahony, C. Bonomi, & J. Stensson (Eds.), *Behind the Scenes: Freud in Correspondence* (pp. 155–201). Oslo: Scandinavian University Press, 1997.

Borgogno, F. (2007). *The Vancouver Interview: Frammenti di vita e opere d'una vocazione psicoanalitica*. Rome: Borla.

Bos, J. (2005). Marginal historiography: on Stekel's account of things. *Psychoanalysis and History, 7*: 81–98.

Bos, J., & Groenendijk, L. (2004). The art of imitation: Wilhelm Stekel's Lehrjahre. *International Journal of Psychoanalysis, 85*: 713–729.

Bos, J., & Groenendijk, L. (2007). *The Self-Marginalization of Wilhelm Stekel: Freudian Circles Inside and Out*. New York: Springer.

Bowlby, J. (1980). *Loss: Sadness and Depression. Attachment and Loss, Vol. 3*. New York: Basic Books.

Brabant, E., Falzeder, E., & Giampieri-Deutsch, P. (Eds.) (1993). *The Correspondence of Sigmund Freud and Sándor Ferenczi, Volume 1, 1908–1914*, P. T. Hoffer (Trans.). Cambridge, MA: Harvard University Press.

Bullough, G. (Ed.) (1973). *Narrative and Dramatic Sources of Shakespeare, Vol. 7. The Major Tragedies*. New York: Columbia University Press.

Clark-Lowes, F. (2001). Freud, Stekel, and the interpretation of dreams: the affinities with existential analysis. *Psychoanalysis and History, 3*: 69–78.

Coltart, N. (1985). The practice of psychoanalysis and Buddhism. In: *Slouching Towards Bethlehem . . . And Further Psychoanalytic Explorations* (pp. 164–175). London: Free Association Books, 2002.

Coltart, N. (1986). Slouching towards Bethlehem . . . or thinking the unthinkable in psychoanalysis. In: *Slouching Towards Bethlehem . . . And Further Psychoanalytic Explorations* (pp. 1–14). London: Free Association Books, 2002.

Coltart, N. (1991a). The analysis of an elderly patient. In: *Slouching Towards Bethlehem . . . And Further Psychoanalytic Explorations* (pp. 144–163). London: Free Association Books, 2002.

Coltart, N. (1991b). The silent patient. In: *Slouching Towards Bethlehem . . . And Further Psychoanalytic Explorations* (pp. 79–94). London: Free Association Books, 2002.

Coltart, N. (1993a). *How to Survive as a Psychotherapist*. London: Sheldon Press.

Coltart, N. (1993b). *Slouching Towards Bethlehem . . . And Further Psychoanalytic Explorations*. London: Free Association Books, 2002.

Coltart, N. (1995). A philosopher and his mind. In: *The Baby and the Bathwater* (pp. 75–90). London: Karnac, 1996.

Coltart, N. (1996a). "And now for something completely different . . ." In: *The Baby and the Bathwater* (pp. 109–124). London: Karnac, 1996.

Coltart, N. (1996b). Blood, shit, and tears: a case of ulcerative colitis. In: *The Baby and the Bathwater* (pp. 91–108). London: Karnac, 1996.

Coltart, N. (1996c). *The Baby and the Bathwater*. London: Karnac.

Coltart, N. (1996d). The baby and the bathwater. In: *The Baby and the Bathwater* (pp. 155–166). London: Karnac, 1996.

Coltart, N. (1996e). Buddhism and psychoanalysis revisited. In: *The Baby and the Bathwater* (pp. 125–139). London: Karnac, 1996.

Coltart, N. (1996f). The man with two mothers. In: *The Baby and the Bathwater* (pp. 1–22). London: Karnac, 1996.

Coltart, N. (1996g). Two's company, three's a crowd. In: *The Baby and the Bathwater* (pp. 41–56). London: Karnac, 1996.

Coltart, N. (1996h). Why am I here? In: *The Baby and the Bathwater* (pp. 23–40). London: Karnac, 1996.

Cooper, A. M. (1985). Will neurobiology influence psychoanalysis? In: E. L. Auchincloss (Ed.), *The Quiet Revolution in American Psychoanalysis: Selected Papers* (pp. 81–94). New York: Brunner-Routledge, 2004.

Cooper, A. M. (1988). The narcissistic–masochistic character. In: E. L. Auchincloss (Ed.), *The Quiet Revolution in American Psychoanalysis: Selected Papers* (pp. 121–139). New York: Brunner-Routledge, 2004.

Cooper, A. M. (1989). Infant research and adult psychoanalysis. In: E. L. Auchincloss (Ed.), *The Quiet Revolution in American Psychoanalysis: Selected Papers* (pp. 95–102). New York: Brunner-Routledge, 2004.

Dupont, J. (1994). Freud's analysis of Ferenczi as revealed by their correspondence. *International Journal of Psychoanalysis, 75*: 301–320.

Eissler, K. R. (1953). Interview with C. G. Jung. Unpublished manuscript, Library of Congress, 61 pp (in German).

Eissler, K. R. (1994). *Three Instances of Injustice*. Madison, CT: International Universities Press.

Eliot, T. S. (1921). Andrew Marvell. In: *Selected Essays* (pp. 251–263). New York: Harcourt, Brace & World, 1964.

Evans, G. B. (Ed.) (1974). *The Riverside Shakespeare*. Boston, MA: Houghton Mifflin.

Fairbairn, W. R. D. (1944). Endopsychic structure considered in terms of object-relationships. In: *Psychoanalytic Studies of the Personality* (pp. 82–136). London: Routledge and Kegan Paul, 1986.

Falzeder, E. (1997). Dreaming of Freud: Ferenczi, Freud and an analysis without end. *Psychoanalytic Inquiry, 17*: 416–427.

Falzeder, E. (Ed.) (2002). *The Complete Correspondence of Sigmund Freud and Karl Abraham, 1907–1925*, C. Schwarzbacher (Trans.), with the collaboration of C. Trollope & K. Majthényi King. London: Karnac.

Falzeder, E., & Brabant, E. (Eds.) (1996). *The Correspondence of Sigmund Freud and Sándor Ferenczi. Volume 2, 1914–1919*, P. T. Hoffer (Trans.). Cambridge, MA: Harvard University Press.

Falzeder, E., & Brabant, E. (Eds.) (2000). *The Correspondence of Sigmund Freud and Sándor Ferenczi. Volume 3, 1920–1933*, P. T. Hoffer (Trans.). Cambridge, MA: Harvard University Press.

Ferenczi, S. (1915). The dream of the occlusive pessary. In: J. Rickman (Ed.), J. I. Suttie (Trans.), *Further Contributions to the Theory and Technique of Psychoanalysis* (pp. 304–311). New York: Brunner/Mazel, 1980.

Ferenczi, S. (1923). The dream of the "clever baby". In: J. Rickman (Ed.), J. I. Suttie (Trans.), *Further Contributions to the Theory and Technique of Psychoanalysis* (pp. 349–350). New York: Brunner/Mazel, 1980.

Ferenczi, S. (1931). Child analysis in the analysis of adults. In: M. Balint (Ed.), E. Mosbacher and others (Trans.), *Final Contributions to the Problems and Methods of Psychoanalysis* (pp. 126–142). New York: Brunner/Mazel, 1980.

Ferenczi, S. (1949). Confusion of tongues between adults and the child: the language of tenderness and passion. In: M. Balint (Ed.), E. Mosbacher and others (Trans.), *Final Contributions to the Problems and Methods of Psychoanalysis* (pp. 156–167). New York: Brunner/ Mazel, 1980.

Ferenczi, S. (1985). *The Clinical Diary of Sándor Ferenczi*, J. Dupont (Ed.), M. Balint & N. Zarday Jackson (Trans.). Cambridge, MA: Harvard University Press.

Forrester, J. (1997). *Dispatches from the Freud Wars: Psychoanalysis and Its Passions*. Cambridge, MA: Harvard University Press.

Freud, E. L. (Ed.) (1960). *The Letters of Sigmund Freud*, T. Stern & J. Stern (Trans.). New York: Basic Books, 1979.

Freud, S. (1899a). Screen memories. *S.E., 3*: 303–322. London: Hogarth.

Freud, S. (1900a). *The Interpretation of Dreams. S.E., 4 & 5*. London: Hogarth.

Freud, S. (1901a). On dreams. *S.E., 5*: 629–684. London: Hogarth.

Freud, S. (1901b). *The Psychopathology of Everyday Life. S.E., 6*. London: Hogarth.

Freud, S. (1908d). "Civilized" sexual morality and modern nervous illness. *S.E., 9* : 177–204. London: Hogarth.

Freud, S. (1910a). Five lectures on psychoanalysis. *S.E., 11*: 9–55. London: Hogarth.

Freud, S. (1910h). A special type of choice of object made by men. *S.E., 11*: 165–175. London: Hogarth.

Freud, S. (1910k). 'Wild' psychoanalysis. *S.E., 11*: 219–227. London: Hogarth.

Freud, S. (1912d). On the universal tendency to debasement in the sphere of love. *S.E., 11*: 179–190. London: Hogarth.

Freud, S. (1913f). The theme of the three caskets. *S.E., 12*: 291–301. London: Hogarth.

Freud, S. (1912–1913). *Totem and Taboo, S.E., 13*: 1–161. London: Hogarth.

Freud, S. (1914b). *The Moses of Michelangelo. S.E., 13*: 211–238. London: Hogarth.

Freud, S. (1914d). On the history of the psychoanalytic movement. *S.E., 14*: 7–66. London: Hogarth.

Freud, S. (1916d). Some character-types met with in psychoanalytic work. *S.E., 14*: 311–333. London: Hogarth.

Freud, S. (1916–1917). *Introductory Lectures on Psychoanalysis. S.E., 15 & 16*. London: Hogarth.

Freud, S. (1919j). On the teaching of psychoanalysis in universities. *S.E.*, *17*: 169–173. London: Hogarth.

Freud, S. (1920g). *Beyond the Pleasure Principle*. *S.E.*, *18*: 7–64. London: Hogarth.

Freud, S. (1923a). Two encyclopedia articles. *S.E.*, *18*: 235–259. London: Hogarth.

Freud, S. (1933a). *New Introductory Lectures on Psychoanalysis*. *S.E.*, *22*: 5–182.

Freud, S. (1937c). Analysis terminable and interminable. *S.E.*, *23*: 216–253. London: Hogarth.

Gadamer, H.-G. (1960). *Truth and Method*, G. Barden & J. Cumming (Trans.). New York: Crossroad, 1975.

Gay, P. (1988). *Freud: A Life for Our Time*. New York: Norton.

Graf, M. (1942). Reminiscences of Professor Sigmund Freud. *Psychoanalytic Quarterly*, *11*: 465–476.

Greenblatt, S. (2004). *Will in the World: How Shakespeare Became Shakespeare*. New York: Norton.

Groenendijk, L. F. (1997). Masturbation and neurasthenia: Freud and Stekel in debate on the harmful effects of autoerotism. *Journal of Psychology and Human Sexuality*, *9*: 71–94.

Guntrip, H. (1968). *Schizoid Phenomena, Object Relations and the Self*. London: Hogarth, 1986.

Hamilton, E., & Cairns, H. (Eds.) (1973). Phaedrus. In: R. Hackforth and others (Trans.), *The Collected Dialogues of Plato* (pp. 475–525). Princeton, NJ: Princeton University Press.

Hampstead and Highgate (1997). Coltart suicide was clear decision, 1 August.

Hanly, C. (1986). Lear and his daughters. *International Review of Psychoanalysis*, *13*: 211–220.

Hanly, C. (2009). On truth and clinical psychoanalysis. *International Journal of Psychoanalysis*, *90*: 363–373.

Irigaray, L. (1974). *Speculum of the Other Woman*, C. C. Gill (Trans.). Ithaca, NY: Cornell University Press, 1985.

Johnson, S. (1781). Life of Cowley. In: *Lives of the English Poets* (2 Volumes), *1*: 1–53. London: Oxford University Press, 1973.

Jones, E. (1913). The God complex: the belief that one is God, and the resulting character traits. In: *Essays on Applied Psychoanalysis* (2 Volumes), *2*: 244–265. London: Hogarth, 1964.

Jones, E. (1955). *The Life and Work of Sigmund Freud, Vol. 2, Years of Maturity, 1901–1919*. New York: Basic Books.

Jorden, E. (1603). *A Brief Discourse of a Disease Called the Suffocation of the Mother*. London: John Windet.

Jung, C. G. (1912). *Psychology of the Unconscious [Transformations and Symbols of the Libido]*, B. M. Hinkle (Trans.). New York: Moffat, Yard.

Jung, C. G. (1952). *Answer to Job*, R. F. C. Hull (Trans.). Princeton, NJ: Princeton University Press, 1973.

Jung, C. G. (1963). *Memories, Dreams, Reflections* (revised edition), A. Jaffé (Ed.), R. Winston & C. Winston (Trans.). New York: Vintage, 1989.

Kahn, C. (1986). The absent mother in *King Lear*. In: M. W. Ferguson, M. Quilligan, & N. J. Vickers (Eds.), *Rewriting the Renaissance: The Discourses of Sexual Difference in Early Modern Europe* (pp. 33–49). Chicago, IL: University of Chicago Press.

Kahr, B. (1996). *D. W. Winnicott: A Biographical Portrait*. London: Karnac.

Kandel, E. R. (Ed.) (1979). Psychotherapy and the single synapse: the impact of psychiatric thought on neurobiologic research. In: *Psychiatry, Psychoanalysis, and the New Biology of Mind* (pp. 5–31). Washington, DC: American Psychiatric Publishing, 2005.

Kandel, E. R. (2005). *Psychiatry, Psychoanalysis, and the New Biology of Mind*. Washington, DC: American Psychiatric Publishing.

Kandel, E. R. (2006). *In Search of Memory: The Emergence of a New Science of Mind*. New York: Norton.

Kanter, J. (Ed.) (2004). *Face to Face with Children: The Life and Work of Clare Winnicott*. London: Karnac.

Kerr, J. (1993). *A Most Dangerous Method: The Story of Jung, Freud, and Sabina Spielrein*. New York: Knopf.

Khan, M. M. R. (1963). The concept of cumulative trauma. In: *The Privacy of the Self: Papers on Psychoanalytic Theory and Technique* (pp. 42–58). London: Hogarth, 1986.

Khan, M. M. R. (1972). The becoming of a psychoanalyst. In: *The Privacy of the Self: Papers on Psychoanalytic Theory and Technique* (pp. 112–128). London: Hogarth, 1986.

Kitcher, P. (1992). *Freud's Dream: A Complete Interdisciplinary Science of Mind*. Cambridge, MA: MIT Press, 1995.

Klein, M. (1930). The importance of symptom-formation in the development of the ego. In: R. Money-Kyrle, B. Joseph, E. O'Shaughnessy & H. Segal (Eds.), *The Writings of Melanie Klein* (4 Volumes), 1: 219–232. New York: Free Press, 1975.

Klein, M. (1935). A contribution to the psychogenesis of manic-depressive states. In: R. Money-Kyrle, B. Joseph, E. O'Shaughnessy & H. Segal (Eds.), *The Writings of Melanie Klein* (4 Volumes), 1: 262–289. New York: Free Press, 1975.

Kohon, G. (Ed.) (1986). *The British School of Psychoanalysis: The Independent Tradition*. London: Free Association Books.

Kris, E. (1956). The recovery of childhood memories in psychoanalysis. *The Psychoanalytic Study of the Child, 11*: 54–88.

Krüll, M. (1979). *Freud and His Father*, A. J. Pomerans (Trans.). New York: Norton, 1986.

Kuhn, P. (1998). "A pretty piece of treachery": the strange case of Dr Stekel and Sigmund Freud. *International Journal of Psychoanalysis, 79*: 1151–1171.

Lacoursiere, R. B. (2008). Freud's death: historical truth and biographical fictions. *American Imago, 65*: 107–128.

Lear, J. (1995). The shrink is in. *The New Republic*, 25 December, pp. 18–25.

Little, M. I. (1957). "R"—the analyst's total response to his patient's needs. In: *Transference Neurosis and Transference Psychosis: Toward Basic Unity* (pp. 51–80). New York: Aronson, 1981.

Little, M. I. (1958). On delusional transference (transference psychosis). In: *Transference Neurosis and Transference Psychosis: Toward Basic Unity* (pp. 81–91). New York: Aronson, 1981.

Little, M. I. (1960). On basic unity (primary total undifferentiatedness). In: *Transference Neurosis and Transference Psychosis: Toward Basic Unity*. (pp. 109–125). New York: Aronson, 1981.

Little, M. I. (1985). Winnicott working in areas where psychotic anxieties predominate: a personal record. *Free Associations, 3*: 9–42.

Little, M. I., & Langs, R. (1981). Dialogue. In: M. I. Little, *Transference Neurosis and Transference Psychosis: Toward Basic Unity*. (pp. 269–306). New York: Aronson.

Maciejewski, F. (2006). Freud, his wife, and his "wife", J. Gaines (Trans.), with the collaboration of P. J. Swales & J. Swales. *American Imago, 63*: 497–506.

Macmillan, M., & Swales, P. J. (2003). Observations from the refuse-heap: Freud, Michelangelo's Moses, and psychoanalysis. *American Imago, 60*: 41–104.

Mahony, P. (1979). Friendship and its discontents. In: P. Mahony, C. Bonomi, & J. Stensson (Eds.), *Behind the Scenes: Freud in Correspondence* (pp. 1–45). Oslo: Scandinavian University Press, 1997.

Marcus, S. (1977). Introductory essay to *The Origins of Psychoanalysis: Letters to Wilhelm Fliess, Drafts and Notes: 1887–1902* by Sigmund Freud (pp. vii–xix), M. Bonaparte, A. Freud & E. Kris (Eds.), E. Mosbacher & J. Strachey (Trans.). New York: Basic Books.

Masson, J. M. (Ed. & Trans.) (1985). *The Complete Letters of Sigmund Freud to Wilhelm Fliess, 1887–1904*. Cambridge, MA: Harvard University Press.

May, U. (2003). The early relationship between Sigmund Freud and Isidor Sadger: a dream (1897) and a letter (1902). *Psychoanalysis and History*, 5: 119–146.

McGuire, W. (Ed.) (1974). *The Freud/Jung Letters: The Correspondence between Sigmund Freud and C. G. Jung*, R. Manheim & R. F. C. Hull (Trans.). Princeton: Princeton University Press.

Meisel, P., & Kendrick, W. (Eds.) (1985). *Bloomsbury/Freud: The Letters of James and Alix Strachey 1924–1925*. New York: Basic Books.

Melville, H. (1852). *Pierre or The Ambiguities*, W. C. Spengemann (Ed.). Harmondsworth: Penguin Books, 1996.

Menaker, E. (1989). *Appointment in Vienna: An American Psychoanalyst Recalls Her Student Days in Pre-War Austria*. New York: St. Martin's Press.

Milner, M. (1969). *The Hands of the Living God: An Account of a Psychoanalytic Treatment*. New York: International Universities Press.

Molino, A. (Ed.) (1997). *Freely Associated: Encounters in Psychoanalysis with Christopher Bollas, Joyce McDougall, Michael Eigen, Adam Phillips, Nina Coltart*. London: Free Association Books.

Moritz, L. (2007). Turning to our work. *The American Psychoanalyst*, 41–2: 3, 15.

Mühlleitner, E. (1992). *Biographisches Lexicon der Psychoanalyse. Die Mitglieder der Psychologischen Mittwoch-Gesellschaft und der Wiener Psychoanalytischen Vereiningung*, in collaboration with Johannes Reichmayr. Tübingen: edition diskord.

Nunberg, H., & Federn, E. (Eds.) (1974). *Minutes of the Vienna Psychoanalytic Society. Vol. 3: 1910–1911*, M. Nunberg (Trans.). New York: International Universities Press.

Parsons, M. (2000). *The Dove that Returns, the Dove that Vanishes: Paradox and Creativity in Psychoanalysis*. London: Routledge.

Parsons, M. (2009a). An independent theory of clinical technique. *Psychoanalytic Dialogues*, 19: 221–236.

Parsons, M. (2009b). Reply to commentaries. *Psychoanalytic Dialogues*, 19: 259–266.

Paskauskas, R. A. (Ed.) (1993). *The Complete Correspondence of Sigmund Freud and Ernest Jones, 1908–1939*. Cambridge, MA: Harvard University Press.

Paul, R. A. (1996). *Moses and Civilization: The Meaning behind Freud's Myth*. New Haven: Yale University Press.

Paul, R. A., & Gamarra, E. A. Jr. (1999). On the establishment of the Emory University psychoanalytic studies program. *Psychoanalytic Studies, 1*: 447–452.

PDM Task Force (2006). *Psychodynamic Diagnostic Manual.* Silver Spring, MD: Alliance of Psychoanalytic Organizations.

Phillips, A. (1988). *Winnicott.* London: Fontana.

Poland, W. S. (2009). Commentary on paper by Michael Parsons. *Psychoanalytic Dialogues, 19*: 253–258.

Rank, O. (1932). *Modern Education: A Critique of Its Fundamental Ideas,* M. E. Moxon (Trans.). New York: Knopf.

Rashkin, E. (2006). Nicolas Abraham and Maria Torok (1919–1975 and 1925–1998). In: L. D. Kritzman, B. J. Reilly, & M. B. DeBevoise (Eds.), *The Columbia History of Twentieth-Century French Thought* (pp. 377–379). New York: Columbia University Press, 2006.

Reeder, J. (2004). *Hate and Love in Psychoanalytical Institutions: The Dilemma of a Profession.* New York: Other Press.

Reeves, C. (2004). On being "intrinsical": a Winnicott enigma. *American Imago, 61*: 427–456.

Reik, T. (1957). *Myth and Guilt: The Crime and Punishment of Mankind.* New York: Grosset and Dunlap.

Riviere, J. (1936). A contribution to the analysis of the negative therapeutic reaction. In: A. Hughes (Ed.), *The Inner World and Joan Riviere: Collected Papers 1920–1958* (pp. 134–153). London: Karnac, 1991.

Roazen, P. (1971). *Freud and His Followers.* New York: Meridian, 1976.

Rodman, F. R. (Ed.) (1987). *The Spontaneous Gesture: Selected Letters of D. W. Winnicott.* Cambridge, MA: Harvard University Press.

Rodman, F. R. (2003). *Winnicott: Life and Work.* Cambridge, MA: Perseus.

Rosenzweig, S. (1992). *Freud, Jung and Hall the King-Maker: The Expedition to America (1909).* St Louis: Rana House Press.

Roth, P. (2001). *The Dying Animal.* New York: Vintage, 2002.

Roudinesco, É. (1994). *Généalogies.* Paris: Fayard.

Rudnytsky, P. L. (1987). *Freud and Oedipus.* New York: Columbia University Press.

Rudnytsky, P. L. (1991). *The Psychoanalytic Vocation: Rank, Winnicott, and the Legacy of Freud.* New Haven: Yale University Press.

Rudnytsky, P. L. (Ed.) (1993). *Transitional Objects and Potential Spaces: Literary Uses of D. W. Winnicott.* New York: Columbia University Press.

Rudnytsky, P. L. (1994). Freud's Pompeian fantasy. In: S. L. Gilman et al. (Eds.), *Reading Freud's Reading* (pp. 211–231). New York: New York University Press.

Rudnytsky, P. L. (1999a). "The darke and vicious place": the dread of the vagina in *King Lear*. *Modern Philology, 96*: 291–311.

Rudnytsky, P. L. (1999b). Wrecking Crews. *American Imago, 56*: 285–298.

Rudnytsky, P. L. (2000). *Psychoanalytic Conversations: Interviews with Clinicians, Commentators, and Critics*. Hillsdale, NJ: Analytic Press.

Rudnytsky, P. L. (2002). *Reading Psychoanalysis: Freud, Rank, Ferenczi, Groddeck*. Ithaca, NY: Cornell University Press.

Rudnytsky, P. L., & Gordon, A. M. (Eds.) (2000). *Psychoanalyses/Feminisms*. Albany, NY: State University of New York Press.

Sadger, I. (1930). *Sigmund Freud: Persönliche Errinerungen*, A. Huppke & M. Schröter (Eds.). Tübingen: edition diskord.

Sadger, I. (2005). *Recollecting Freud*, J. M. Jacobsen & A. Dundes (Trans.). Madison, WI: University of Wisconsin Press.

Schacht, L. (Ed.) (1977). *The Meaning of Illness: Selected Psychoanalytic Writings by Georg Groddeck*, G. Mander (Trans.). London: Maresfield Library.

Schwartz, M. M., & Kahn, C. (Eds.) (1980). *Representing Shakespeare: New Psychoanalytic Essays*. Baltimore, MD: Johns Hopkins University Press.

Shapiro, E. R. (2007). From the medical director. *The Austen Riggs Center Review, 19–1*: 1.

Sharpe, E. F. (1946). From *King Lear* to *The Tempest*. *International Journal of Psychoanalysis, 27*: 19–30.

Simon, B. (1988). All germains spill at once: Shakespeare's *King Lear*. In: *Tragic Drama and the Family: Psychoanalytic Studies from Aeschylus to Beckett* (pp. 103–139). New Haven, CT: Yale University Press.

Simon, B. (2006). It's really more complicated than you imagine: narratives of real and imagined trauma. In: P. L. Rudnytsky & R. Charon (Eds.), *Psychoanalysis and Narrative Medicine* (pp. 119–136). Albany, NY: State University of New York Press.

Slochower, H. (1981). Freud as Yahweh in Jung's *Answer to Job*. *American Imago, 38*: 3–39.

Sprengnether, M. (1990). *The Spectral Mother: Freud, Feminism, and Psychoanalysis*. Ithaca, NY: Cornell University Press.

Stanton, M. (1988). Wilhelm Stekel: a refugee analyst and his English reception. In: E. Timms & N. Segal (Eds.), *Freud in Exile: Psychoanalysis and Its Vicissitudes* (pp. 163–174). New Haven, CT: Yale University Press, 1988.

Stekel, W. (1926). Zur Geschichte der analytischen Bewegung. *Fortschritte der Sexualwissenschaft und Psychoanalyse*, 2: 539–575.

Stekel, W. (1950). *The Autobiography of Wilhelm Stekel: The Life Story of a Pioneer Psychoanalyst*, E. Gutheil (Ed.). New York: Liveright.

Stekel, W. (2005). On the history of the analytical movement, J. Bos (Trans.). *Psychoanalysis and History*, 7: 99–130.

Stevens, W. (1942). Notes toward a supreme fiction. In: *Complete Poems* (pp. 380–408). London: Faber & Faber, 1971.

Sullivan, H. S. (1953). *The Interpersonal Theory of Psychiatry*. New York: Norton, 1997.

Swales, P. J. (1982). Freud, Minna Bernays, and the conquest of Rome: new light on the origins of psychoanalysis. *New American Review*, Spring/Summer, pp. 1–23.

Swales, P. J. (1986). Freud, his teacher, and the birth of psychoanalysis. In: P. E. Stepansky (Ed.), *Freud: Appraisals and Reappraisals: Contributions to Freud Studies, Volume 1* (pp. 1–82). Hillsdale, NJ: Analytic Press.

Swales, P. J. (2005). Sex in the life of Sigmund Freud. Unpublished manuscript.

Tögel, C. (Ed.) (2002). *Unser Herz zeigt nach dem Süden: Reisebriefe 1895–1923*. In collaboration with M. Molnar. Berlin: Aufbau-Verlag.

Trilling, L. (1940). Freud and literature. In: *The Liberal Imagination: Essays on Literature and Society* (pp. 32–54). Garden City, NY: Anchor Books, 1953.

Vida, J. E. (1996). The "wise baby" grows up: the contemporary relevance of Sándor Ferenczi. In: P. L. Rudnytsky, A. Bókay, & P. Giampieri-Deutsch (Eds.), *Ferenczi's Turn in Psychoanalysis* (pp. 266–286). New York: New York University Press, 1996.

Westen, D. (1998). The scientific legacy of Sigmund Freud: toward a psychodynamically informed psychological science. *Psychological Bulletin*, 124: 333–371.

Wheelis, A. (1956). The vocational hazards of psychoanalysis. *International Journal of Psychoanalysis*, 37: 171–184.

Wheelis, A. (1959). *The Quest for Identity*. London: Victor Gollancz.

Wheelis, A. (1999). *The Listener: A Psychoanalyst Examines His Life*. New York: Norton.

Willoughby, R. (2005). *Masud Khan: The Myth and the Reality*. London: Free Association Books.

Wilson, E. O. (1998). *Consilience: The Unity of Knowledge*. New York: Knopf.

Winnicott, C. (1945). Children who cannot play. In: J. Kanter (Ed.), *Face to Face with Children: The Life and Work of Clare Winnicott* (pp. 112–121). London: Karnac, 2004.

Winnicott, C. (1978). D. W. W.: a reflection. In: J. Kanter (Ed.), *Face to Face with Children: The Life and Work of Clare Winnicott* (pp. 237–253). London: Karnac, 2004.

Winnicott, C. (1982). D. W. Winnicott: his life and work. In: J. Kanter (Ed.), *Face to Face with Children: The Life and Work of Clare Winnicott* (pp. 254–277). London: Karnac, 2004.

Winnicott, C. (1983). Interview with Michael Neve. In: P. L. Rudnytsky, *The Psychoanalytic Vocation: Rank, Winnicott, and the Legacy of Freud* (pp. 180–193). New Haven: Yale University Press, 1991.

Winnicott, C. (1984). Introduction to *Deprivation and Delinquency*. In: J. Kanter (Ed.), *Face to Face with Children: The Life and Work of Clare Winnicott* (pp. 122–126). London: Karnac, 2004.

Winnicott, D. W. (1945). Primitive emotional development. In: *Through Paediatrics to Psycho-Analysis* (pp. 145–154). New York: Basic Books, 1975.

Winnicott, D. W. (1947). Hate in the countertransference. In: *Through Paediatrics to Psycho-Analysis* (pp. 194–203). New York: Basic Books, 1975.

Winnicott, D. W. (1949a). Birth memories, birth trauma, and anxiety. In: *Through Paediatrics to Psycho-Analysis* (pp. 174–193). New York: Basic Books, 1975.

Winnicott, D. W. (1949b). Mind and its relation to the psyche–soma. In: *Through Paediatrics to Psycho-Analysis* (pp. 243–254). New York: Basic Books, 1975.

Winnicott, D. W. (1950–1955). Aggression in relation to emotional development. In: *Through Paediatrics to Psycho-Analysis* (pp. 204–218). New York: Basic Books, 1975.

Winnicott, D. W. (1952). Psychoses and child care. In: *Through Paediatrics to Psycho-Analysis* (pp. 219–228). New York: Basic Books, 1975.

Winnicott, D. W. (1953). Transitional objects and transitional phenomena. In: *Playing and Reality* (pp. 1–25). London: Tavistock, 1984.

Winnicott, D. W. (1956). The antisocial tendency. In: *Through Paediatrics to Psycho-Analysis* (pp. 306–321). New York: Basic Books, 1975.

Winnicott, D. W. (1957). Excitement in the aetiology of coronary thrombosis. In: C. Winnicott, R. Shepherd, & M. Davis (Eds.), *Psycho-Analytic Explorations* (pp. 34–38). Cambridge, MA: Harvard University Press.

Winnicott, D. W. (1959–1964). Classification: is there a psycho-analytic contribution to psychiatric classification? In: *The Maturational Processes and the Facilitating Environment: Studies in the Theory of Emotional Development* (pp. 124–139). New York: International Universities Press, 1966.

Winnicott, D. W. (1960a). Ego distortion in terms of true and false self. In: *The Maturational Processes and the Facilitating Environment: Studies in the Theory of Emotional Development* (pp. 140–152). New York: International Universities Press, 1966.

Winnicott, D. W. (1960b). The theory of the parent–infant relationship. In: *The Maturational Processes and the Facilitating Environment: Studies in the Theory of Emotional Development* (pp. 37–55). New York: International Universities Press, 1966.

Winnicott, D. W. (1963a). Communicating and not communicating leading to a study of certain opposites. In: *The Maturational Processes and the Facilitating Environment: Studies in the Theory of Emotional Development* (pp. 179–192). New York: International Universities Press, 1966.

Winnicott, D. W. (1963b). D. W. W.'s dream related to reviewing Jung. In: C. Winnicott, R. Shepherd, & M. Davis (Eds.), *Psycho-Analytic Explorations* (pp. 228–230). Cambridge, MA: Harvard University Press, 1989.

Winnicott, D. W. (1964). Review of *Memories, Dreams, Reflections*. In: C. Winnicott, R. Shepherd, & M. Davis (Eds.), *Psycho-Analytic Explorations* (pp. 482–492). Cambridge, MA: Harvard University Press, 1989.

Winnicott, D. W. (1969). The use of an object and relating through identifications. In: *Playing and Reality* (pp. 86–94). London: Tavistock, 1984.

Winnicott, D. W. (1974). Fear of breakdown. In: C. Winnicott, R. Shepherd, & M. Davis (Eds.), *Psycho-Analytic Explorations* (pp. 87–95). Cambridge, MA: Harvard University Press, 1989.

Winnicott, D. W. (1988). *Human Nature*, C. Bollas, M. Davis, & R. Shepherd (Eds.). London: Free Association Books.

Winnicott, D. W., & Britton, C. (1944). The problem of homeless children. In: J. Kanter (Ed.), *Face to Face with Children: The Life and Work of Clare Winnicott* (pp. 97–111). London: Karnac, 2004.

Winter, S. (1999). *Freud and the Institution of Psychoanalytic Knowledge*. Stanford, CA: Stanford University Press.

Wittels, F. (1924). *Sigmund Freud: His Personality, his Teaching and his School*, E. Paul & C. Paul (Trans.). London: Allen & Unwin.

Wordsworth, W. (1815). Essay, supplementary to the Preface. In: E. de Selincourt (Ed.), *Poetical Works* (2nd edn.), 5 Volumes, 2: 409–430. Oxford: Clarendon Press, 1965.

Young-Bruehl, E. (1988). *Anna Freud: A Biography*. New York: Summit Books.

INDEX